The three-volume *Encyclopedia of Rock* is a unique reference work. There is nothing available that can approach it in quality or price. Clearly arranged, enormously comprehensive and packed with triple-checked facts, it is the best reference book on Rock ever published.

The Sounds of the Seventies brings the *Encyclopedia of Rock* up to date. From Elton John to Joni Mitchell, from Yes to the Bay City Rollers, a kaleidoscope of styles is accurately documented for the first time. Included are all the fascinating facts and behind-the-scene details about the frenzied musical scene of today with its supergroups and obscure groups, record companies, producers, performers and manipulators.

The Encyclopedia of Rock
Edited by Phil Hardy and Dave Laing

Consultant Editors:
Charlie Gillett
Greil Marcus
Bill Millar
Greg Shaw

The Encyclopedia of Rock

Volume III
The Sounds of the Seventies

Edited by Phil Hardy and Dave Laing

Panther

Granada Publishing Limited
Published in 1976 by Panther Books Ltd
Frogmore, St Albans, Herts AL2 2NF

Made and printed in Great Britain by
Hazell Watson & Viney Ltd
Aylesbury, Bucks
Set in Linotype Times

This book is dedicated to *Let It Rock* magazine, 1972–75

Contributors to this volume:

STEPHEN BARNARD
JOHN COLLIS
TONY CUMMINGS
DAVID DOWNING
MIKE FLOOD PAGE
DAVE GELLY
JERRY GILBERT
MICK GOLD
PHIL HARDY
MARTIN HAWKINS
MICK HOUGHTON
JOHN INGHAM
DAVE LAING
DAVID MCGILLIVRAY
PHIL MCNEILL
BILL MILLAR
JONATHAN MORRISH
JOHN PIDGEON
CLIVE RICHARDSON
GREG SHAW
PETER SIMONS
GRAHAM TAYLOR
JOHN TOBLER
DAVID WALTERS
CLIFF WHITE

ACKNOWLEDGEMENTS

The editors and contributors freely acknowledge the considerable debt they owe to the following:
Bigtown Review, Billboard, Bim Bam Boom, Blues & Soul, Blues Research, Blues Unlimited, Blues World, Boppin' News, Cashbox, Barrett Hansen, *Jazz & Blues, Let It Rock, Living Blues, Melody Maker, New Musical Express, Penniman News, Record Mirror, Rock File, R&B Monthly, R&B Magazine, Rollin' Rock, Rolling Stone, Shout, Soul Bag,* Joel Whitburn and *Who Put the Bomp.*

INTRODUCTION

This is the third and final volume of the Encyclopedia of Rock. It brings the story of the music up to the beginning of 1976. The emergence and growth of rock music in the Fifties and Sixties are covered in the previous volumes of the series.

Inclusion in the Encyclopedia depends, firstly, on an artist's commercial success. Artists with a consistent record of hits in Britain and/or America during the Seventies will almost invariably be discussed in the following pages. The major exceptions are artists whose work is unconnected with rock music, such as Laurel and Hardy and Les Crane, who made the novelty spoken record 'Desiderata'. In addition, and perhaps more importantly, artists are included whose work, in the judgement of the Editors and Consultant Editors, is of historical influence and significant musical quality. These judgements have been carefully considered: the Consultant Editors and contributors to the Encyclopedia of Rock are acknowledged experts in the field.

In general, the length of each entry has been dictated by an estimate of the importance of its subject to rock music as a whole. Often, the people behind the scenes have been as influential as the performers, so here, in many cases for the first time, is recognition of the contribution made by the record companies, producers, session musicians and songwriters. The Encyclopedia gives due weight to the work of these figures, as well as to musicians from areas of music which border on rock and have exerted considerable influence on it. In the case of the present volume, many leading figures in jazz and reggae are covered.

Mainly because we are still in the midst of it, the Seventies is a difficult period in which to see rock music as a whole. During the last few years, popular music has firmly established itself as the leading section of the entertainment industry in both America and Britain. One sign of this is simply the size of its turnover, in record and ticket sales, but, more significantly, other arts have begun increasingly to feed off rock. It is now commonplace to find films using rock soundtracks and taking their themes from the world of rock. In the theatre, rock musicals proliferate, while television plays and commercials frequently use rock as incidental music.

The expansion of popular music and the growth of its audience has meant that many different streams of music exist side by side, on the radio waves and in the charts. This is most apparent in America, where the singles charts and album charts during the Seventies have often included singer-songwriters, heavy metal groups, updated crooners, soul singers and novelty records. British charts have been more insular, with the emergence of a new teenage pop music, often leaning heavily on modified images from earlier decades.

Some more general trends can be glimpsed, however. 'Glam-rock', as such, may have been more of a marketing concept than a description of a musical style, but artists like David Bowie and Bryan Ferry managed to appeal equally to dancing and thinking audiences. And black music, as a whole, was transferred from merely a section of the pop spectrum into something which spread throughout it, providing major artists in dance music, progressive rock and even middle-of-the-road music.

Some of the most successful artists of the Seventies do not appear in the current volume, simply because their major or most significant contribution to rock was made in the Sixties or even the Fifties. Thus, even though Elvis Presley has continued to have hits in the last five years, his career is discussed and evaluated in our first volume, since his true importance lay in his part in the emergence of rock'n'roll and modern pop music.

Further, the rapidly changing kaleidoscope of popular music in the Seventies inevitably means that the picture of the decade presented in these pages may soon come to seem somewhat lopsided. When this volume was first planned in

1974, its shape was very different to the one it has now assumed. However, the Encyclopedia of Rock is intended to be an evolving work, and we would be pleased to hear from readers about any errors or omissions they discover in it.

PHIL HARDY
DAVE LAING
December 1975

A&M Records was formed in the summer of 1962 by band leader Herb Alpert and West Coast promotion man Jerry Moss – thus A&M. Their first single release was 'Lonely Bull' by Herb Alpert and the Tijuana Brass. It was a world-wide hit, immediately establishing the Los Angeles-based company, which was then housed in a converted garage. By 1966 Herb and the Tijuana Brass had five albums in the Top Twenty and had signed Sergio Mendes and Brasil '66, another big-selling easy listening group, produced by Alpert. Other successes that year included 'The More I See You' by Chris Montez and 'Guantanamera' by The Sandpipers. Of the 25 albums released by A&M, 16 went Gold.

By 1968 A&M had acquired wholly-owned subsidiaries in London and Toronto, signed their first rock-oriented band, The Flying Burrito Brothers, and opened their own studios on the West Coast. In 1969 Joe Cocker signed to the label and Phil Spector also returned as a producer in conjunction with his own Phil Spector Productions. Ike and Tina Turner's 'River Deep – Mountain High' was issued under this agreement.

By 1970 Lou Adler had brought his Ode label to A&M for distribution, which resulted in solo success for Carole King and Cheech and Chong. Leon Russell's Shelter Records also signed a distribution deal with A&M, releasing several solo albums plus albums by Freddie King. The Carpenters were also contracted to the label, becoming A&M's biggest-selling act. Other major signings included Humble Pie and Joan Baez, Rick Wakeman and distribution of George Harrison's Dark Horse label. A&M was now a leading independent company, and its British arm enjoyed success with the Strawbs, Stealers Wheel and Supertramp.

Abba, formed in 1973 when Bjorn and Benny, a popular Swedish duo, decided to bring their girlfriends into the group, became an immediate sensation, with 'Ring Ring' topping charts all over Europe and the follow-up, 'Waterloo', winning the Eurovision Song Contest and becoming a worldwide hit. The airy female vocals merged effectively with the group's pounding pop-rock sound which was strongly influenced by Roy Wood's production style. While the girls (Agnetha Faltskog and Annifrid Lyngstad) had several years' prior singing experience, the core of the group was the team of Bjorn and Benny, who had recorded under that name since 1966, before which Bjorn Ulvaeus had been a member of the Hootenanny Singers while Benny Anderson had played keyboards with the Hep Stars, who for years were Sweden's most popular rock group. Their accumulated experience enabled Abba, the name coming from the members' initials, to make a powerful first impression which, unfortunately, failed to carry over into 1975 when 'So Long', a record reminiscent of early Phil Spector, failed to arouse much interest. The follow-up, a ballad called 'I Do, I Do, I Do, I Do' was a European hit. However, by the end of 1975 they returned to both the American and British Top Tens with the engaging 'S.O.S.' and 'Mama Mia' (on Atlantic and Epic respectively).

Ace are Alan 'Bam' King (guitar, born in London in 1946), a former member of the Action, a Mod group that recorded for Parlophone in the mid-Sixties ('Land Of 1000 Dances', 1965, 'Never Ever', 1967) and Mighty Baby in the late Sixties, Phil Harris (guitar, born in London in 1948), Paul Carrack (vocals, born in Sheffield in 1951), Terry 'Tex' Comer (bass, born in Burnley in 1949), both ex-members of Warm Dust, and Fran Byrne, from Bees Make Honey (drums, born in Dublin in 1948). Harris, King and Comer formed the group at Christmas 1972, Carrack joined in April, 1973 and Byrne in September, 1974. Signed to Ian Ralfini's newly formed Anchor label in 1974, Ace were the first pub band to achieve major success when the gently soulful 'How Long' from *Five-A-Side* became a British Top Twenty hit in 1974 and topped the American charts in 1975. Subsequent records, including the disappointing *Time For Another* (1975) failed to repeat Ace's initial success.

Aerosmith comprise Steve Tyler (vocals, born in 1950 in New York), Joe Perry (guitar, born in Boston), Brad Whitford (guitar, born in 1954 in Winchester, Mass.), Tom Hamilton (bass, born in 1954 in Colorado Springs) and Joey Kramer (drums, born in 1952 in New York). Formed in Boston in 1970, they signed to Columbia in 1972 after an impressive appearance at Max's Kansas City in New York.

Less ostentatious than other younger-generation heavy metal bands, Aerosmith's first two albums, *Aerosmith* (1973) and *Get Your Wings* (1974), made little impact. In 1975, however, the group had a Top Twenty hit with *Toys In The Attic.*

Alice Cooper is the name of both the group and the stage persona of its leader, Vincent Furnier. Born in Detroit on December 25, 1945, he spent most of his early life in Phoenix, forming his first band, the Earwigs, in 1965 with Glen Buxton (lead guitar), Dennis Dunaway (bass guitar), John Tatum and John Speare. Later that year they changed to the Spiders, losing Tatum and Speare and adding Michael Bruce (piano, guitar). Basing their activity on outrage and a Who/Stones/Kinks repertoire they had a local hit with 'Don't Blow Your Mind'. The group dressed more outrageously and began using props, day-glo, ultra-violet lights and started writing their own songs. In late 1966 they changed to the Nazz (not the Philadelphia group), beginning sporadic lunges towards Los Angeles. Neal Smith (drums) joined. Legend has it through a Ouija board they made contact with a spirit named Alice Cooper; when asked who Alice Cooper was, the insistent reply was, 'Alice Cooper is Vincent Furnier.' Going nowhere, they decided on a further name change; with hesitation they accepted Alice, trading on the ambiguity and outrage. Playing at a Lenny Bruce Memorial Party one week later they drove the audience from the club, leaving only Shep Gordon and Frank Zappa, who were both fascinated by the spectacle. Gordon managed them, Zappa signed them to his Straight Records.

Their first album wasn't released until 1969 with the second a year later. Gaining a contractual release they eventually signed with Warner Bros Records, touring the country, working out the right balance of violence and outrage for their stage show, gaining invaluable publicity over simulated chicken and baby killing. In 1970 they found their first appreciative audience in Detroit and in early 1971 'I'm Eighteen' became their first hit. Teamed with producer Bob Ezrin they devised the first of three thematic records/acts, *Killer*, wherein Alice fondled snakes, threw money at the crowd, dismembered a baby doll and was hung for his sins. This ritualistic violence atoned by death became a mainstay of the Cooper show: from the gallows to the electric chair to the guillotine.

By mid-1972 Cooper was a world act on the strength of hits like 'School's Out' and 'Elected', slowly revealing himself to be a decidedly normal person who constantly drank beer and watched TV. In early 1973 the group embarked on a three-month *Billion Dollar Babies* tour of America, leaving them a shambles, disgusted with the violence of their audience. Alice spent the next year playing golf and appearing in television shows, becoming a personality. A film of the last tour was released in 1974 and Alice filmed a television special with subsequent record and live tour in 1975 which resulted in an American Top Twenty hit with 'Only Women Bleed' (ABC) and the *Welcome To My Nightmare* album. The rest of the group continued to work on solo projects.

The Allman Brothers Band spearheaded a salutary return to blues and country roots in rock music in the early Seventies. They stood out from the many basic boogie bands of the era because of the skill and sensibility of twin lead guitarists Duane Allman and Richard Betts.

The group was formed by Duane Allman (born on Nov. 20, 1946). Raised in Nashville and then Daytona Beach, Florida, he recorded first in Los Angeles in 1968 with Hour Glass, a group which included his brother Gregg (born Dec.

8, 1947) on keyboards. A first album on Liberty led to further sessions at Rick Hall's studio in Muscle Shoals. When these tapes were rejected by Liberty, Duane returned at Hall's request to play on sessions by Wilson Pickett, Percy Sledge, Aretha Franklin, Boz Scaggs and others. Many examples of his solos for other artists crop up on *Duane Allman: An Anthology* (Capricorn, 1972).

An abortive solo album was cut at the insistence of Atlantic's Jerry Wexler, following which Duane signed to Phil Walden's Capricorn Records of Macon, Georgia and set about forming a band. From Jacksonville, Florida came bass-player Berry Oakley (born April 4, 1948) and guitarist Richard Betts (born Dec. 12, 1943, formerly with Tommy Roe's Romans). Gregg Allman returned from California and twin drummers Jai Johnny Johanson (born July 8, 1944) and Butch Trucks completed the line-up.

They began to tour extensively in the South, forming the kind of relationship with the region that the Grateful Dead had with the West Coast. Their first album (*The Allman Brothers Band*, 1969) found them, like the Stones and Butterfield before them, reworking rock's blues inheritance, but with far greater fluidity and assurance. Central to the Allmans' sound on this and *Idlewild South* (1970) was the combination of Duane Allman's slide guitar and Betts' more delicate electric patterns. The latter, which included the original version of 'Midnight Rider' with vocals from Gregg, broke nationally, earning the group a gold album.

Duane continued to play some sessions, notably those for Eric Clapton's *Layla* album. Their duets on the title track and others were among Allman's finest work, though the emotional power of his live playing with the Allman Brothers Band was preserved on *Live At The Fillmore East* (1971). These were virtually Duane Allman's last recordings before he died in a motorcyle accident on October 29, 1971 in Atlanta.

Wisely, no attempt was made to replace Duane who had been, in many respects, the most complete guitarist of his generation. The remainder of the band went on to complete *Eat A Peach* (1972), another Top Ten album. Without

Duane, the group gravitated towards a more melodic, country-influenced sound exemplified on 'Ramblin' Man' and Betts' instrumental 'Jessica' from the next album, *Brothers And Sisters* (1973). In 1972, Berry Oakley died, in a similar way to Duane (on November 11), and the band gained two new members: Chuck Leavill (keyboards) and Lamar Williams (bass).

The success of 'Ramblin' Man' and 'Jessica' established the Allman Brothers Band as a singles group and by now they had fostered the acceptance of a whole host of Southern rock bands. Next, both Gregg Allman and Betts cut solo albums, with Gregg also forming a band to tour in 1974, later releasing a live double album. By the mid-Seventies, the band itself no longer seemed the central force it had been during Duane's lifetime, something the selection of tracks for their double greatest-hits album (*The Road Goes on Forever*, Capricorn, 1975) emphasized.

America was formed by three Americans living in London – Gerry Beckley (born Sept. 12, 1952), Dan Peek (born in 1950) and Dewey Bunnell (born in 1951). Their first album, *America* (Warner Bros, 1971), which was introduced to the world by two million-selling singles, 'A Horse With No Name' and 'I Need You', featured a softer version of the acoustic guitar/vocal harmony style pioneered by Crosby, Stills and Nash. All three members write, play guitar and sing, sometimes remarkably like Neil Young. Their later work, *Hat Trick* and *Hearts*, which has seen them expanding their musical range, has been consistently successful in America where they have 'introduced' each album with a hit single, 'Tin Man' (1974) and 'Sister Golden Hair' (1975).

American Pop. As in Britain, 1967 brought a schism between commercial pop and so-called 'underground' or 'progressive' music in America. The latter, developed in the psychedelic ballrooms, was chiefly live music, given to extended songs (seldom under 15 minutes) that, when it began to be recorded in 1967–68, could only receive airplay on the new FM stations that were beginning to appear. The progressive audience scorned AM radio, the 3-minute limit and the screaming jocks, which meant that the unified pop scene in which AM radio was the sole outlet for everything vanished, and with it all pretence of a unified audience.

One result of this was that the AM radio audience, comprised mainly of housewives and younger teenagers, was largely excluded from the rock'n'roll process and left with the products of studio groups and rock groups that didn't appeal to the progressive faction such as the Box Tops, Tommy James and the Shondells, Paul Revere and the Raiders, the Monkees, the Buckinghams, the Grass Roots, the Guess Who, Three Dog Night, the Association, Tommy Boyce and Bobby Hart, Neil Diamond, John Fred, Andy Kim, Johnny Rivers, Tommy Roe, B. J. Thomas and the Turtles. These were the most consistently popular acts of the late Sixties and, with certain exceptions, they set a fairly impressive standard.

By the end of the Sixties, the rock element had all but disappeared from pop, the only 'pop' act using primarily rock instrumentation being Three Dog Night. The trend by now was towards 'soft rock', either heavily orchestrated (the Carpenters) or more folkish, semi-acoustic rock (Loggins and Messina, John Denver, Lobo), probably best epitomized by Bread, whose records were pure melody and production.

By far the most successful pop artists of the early Seventies were the Partridge Family and the Osmonds, in all their various permutations. Produced respectively by Wes Farrell and Mike Curb (two of America's foremost pop masterminds) these acts virtually cornered the subteen market, which reached a peak in the years 1971–73.

Around 1973, a new trend began developing in American pop. Creative musicians with progressive appeal once again turned to pop as a vehicle for their music. This was inevitable, as FM radio became more commercial, and as total freedom ran its course and a bit of structure began to seem like not such a bad idea. Some of the more noted rock artists who produced successful pop singles in this period included Todd Rundgren, Alice Cooper, Maria Muldaur, Carly Simon, Jim Croce, Aerosmith, and Nilsson. Also, a new generation of pop, AM-radio-oriented rock bands appeared, ranging from the Raspberries to Bachman Turner Overdrive. They played hard rock, but they thought in terms of hit singles, heavily structured and flashy.

While hard rock was returning to the pop spectrum with these acts and other, so-called 'underground' bands were making the charts more than ever before, the mid-Seventies brought a decreased number of ultra-pop recordings. Discounting Soul, the leading pop acts of 1974–75 included Paul Anka, Neil Sedaka, Charlie Rich, Tony Orlando and Dawn, the Carpenters, B. J. Thomas, Barry Manilow and Frankie Valli. Interestingly, most of these were carry-overs or comebacks from a previous era, while by the mid-Seventies the trend among younger musicians was away from both traditional pop and uncompromising rock, and towards some new synthesis of the two.

American Rock. When rock first broke free of the restrictions of AM radio commercialism, for a while (1967–69) it swung to the opposite extreme. This was the era of 'underground' rock, coinciding with the emergence of FM radio, the ballroom dances, and the great psychedelic and radical movements which swept up the youth of this era. Novelty, experiment, and the rejection of all tradition and structure became fashionable, and nearly anything that hadn't been tried before seemed worth doing for that reason alone. It was rock's most eclectic period, grafting on influences from jazz, blues, the Middle East, the Far East, ethnic styles from Bulgaria, Tibet, anywhere. Out of this first eruption of 'progressive' rock (1966–67) came many startling new ideas and intriguing possibilities, but soon the scene was cluttered with dull, overbearingly pretentious imitators, who spent much of the remainder of the decade driving the original vision of progressive rock into the ground, fragmenting the music into various trends, each with its own separate audience. There was the country rock trend, which included, among others, the Byrds, Poco, Jackson Browne, the Flying Burrito Brothers, Rick Nelson, Crazy Horse, and Linda Ronstadt. Also there were singer-songwriters ranging from Randy

Newman, Bob Dylan, Joni Mitchell, James Taylor to Crosby, Stills, Nash and Young, but the vast majority of rock fans supported the hard rock bands of the era, which fell into several categories.

There were the San Francisco groups, of second and third generation, and their imitators: Moby Grape, Country Joe, Steve Miller, Blue Cheer, Lee Michaels, Cold Blood, Electric Flag, Quicksilver, Santana, Tower of Power, Iron Butterfly, Youngbloods, Blues Magoos, Steppenwolf, Blood, Sweat And Tears, Chicago, Fever Tree, Creedence Clearwater, Kaleidoscope, Lothar and the Hand People, Captain Beefheart, Ultimate Spinach, Doors, and hundreds more.

There were also a number of blues-based groups, notably Canned Heat, Paul Butterfield, Siegel-Schwall, the J. Geils Band, and the early Allman Brothers. This form of progressive, drawn-out blues riffing led to the 'boogie' trend, which produced dozens of bands playing repetitive music that was located somewhere between blues and rock, and had its heyday at the massive rock festivals of the late Sixties. These festivals gave exposure to and launched many bands who became mainstays of this period (roughly 1969–71), such as Grand Funk, Rare Earth, Johnny and Edgar Winter, Blues Image, Alice Cooper, Z.Z. Top, Black Oak Arkansas, Cactus, the Amboy Dukes, Bob Seger, and the James Gang.

This approach to rock remained popular, particularly in the South and the Midwest, well into the mid-Seventies. With regional scenes beginning to return in 1972, Georgia emerged as a mecca for Southern boogie bands. The Allman Brothers, Wet Willie, the Marshall Tucker Band, Lynyrd Skynyrd, Hydra, Charlie Daniels and many others came out of this sudden upsurge of Southern music, and most had hits during 1974, although by 1975 the trend had sharply declined. Even in these bands, a strong commercial element and sense of structure was felt towards the end, a reversal of the endless shuffles most had begun with. Instead of shunning AM radio, these bands were purposely trying to record hit singles. It was a sign of the times.

The growth of regional scenes in the Seventies produced

other localized styles, from the country and western Tex-Mex swing bop of Austin (embracing Commander Cody, Asleep at the Wheel, Doug Sahm, Michael Murphey, B. W. Stevenson, Willie Nelson, Jerry Jeff Walker), to the Angloid pop of Ohio (Raspberries, Circus, Rainbow, Left End, Blue Ash, Glass Harp) to the glitter and outrage of New York (the Dolls, Kiss, Blue Oyster Cult). These and dozens of other groups thrived and built national followings in the early years of the decade, with little support from radio but plenty of exposure via the concert circuit, which was becoming a much larger and better organized part of the music industry than ever before.

Aside from blues boogie, the other predominant style was heavy metal, which tended to be harder, louder, and more given to riffs than individual soloing. Other than that, however, it was the same noise, and its leading purveyors included Grand Funk, Alice Cooper, the James Gang, Cactus, Mountain, Kiss, Black Oak Arkansas, Blue Oyster Cult, R. E. O. Speedwagon, Montrose, and Joe Walsh. Oddly enough, the American originators of the style, such as the MC5 and the Stooges, did poorly and eventually broke up.

The popularity of these boogie bands was so entrenched that it acted to prevent new styles from catching on. The glitter movement which swept Britain in 1971–73 should logically have spread across the Atlantic, but such chart-toppers as Slade, Suzi Quatro and T. Rex were virtually ignored in America. The American trendies who flirted with glitter and pop revival (New York Dolls, Raspberries, Big Star, etc.) were never really accepted, although some of the boogie bands did take to wearing makeup and flashier clothes (Kiss, Edgar Winter, Fanny).

The general trend towards commercial pop was impossible to resist, however, and by 1975 most of the top American bands were also regulars on the singles charts, including country rockers (the Eagles, the Ozark Mountain Daredevils, Linda Ronstadt), Southern boogie bands (Allmans, Wet Willie, Lynyrd Skynyrd, Z.Z. Top) and heavy metal bands (Kiss, Fanny, Grand Funk, Styx, Rick Derringer, etc.). Other, less classifiable rock bands from the Doobie

Brothers and Loggins and Messina to Dr Hook and the Medicine Show, have also depended heavily on AM radio exposure, which is probably the most meaningful development in American rock since the late Sixties.

American Spring, originally called Spring, were met with great critical acclaim when their debut album, *American Spring*, was issued by United Artists in 1972. The two sisters, Marilyn Wilson and Diane Rovell, produced by Marilyn's husband Brian Wilson, had been singing together since 1963. As the Honeys (including their cousin Ginger Blake) they had sung background on many early records by the Beach Boys and other surfing groups, in addition to having five singles of their own released. Spring had a light, gentle, subtly produced sound that went over well with their fans but failed to set off the mass following Wilson had envisaged. A subsequent deal with Columbia resulted in a productive recording session in Idaho, but following one fine single ('Shyin' Away') nothing further was issued.

American Television. With the exception of the two years (1965–66) when teenage mania was at such a peak that prime-time rock shows were viable, TV has always confined rock to Saturday afternoon dance formats. Paradoxically, although rock is a considerably bigger industry than, for instance, movies, there are simply not enough rock fans to attract the quantity of viewers (a minimum of 40 million) needed to support a prime-time programme. Thus, television has never supplied the opportunity or the budgets for any attempt to see how far rock could be adapted to the TV medium.

All through the late Sixties, as rock became a more profound influence on American youth, attempts were made to find a suitable format for it on TV. Guest spots on variety shows (such as the *Smothers Brothers Comedy Hour*) were popular, but the new generation of progressive groups found it difficult to get their sound across in a TV studio. In 1969 ABC, always the most experimental network, launched *Music Scene*, presenting a potpourri of rock, comedy and 'progressive' variety in an early evening time slot. The show didn't attract enough viewers, however, and despite a steadily growing mass audience, it was years before TV would take another chance on a rock music show.

Dick Clark, the perennial giant of TV rock, was the first to propose a series devoted to broadcasting live concerts, in 1973. His idea was shelved, but several months later ABC initiated a series of late-night specials under the 'Wide World of Entertainment' banner, among them a rock show entitled *In Concert.* Although Don Kirshner was originally brought in to produce *In Concert*, he turned it over to Dick Clark after the first few shows and went on to launch *Don Kirshner's Rock Concert*, a syndicated package in which he attempted to retain more freedom and realism than the network allowed. The secret of the success of both these shows was the use of late-night time, when the rock audience was a larger share of the overall viewing populace. *In Concert*, which aired at 11.30, gave ABC its highest ratings ever for that time period. Even more successful was NBC's *Midnight Special*, which came on at 1 a.m., an hour at which network broadcasting had previously not existed. With almost no competition, *Midnight Special* did extremely well, with a slick variety-rock format presenting many little-known groups in addition to the second and third echelon artists seen on *In Concert* and *Rock Concert* (because of the low pay scale, few really major artists have appeared on the late-night rock shows).

By 1974, these shows had become an established forum for exposing the hundreds of popular recording groups. Predictably, however, the format became repetitive, and with the added drawback of poor sound reproduction (only *In Concert* had their soundtrack simulcast, over FM stations in larger cities) public interest began to drop. *In Concert* went off the air in early 1975, and the others were expected to follow suit. The growing importance of soul music was reflected in the success of *Soul Train*, in essence a Seventies equivalent to *American Bandstand*.

Amon Duul II include Renate Knaup (vocals), John Weinzier (guitar), Chris Karrer (guitar, violin, sax), Falk Rogner (keyboards), Lothard Meid (bass) and Danny Fischelscher (drums). Formed in 1968 as the musically inclined half of a politico-musical Munich commune, Amon Duul II were the first German group to make an impact in the North Atlantic market. Their music originally owed much to the early Pink Floyd space songs, but Syd Barrett's sense of awe in the face of the Universe was transformed by Amon Duul II into a harsher vision of fearful mysteries lying in wait just beyond the boundaries of normal experience. The solid rock base was complemented by electronic effects and *avant-garde* jazz improvisation, not least in the vocals. The two albums that best exemplified this approach were *Yeti* and *Dance Of The Lemmings* in 1970 and 1971 on Liberty. Since then their music has gained in sophistication but lost, more significantly, much of its eerie power.

Lynn Anderson had her biggest hit with one of the international bestsellers of 1970, 'Rose Garden' (Columbia), a Joe South song. She belongs to a country music family, daughter of RCA artist Liz Anderson and wife of songwriter Glen Sutton. Born in Grand Forks, North Dakota on Sept. 26, 1947, she works out of California but keeps in touch with Nashville. She began recording with Chart Records in 1966, and made the successful switch to Columbia/Epic (for whom she has recorded many hits) in 1970.

Argent was formed in 1969 by Rod Argent (born June 14, 1945), former keyboards player with the Zombies. The other members were Russ Ballard (guitar, vocals, born Oct. 31, 1947) and Robert Henrit (drums, born May 2, 1946), both from the Roulettes and Unit 4+2, and Jim Rodford (bass, born July 7, 1945). The recording of their first album (*Argent*, CBS, 1970, which included 'Liar', later a hit for Three Dog Night) was followed by a lengthy American tour.

Ring Of Hands (1971) and *All Together Now* (1972) saw Argent developing a distinct persona and 'Hold Your Head Up' from the latter was a Top Ten hit on both sides of the Atlantic. On *In Deep* (1973) and *Nexus* (1974), Rod Argent's mellotron and synthesizer playing began to dominate. 'God

Gave Rock And Roll To You' reached the British Top Twenty in 1973.

Following a double live-album (*Encore*, 1974), Ballard left to follow a solo career. He was replaced by John Grimaldi (guitar, born May 25, 1955) and John Verity (vocals, guitar, born May 2, 1944). By 1975 the revised line-up had made two albums, *Circus* (Epic) and *Counterpoints* (RCA).

Arrival began singing together in October 1969 as a four-piece vocal group from Liverpool. Dyan Birch, Carroll Carter, Frank Collins and Paddy McHugh displayed a tight and well-textured vocal combination with a mixture of soul and gospel influences. A record deal with Decca led to hits in 1970 with 'Friends' and 'I Will Survive'. Carroll Carter left the band in 1972 and despite an album, *Arrival*, the following year the group disbanded. Dyan Birch, Paddy McHugh and Frank Collins together with Tony O'Malley, their regular keyboards player, formed the nucleus of Kokomo in 1974 – now a solid eight-piece white soul band recording for CBS.

Ashford and Simpson – Nicholas Ashford and Valerie Simpson – are black singers/songwriters *extraordinaire*. Nick moved from Detroit to New York, meeting Valerie at Harlem's White Rock Church where she sang in the choir and had formed a gospel group, the Followers. Valerie and Nick became a singing duo (recording with Glover) and songwriting team (penning 'Let's Go Get Stoned', eventually a hit for Ray Charles in 1966, and others for Maxine Brown and Chuck Jackson). Signed to Motown Records as staff writers the duo began a fruitful period of working with such as Marvin Gaye ('You're All I Need To Get By') and Diana Ross ('Ain't No Mountain High Enough'), and moving into production before Valerie was eventually launched by Motown as a solo recording artist. Despite two brilliant albums, the critical acclaim wasn't matched in sales. Nick and Valerie left Motown in 1973, to sign with Warner Bros Records, where two albums, *Gimme Something Real* and *I Wanna Be Selfish*, displayed their subtle, warm, sensitive music.

Asylum Records was started by David Geffen (born in New York on Feb. 21, 1943) in 1971 with $400,000 and an artist roster that included Jackson Browne, Jo Jo Gunne, David Blue and Judee Sill. A year later he sold out to Warner Communications for $5 million, though still remaining company president. In July 1973 he took over the running of Elektra Records (also part of Warner Communications) and merged it with the Asylum label, dropping 25 of its 35 recording artists. By this time he had signed the Eagles and Linda Ronstadt to Asylum. Then he spirited Bob Dylan (briefly) away from Columbia and Joni Mitchell from Reprise. In the first year of Geffen's tenure, Elektra-Asylum sales were in excess of $18 million, climbing even higher in subsequent years. In 1975 Geffen moved into films and Joe Smith replaced him as president.

Audience were one of the London-based bands who looked set for success on the thriving college and club scenes of the late Sixties. The group – originally Howard Werth, Trevor Williams, Keith Gemmell and Tony Connor – won critical acclaim with their first two Charisma albums *Friend's Friend's Friend* (1969) and *House On The Hill* (1970) and they built up a large underground following in America as a result of touring with the Faces. However by this time friction between saxophonist Keith Gemmell and the rest of the band was rife and despite the arrival of Nick Judd and top American session men Bobby Keyes and Jim Price for the *Lunch* sessions, this proved to be Audience's final album and only producer Gus Dudgeon and singer Howard Werth succeeded in furthering their own careers when Audience split in 1972.

The Average White Band were six experienced Scottish musicians who had first met and played together in and around the Dundee and Glasgow areas in the mid-Sixties. The members were: Alan Gorrie, bass, lead vocals; Hamish Stuart, guitar, lead vocals; Onnie McIntyre, lead guitar; Robbie McIntosh, drums; Roger Ball, alto and baritone saxes, keyboards; and Malcolm Duncan, tenor and soprano saxes. Formed in 1972, their first real break came playing support to Eric Clapton at his comeback Rainbow performance in January, 1973. The AWB consolidated this success with an impressive debut album, *Show Your Hand* (MCA), a few months later.

Their music is a derivation of modern black soul, their near-perfect recreations as close as any British band has come to emulating the real thing. They bring to mind certain British R&B groups of the mid-Sixties in their striving for authenticity. With their second album *Average White Band* (Atlantic) they broke into the American market in a big way, and spent most of 1974 and 1975 living and touring there. In September 1974 Robbie McIntosh died after an accidental overdose of heroin. The group was stunned. They had always been close friends as well as a well-integrated musical unit. But within a couple of weeks they were back on tour with pick-up drummers, before adding Steve Ferrone. A third, less exceptional but more commercially successful album *Cut The Cake* (1975) followed, introduced to America by a Top Twenty single, 'Pick Up The Pieces'.

Hoyt Axton was born in Oklahoma in 1938. Like his mother, Mae Boren, composer of 'Heartbreak Hotel', he is best known as a songwriter. After a spell as an itinerant folk singer, he co-wrote 'Greenback Dollar' with Ken Ramsey. It was a Top Thirty hit for the Kingston Trio in 1964.

Two of Axton's songs dealing with drug abuse – 'The Pusher' and 'Snowblind Friend' – were recorded by Steppenwolf, the former appearing on the best-selling *Easy Rider* soundtrack album. Later pop single hits came with 'Joy To The World' (Three Dog Night) and 'No No Song' (Ringo Starr), while 'Never Been To Spain' is perhaps his most-recorded song.

Axton's compositions span the divide between folk, country and rock, with the result that over thirty artists have recorded his material, ranging from Tiny Tim to Joan Baez. He has cut a dozen albums as a solo artist, most recently for A&M.

Kevin Ayers, founder member of Soft Machine and self-confessed professional eccentric, was born in Malaya on August 16, 1945. He began his solo career with the Harvest album *Joy Of A Toy* (1969). It contained the themes which have remained central to his work, presented with subversive wit and frequently disturbing effect: dreams, relationships with the audience, and personal relationships.

In 1970 he formed The Whole World, including Lol Coxhill, David Bedford and Mike Oldfield, the first of a series of freewheeling agglomerations such as Banana Follies (1973) and the Soporifics (1974) which have contained many of the key figures of the British *avant-garde*, among them Steve Hillage, Archie Leggett, Robert Wyatt, and Ollie Halsall. An erratic performer, he has also guested with Gong and Henry Cow, while continuing to represent the spirit of 1967 as in songs like 'Stranger In Blue Suede Shoes' from *Whatevershebringswesing* (1971), though often despairing of its viability as in 'Shouting In A Bucket Blues' from *Bananamour* (1973). In 1974 he moved to Island and recorded *The Confessions Of Dr Dream*, containing a remake of his classic 'It Begins With A Blessing . . .', and teamed up with the disparate talents of John Cale, Eno and Nico for a concert at London's Rainbow Theatre which yielded a live album *June 1, 1974*. A cult figure with a strong European following, he continues to record and tour occasionally.

Bachman Turner Overdrive. Randy Bachman was a founder member of the Guess Who, their lead guitarist and the songwriter responsible for their long string of hits. His last, 'American Woman', was still riding the charts when he quit in 1970. With bass player CF (Fred) Turner and brother Robbie Bachman on drums, he teamed up with the original Guess Who singer (when they were Chad Allan and the Expressions), Chad Allan, to form Brave Belt. They made two albums for Warner Bros, dabbling in the country end of rock, the second with Tim Bachman replacing Allan. Both were indifferently received and it was only after some persuasion that Mercury signed the group with a third album already in the can which was released under the name of

Bachman Turner Overdrive. Within a year they'd notched up monster hits 'Takin' Care of Business' (1973), 'You Ain't Seen Nothing Yet' (1974), and 'Let It Ride' (1975) – all compelling examples of the pop end of the heavy-rock spectrum – and had seen *BTO* (1973) and *BTO II* (1973) go gold.

Tim Bachman departed and the group brought in guitarist and sex symbol – the rest of them are somewhat overweight – Blair Thornton. Things went from better to better still with two more platinum albums, *Not Fragile* (1974) and *Four Wheel Drive* (1974). BTO give their audiences what they want. They work hard, put themselves about a lot, giving out massive doses of primal energy lapped up by millions. They laugh all the way to the bank and back again with a philosophy that a rock group's life span is short – so make the most of it while you can.

Badfinger. During the Beatles' eclipse the public (particularly in America) took Badfinger to its bosom as a reincarnation of the moptops. In fact only two of the group – Tom Evans and Joe Molland, both born in 1947 – were Liverpudlians; the others – Pete Ham (born April 27, 1947) and Mike Gibbins (born in 1949) – came from Swansea. But they had played at the Cavern (as the Iveys) and, in 1970, they had Top Ten hits with McCartney's 'Come and Get It' and their own 'No Matter What'.

1971 and 1972 saw them in the Top Twenty with 'Day After Day' and 'Baby Blue' respectively, but the group fell out of favour following their move to Warner Bros in 1973. By 1975, when Pete Ham, the group's founder and chief songwriter committed suicide, Badfinger had all but been forgotten by the record-buying public.

Barclay James Harvest. In spite of their perseverance and the fashionably opulent presentation of their work, Barclay James Harvest have remained a cult band since their formation in 1967 – probably one reason for this has been their refusal to leave Manchester.

The group – Woolley Wolstenholme (keyboards, vocals,

born April 15, 1947), Melvin Pritchard (drums, born Jan. 20, 1948), Les Holroyd (bass, born March 12, 1948) and John Lees (guitar, born Jan. 13, 1948) were one of the first bands to use mellotron. On selected gigs they also presented their own orchestra.

Despite being launched on the new Harvest label, which was reputedly named after them, and winning large critical acclaim with their second album *Once Again* (1971), the band's classically oriented music never really found favour with large audiences. In 1973 front liners Woolley Wolstenholme and John Lees embarked on solo projects but in 1975 the group's new album *Time Honoured Ghosts* (Polydor), which was produced by Elliot Mazer, saw them once more progressing musically.

Mike Batt, born Feb. 6, 1950, rose from staff songwriter to A&R manager at Liberty Records, producing the Groundhogs' first album and Hapshash And The Coloured Coat's psychedelic noises. Eventually he went independent to produce a series of cheap orchestral albums of Beatles/Stones material, a synthesizer album, and advertising jingles, etc. Success came early in the Seventies when he wrote the theme for Elizabeth Beresford's creation *The Wombles*, a British TV series featuring woolly creatures who won millions of kids' hearts collecting litter on Wimbledon Common. The record was a hit, and Batt churned out Wombles records – possibly Britain's only genuine bubblegum – in a wide variety of pastiches on CBS: 'Wombles Beach Party' (surf), 'Wombling White Tie And Tails' (Fred Astaire), a Womble minuet, Womble rock'n'roll, 'Superwomble' . . .

Despite singing, playing piano, producing and arranging all the Wombles records, Batt's own 1975 hit, 'Summertime City' – more clever, disposable pop, another TV theme – marked the first time his name and face became well known.

The Bay City Rollers are, with Sweet, the only British pop phenomenon of the Seventies to have found success in America. All the group – Derek Longmuir (drums, born March 19, 1955), Alan Longmuir (bass, born June 20, 1953),

Eric Faulkner (guitar, Oct. 21, 1955), Stuart 'Woody' Wood (guitar, Feb. 25, 1957) and Leslie McKeown (vocals, Nov. 12, 1955) – were born in Edinburgh where, under the management of Tam Paton, they secured a series of residencies in 1969–70 reproducing Top Twenty hits. In 1971 they were signed to Bell Records and secured a Top Ten hit with their Jonathan King-produced version of the Gentrys hit 'Keep On Dancin''.

Subsequent records, produced by King and by Howard and Blaikley, failed, and it was not until they were united with Bill Martin and Phil Coulter, who had previously specialized in Eurovision Song Contest numbers (Sandie Shaw's 'Puppet On A String', 1967, Cliff Richard's 'Congratulations', 1968, and Dana's 'All Kinds Of Everything', 1970), in 1974 with 'Remember', that they again entered the charts. In the interim period, two original members of the group, John Devine (guitar) and Nobby Clarke (vocals), left and Tam Paton created an image for the group by adapting the clothes worn by football's 'bovver boys' and emphasizing their Scottish origins through an excessive use of tartan. The result was a string of Top Ten hits, 'Shang-A-Lang', 'Summerlove Sensation' and 'All Of Me Loves All Of You', and a growing teenybopper following that by the end of the year was comparable to that of the Osmonds.

In 1975 they switched producers again, to Phil Wainman, and the first single under his direction, a re-make of the Four Seasons' 'Bye Bye Baby' which crystallized the group's light pop sound, was an immediate No. 1. Suddenly, the Rollers were the pop sensation of the year, selling albums (*Once Upon A Star*, *Bay City Rollers*), singles ('Give A Little Love') and photographs and mementoes of themselves in vast quantities. Everything they did, be it a car accident or a near riot at one of their shows, was news, and they spawned a whole host of imitations, most of whom lacked even the basic musical abilities of the Rollers. In 1976, against all predictions, the release of 'Saturday Night' gave them a No. 1 American single hit on Arista, and *Bay City Rollers* entered the Top Twenty of the album charts there.

Jeff Beck. When Eric Clapton left the Yardbirds in March, 1965, the Tridents' lead guitarist, Jeff Beck (born in Surrey on June 24, 1944), was recommended by Jimmy Page to replace him. He remained with the group until December, 1966 and contributed much to the 'new' sound of the Yardbirds on records like 'Shapes Of Things' and 'Over Under Sideways Down' (Columbia, 1966), experimenting with electronic sounds and exploring Eastern as well as Western influences. He formed his own Jeff Beck Group with Rod Stewart (vocals), Ron Wood (bass) and Ray Cook (drums), who was replaced by Mickey Waller following a disastrous debut on a Roy Orbison/Small Faces package tour in March, 1967 from which the group was immediately removed. During the next two and a half years the group – subsequently joined by Nicky Hopkins (keyboards) – released two albums, *Truth* (Columbia, 1968) and *Beck-Ola* (1969), and earned a strong reputation in America. Beck's plans to re-form the group with Stewart and Vanilla Fudge's Tim Bogart (bass) and Carmine Appice (drums) fell through and a car smash forced him to retire for some eighteen months before a second Jeff Beck Group appeared in 1971 with *Rough And Ready* (Epic) and new personnel: Bob Tench (vocals), Max Middleton (piano), Clive Chaman (bass), and Cozy Powell (drums). The break-up of Bogart and Appice's band, Cactus, led to the formation of Beck, Bogart and Appice in 1972. An album and a tour later, Beck was again solo, returning in 1975 with his best playing for several years on *Blow By Blow*, produced by George Martin.

Bell Records began as the record outlet of Columbia Pictures in the mid-Fifties, releasing mainly jazz and show tunes. It was the subsidiaries Mala and Amy that went after the rock and R&B market.

Bell's hits included 'Little Girl' by the Syndicate of Sound, and James and Bobby Purify's 'I'm Your Puppet', through an arrangement with Dan Penn and Spooner Oldham that brought them many more R&B hits over the next few years. Other R&B masters were obtained from Marshall Sehorn in New Orleans and Goldwax in Memphis, while many odd singles from all parts of the world found their way onto the Bell label. Merrilee Rush's 'Angel of the Morning' was Bell's biggest hit of 1968, while Amy with Del Shannon and Lee Dorsey, and Mala with Ronny and the Daytonas and the Box Tops, did well through the mid-Sixties. Towards the end of the Sixties, most sub-labels (including Maxx, New Voice, Page One and many smaller ones) were discontinued, and from that point Bell became perhaps America's most prolific pop singles label.

Headed by Larry Uttal (who had run Madison Records in the early Sixties before coming to Bell), they released over 650 singles between 1969 and the label's demise in 1974. Few artists were ever signed to or developed by Bell; it was one of those companies, like 20th Century under Russ Regan today, that survives by putting out so many cheaply purchased masters that a few inevitably become hits. Most of Bell's hits in the early Seventies (Crazy Elephant, Fifth Dimension, the Bay City Rollers, the Stampeders, etc.) came through deals with production companies or foreign labels. Distribution of Big Tree Records (April Wine, Lobo, Brownsville Station) and the licensing of Mickie Most's RAK productions (Sweet, Mud, Peter Noone, Suzi Quatro) added substance to the label, while David Cassidy and the Partridge Family kept profits flowing. Melissa Manchester, Alvin Stardust, Barry Blue, Mungo Jerry, Gary Glitter, the Drifters and the Troggs were also on Bell towards the end, and several big hits including 'Seasons in the Sun' by Terry Jacks, 'Mandy' by Barry Manilow and 'Emma' by Hot Chocolate, plus many by Tony Orlando and Dawn, kept things afloat until Clive Davis, who took over in the spring of 1974, could complete the changeover to Arista, as the label became in early 1975 and pursue a policy of 'rock' (Patti Smith, Eric Anderson) rather than 'pop' signings. Uttal, who left when Davis came in, subsequently launched a label of his own called Private Stock, taking along much of his Bell staff, and has done quite well.

In England, under the direction of Dick Leahy, Bell had a similar policy and released many good, ephemeral pop records. Leahy left in 1974 along with Uttal, later going to GTO Records.

Archie Bell and the Drells played together in Houston, Texas, even releasing a single on the local Ovid label – before topping the American charts with the largely instrumental 'Tighten Up' (Atlantic) in 1968. It was a rhythmic, if unspectacular, dance disc. Under the auspices of Gamble and Huff, the hits kept coming for the group – Archie, born in Henderson, Texas in 1946, brother Lee Bell, Willie Parnell and James Wise – 'I Can't Stop Dancing', 'Do The Choo Choo', 'There's Gonna Be A Showdown' (1968) and 'You're Too Young' (1969). When Gamble and Huff lost interest, Atlantic tried other producers with less success. In 1974 the group briefly moved to Henry Stone's Glades label but in 1975 they re-signed with Gamble and Huff's TSOP label.

Maggie Bell was born in Glasgow on Jan. 12, 1945. With a singing style heavily influenced by soul and blues, she joined the Power, a local group led by Alex Harvey's brother Leslie. Signed in 1969 by Led Zeppelin manager Peter Grant, their name was changed to Stone The Crows. Two albums for Polydor – *Stone The Crows* and *Ode To John Law* – followed, with Colin Allen (drums), Jim Dewar (bass) and John McGinniss (keyboards).

In 1971, Ronnie Leahy and Steve Thompson replaced McGinniss and Dewar as Bell was being acclaimed as the most powerful female singer in Britain, with the inevitable comparisons with Janis Joplin. *Teenage Licks*, in the same year, was the most assured album to date, but in between sessions for *Ontinuous Performance* (1972), Harvey was killed in an on-stage accident at Swansea.

Maggie Bell determined to carry on, bringing in Jimmy McCullough after an abortive attempt to lure Peter Green back into live performance. Stone The Crows split in 1973, since when Bell has released two solo albums – *Queen Of The Night* (1973) and *Suicide Sal* (1975), the former produced by Jerry Wexler.

Thom Bell. Soul music has seen few more intriguing developments than the infusion of 'classical' orchestrations into the hovering soft vocal styles which were the direct successor of the Fifties doowop groups. Thom Bell, more than any other single producer/arranger recognized the full potential of this synthesis and thus broadened the whole spectrum of the black music experience. Born in Philadelphia, Bell came from a middle-class background and grew up studying classical piano and playing 'serious music' with his brother and sister.

In 1959 he teamed up with a school friend, Kenny Gamble, and recorded a vocal duet for Jerry Ross's Heritage label. It flopped, but a seed had been sown. Bell then joined Kenny Gamble's Romeos, playing little clubs and doing some recording (for Jimmy Bishop's Arctic Records). They were to become the nucleus of Philly's famed MFSB session band. While doing session work at Cameo Records the young Bell was brought a vocal group by Stan Watson – the Delfonics. Bell's productions and arrangements for the group (discs on Moon Shot and Cameo) were unsuccessful but when Cameo went bust, Watson formed a label of his own – Philly Groove. Suddenly Bell's Delfonics productions for Philly Groove proved immensely successful. Smashes like 'La La Means I Love You' and 'Break Your Promise' (1968) poured forth. In 1969 Bell teamed up with the flourishing production team of Gamble/Huff and his arrangements for acts like Jerry Butler brought more success. Teaming up with a French lyricist, Linda Creed, Bell began to write a series of beautiful new songs for his next major venture, the Stylistics, whom Avco commissioned him to arrange for and produce in 1971. 'Stop Look And Listen', 'You Are Everything' (1971), 'Betcha By Golly, Wow', 'Stone In Love With You' (1972): the string of quivering falsetto-led hits continued. At the same time, Bell did some of Gamble/Huff's arrangements (including stunning charts for the O'Jays) and produced such Columbia acts as Ronnie Dyson and Johnny Mathis. Another run of hit productions occurred with the Spinners (Atlantic hitting gold from 1972 with 'I'll Be Around' through to 1975 with 'Games People Play').

Thom Bell still seems capable of exerting aesthetic judgement over the use of lush orchestrations in soul and has seldom descended to the vapid muzak of his imitators. That maintenance of real artistic integrity is Bell's ultimate triumph.

Marc Benno. In spite of the encouragement he received from Rita Coolidge, David Anderle and friends in Hollywood, Marc Benno (born in Dallas, Texas on July 1, 1947) faded into obscurity after the release of *Asylum Choir II* (Phillips, 1971) with Leon Russell.

He settled briefly in Los Angeles but soon returned home to Dallas and later moved to Austin, recording three patchy solo albums on A&M. The last, *Ambush*, was co-written with his brother Irvin (who later committed suicide). He recorded an album with a Texan band, the Nightcrawlers, but A&M dropped him and failed to issue it.

Benno worked on sessions with Georgie Fame and then moved to Northern Carolina where he worked with John Collins before returning to Hollywood to put a band together for Bonnie Bramlett in early 1975. However, he has yet to match the artistic success of his first album, *Look Inside The Asylum Choir* (Mercury, 1968).

Big Star was formed out of the remnants of the Box Tops and other stalwarts of the local Memphis pop scene in 1972. The group was the most successful product of Ardent Studios, which in three years produced several excellent records by other groups such as Cargoe and the Hot Dogs on the Ardent label. All these groups, and the producers and musicians who made up the Ardent crew, shared a deep interest in British pop, banding together to form a small minority in the predominantly black-oriented Memphis recording scene.

The first Big Star album, *No. 1 Record* (1972), featuring Alex Chilton's Byrds-like vocals and the distinctive tunes of co-leader Chris Bell, with Andy Hummel (bass) and Jody Stephens (drums), was a critical success, and Big Star became one of the city's most popular live attractions. They suffered a setback following Bell's departure (a result of personality conflict) but came back with an interesting second album, *Radio City*. Sales on both were poor, however, and three impressive singles ('When My Baby's Beside Me', 'Don't Lie To Me', and 'September Girls') failed to take off, which along with other factors led to the group's disbanding when the Ardent label folded in 1975. A solo album by Chilton remains unissued.

Black Oak Arkansas comprises Jim Dandy (vocals, born March 30, 1948, in Black Oak, Arkansas), Stanley Knight (guitar, born in Little Rock, Arkansas, on Feb. 12, 1949), 'Little' Jimmy Henderson (lead guitar, born in Jackson, Mississippi on May 20, 1954), Pat Daugherty (bass, born in Jonesboro, Arkansas, on Nov. 11, 1947), Tommy Aldridge (drums, born in Nashville, Tennessee, on Aug. 15, 1950) and Rickie Lee Reynolds (guitar, born in Manilla, Arkansas, on Oct. 28, 1948). Formed in 1964, the group only took the name Black Oak Arkansas when they moved to Los Angeles in 1969. Signed to Atlantic in 1970 after a brief spell with Stax (*The Knowbody Else*, 1969), they released a clutch of crude Southern Boogie albums including *Keep The Faith* (1971) and *Raunch'n'Roll Live* (1973) and toured extensively, before the Richard Podolor-produced *High On The Hog* (1974) gave them their first gold album. A communal band – their songs are credited to the band and they all live in 'Heaven', Arkansas – their records and stage act, which features Dandy's machismo histrionics, have endeared them to teenage audiences. *Ain't Life Grand* (1975) suggested a mellowing of the group's sound.

Black Sabbath are consummate masters of singleminded apocalyptic heavy metal rock. They comprise Geezer Butler, bass (born July 17, 1949), Tony Iommi, guitar (Feb. 19, 1948), Bill Ward, drums (May 5, 1948), and Ozzie Osbourne, vocals (Dec. 3, 1948). All from Aston, Birmingham, they changed their name from Earth in 1969 to launch upon an astonished world an act remarkable for its use of sheer volume, extreme musical simplicity and overtones of black magic.

Touring Europe for a year, Sabbath returned to Britain in 1970 with a first album *Black Sabbath* (Vertigo) which with a single, 'Paranoid', became an instant hit. *Black Sabbath* set the format for the albums which followed one a year until 1974. Musically it consisted of sub-Cream power chords and riffs delivered with sledge-hammer relentlessness; lyrically it combined the themes of atomic war, death, doom and destruction, with drugs and teenage revolt. The group's appeal, particularly in America, based upon a one-to-one identification with a young audience defied a barrage of negative criticism and virtually no radio air-play to gain the band gold albums – notably *Masters Of Reality* (1971) and *Sabbath Bloody Sabbath* (WWA, 1973) – and sell-out audiences for their almost non-stop world tours, until their semi-retirement in mid-1974, the year when their management company World Wide Artists collapsed. In 1975 Black Sabbath, the precursors of Blue Oyster Cult, returned with a sixth album *Sabotage* (NEMS) and toured America and Britain.

Bloodstone. Charles McCormick, Henry Williams, Charles Love and Williss Draffen all grew up together in Kansas City. They worked as the Sinceres, before moving to Los Angeles where they recorded for Pzazz Records. Returning to Kansas and learning instruments, they moved into Sly-influenced black rock with a new name, Bloodstone. Coming to Britain in 1972, unknown and unrecorded, they appeared on a soul package and created a storm. Subsequently signed to English Decca, their first album was a disaster but their second, brilliantly produced at Chipping Norton by Mike Vernon, brought forth a classic sweet soul ballad, 'Natural High', a double million-seller in America in 1973. Their follow-up albums, *Unreal* and *Riddle Of The Sphinx*, have also been successful in the soul market.

Blue Magic, a sweet-voiced Philly Sound vocal group, was formed out of the Topics and another Philadelphia group Shades Of Love. The group comprises Theodore 'Ted' Mills, Vernon and Wendell Sawyer, Keith Beaton, and Richard Pratt. Signed to an indie production company, WMOT Inc, in 1973, and produced by MFSB guitarist Norman Harris, they succeeded with a series of outstanding soul hits for Atco Records including 'Look Me Up', 'Sideshow' (a million-seller) and 'Three Ring Circus'. On often outstanding songs, Ted Mills' poignant falsetto clearly showed that the sweet soul genre could avoid the cloying saccharin excesses of the Stylistics.

Blue Öyster Cult, originally the Soft White Underbelly, were formed in 1970 in New York under the auspices of *Crawdaddy* critic Sandy Pearlman. They went out on the road, joined and left Elektra, and eventually were signed by Columbia. The group – Donald (Buck Dharma) Roeser, lead guitar, vocals; Eric Bloom, stun guitar, synthesizer; Albert Bouchard, drums, vocals; Joe Bouchard, bass vocals and Allen Lanier, rhythm guitar, keyboards – quickly gained a deserved reputation as *the* intelligent heavy-metal band, partly through their relationship with Pearlman and critic and occasional lyricist Richard Meltzer, partly through their use of extravagant symbolism in their stage act and on their album covers. Their lyrics have always been undecipherable, apart from title lines like 'OD'd On Life Itself' and 'Hot Rails To Hell'; the music, at its best on *Blue Öyster Cult* (1972) and *Tyranny And Mutation* (1973), is quintessential heavy-metal – layers of vicious guitar riffs over a thudding rhythm section, growled and screeched vocals.

Once called 'a portable Altamont', they themselves attribute their music to the 'primal paranoia' in the air. Certainly, with the odd exception like the lyrical 'Last Days Of May' on their first album, their music has little of the light or sense of joy possessed by their predecessors, Cream and Jimi Hendrix. It is usually fast, always powerful and clear, like a well-tuned motorcycle.

Colin Blunstone, born June 24, 1945, enjoyed early success as lead singer with the Zombies. When the group broke up in 1967 he quit the music business, returning only to re-cut the Zombies classic 'She's Not There' and to record for Decca as Neil MacArthur, before his eventual re-emergence as a solo singer with *One Year* (Epic) in 1971 and the hit single, 'Say You Don't Mind', the following year. The formation of a permanent backing group – Pete Wingfield (piano), Derek Griffiths (guitar), Terry Poole (bass), Jim Toomey (drums) – caused a divergence between his recorded work, which tended towards lush arrangements to highlight his airy, floating vocals, and his live performances fronting a band that wanted to rock more than he did. He broke up the band, after the release of *Journey* in 1974, to work alone.

Bob and Marcia. In 1969 Bob Andy, a Jamaican music veteran of the bluebeat/rock steady era and sugar-voiced Marcia Griffiths recorded a reggae version of Nina Simone's plea for black awareness, 'Young Gifted And Black'. It was an international million-seller. Andy had had solo West Indies hits as far back as 1962 with 'I Want To Go Back Home' before signing with the leading rock steady group The Paragons (John Holt's former group). His later teaming with Marcia Griffiths was distinctly pop oriented with British dubbed strings on, for example, 'Pied Piper', their British Top Twenty hit of 1971. Soon afterwards the singers went solo again.

Andy (real name Keith Anderson) cut *Songbook*, an album of his own material, while Griffiths recorded sophisticated reggae tunes like 'Play Me', 'Questions' and the *Sweet Bitter Love* album. She also spent some time in I Three, the female back-up chorus for the Wailers.

Curt Boetcher first enjoyed success as the producer of the first Association album *And Then . . . Along Comes The Association* (1966). Since that time, he has produced a number of minor classics which are notable for their finely wrought harmonies. As a performer, Boetcher (he changed his name from Boettcher after being told it was a 'jinx'), was leader of Sagittarius and the Millennium, both harmony-based groups with good reviews and low sales, and in 1972 released a solo album for Elektra, *There's An Innocent Face*.

Also, he can be heard on several dozen obscure singles as backing vocalist and vocal arranger.

As a producer, apart from the Association, he has worked with Tommy Roe, Song (a group led by Mickey Rooney Junior), and Emitt Rhodes, as well as many lesser names. As an entrepreneur, Boetcher was one of the three founders of Together Records, with Gary Usher and Keith Olsen. The label operated for about three years from 1969, released a number of important archive records, such as *Preflyte*, the first Byrds' recording, *The Hillmen* (featuring Chris Hillman) and such anthology albums as *Early L.A.*, containing contributions from Canned Heat, the Dillards and the Byrds.

Marc Bolan, born on July 30, 1947, in London as Mark Feld, was a leading Mod and occasional male model in the early Sixties. He changed his name to Bolan for his first record, 'The Wizard' (Decca, 1965), after which he briefly joined John's Children and then formed Tyrannosaurus Rex with Steve Peregrine Took (percussion, born July 28, 1949, in London) in 1967, which rapidly became an underground cult band. With Took, he recorded three albums, *My People Were Fair And Had Sky In Their Hair But Now They're Content To Wear Stars On Their Brows* (Regal Zonophone, 1968), *Prophets, Seers And Sages, The Angels Of The Ages* (1969) and *Unicorn* (1969), all a mixture of flower-power philosophy and magic. During this period Bolan also published a book of poetry.

In 1970, Took left and was replaced by Mickey Finn (congas, born June 3, 1947) with whom Bolan recorded *Beard Of Stars* (1970). On that album Bolan began to make the transition to electric guitar, a process that was accelerated when later that year, having shortened the group's name to T. Rex, Bolan had a surprise No. 2 hit with 'Ride A White Swan' (Fly). He immediately added a drummer, Bill Legend (born May 8, 1944 in Essex) and bassist, Steve Currie (born May 21, 1947 in Grimsby), and aimed his next single, 'Hot Love', directly at the emerging teenybopper audience.

A British No. 1, 'Hot Love' was followed by a string of nine successive Top Ten records, including 'Get It On'

(1971) – this record, which featured back-up vocals from Mark Volman and Howard Kaylan, was Bolan's only substantial American hit when it appeared under the title of 'Bang A Gong' on Reprise in 1972 – 'Telegram Sam', 'Children Of The Revolution' (T. Rex, 1972) and '20th Century Boy' (EMI-Marc, 1973) and a stream of albums. Each single consolidated Bolan's temporary preeminence in the British world of glam and glitter rock. However, unlike Bowie, then mining the same genre, Bolan brought neither perception nor mystery to his work and by the end of 1973, when his teenybopper audience began deserting him for more exciting images like Slade, his songs and his act became even more hysterical. He attempted a series of comebacks but seemed unlikely to re-establish himself as the teenage guru.

Ken Boothe, born in Denham Town, Jamaica, in 1949, recorded as one half of the Stranger (Cole) and Ken duo in the Sixties before scoring solo – as 'Mr Rock Steady' – with 'Puppet On A String' (1967) and the reggae anthem 'Freedom Street' (1970). With albums *Black, Gold And Green* (1973) and *Let's Get It On* (1974), Boothe achieved idol status amongst West Indian girls in Britain, leading to a No. 1 pop hit with 'Everything I Own' (Trojan, 1975). Further efforts such as 'Let's Go' and 'Crying Over You' have consolidated his popularity in the reggae and pop markets.

David Bowie, born in London on Jan. 8, 1947 as David Jones, started his musical career playing tenor saxophone for a school group at the age of fifteen. A year later he was in a progressive blues group, the Lower Third, until, 'frustrated by amps', he went solo with an acoustic guitar and recorded a series of confessional love songs sung in an Anthony Newley style for Decca; these were re-released in 1973 as *Images 1966–67*.

The music didn't set the world on fire, and Bowie dropped out of the music business for almost two years, pursuing his involvement with Buddhism almost to the point of a head-shave, and writing and performing for Lindsay Kemp's mime company. In 1969 he went out again with a guitar and started an arts lab in Beckenham to 'try and promote the ideals and creative processes of the underground'. At the same time he recorded the mysterious 'Space Oddity' for Mercury, which surprisingly became an international hit. However, Bowie, going on tour as a support act, did not enjoy the experience, and went back to his one-man show in Beckenham.

So by the turn of the decade there was little sign of the superstar to come. The ingredients of his music, though, were slowly gathering, and the ideological themes of the *Space Oddity* album would be followed, in a logical enough way, right through to the Orwellian cataclysm of *Diamond Dogs* in 1974. The ideals of the Underground provided the social framework, the commitment to change. Buddhism supplied the paradoxes and vicious circles that made a mockery of those hopes. His interest in mime suggests the theatrical context in which the themes would be presented. An actor in a society both unchangeable and unacceptable. From 1969 onwards Bowie was aimed towards 1984.

The music to complement the vision – that is always how Bowie has seen music – was also coming together. His second, and last, album for Mercury, *The Man Who Sold The World* (1970), featured Mick Ronson and Mick Woodmansey on guitar and drums; they would later form his backing group with Trevor Bolder. *The Man Who Sold The World* was a far cry fom the acoustic *Space Oddity*, featuring music dark and heavy, Ronson's vicious guitar riffs and a spacey moog, Bowie's voice at its coldest and most metallic. The music suited the subjects: outsiders drifting on the edge of sanity, through a netherworld of sexual doubts and death-wishes.

The album started a cult following for Bowie, particularly in America which he toured as a latter-day Garbo, complete with long dresses and flowing hair. But a cult following was not what he wanted, and the next album saw the pendulum wrenched violently to the other extreme. *Hunky Dory* (1971), the first RCA album, saw his voice at its warmest and his tunes at their most melodic. It was still a tortured vision but it didn't *sound* it. And it started the bandwagon rolling in earnest. By early 1972 Bowie was the coming star. He had the image and the album ready to make the most of it. Not that *The Rise And Fall Of Ziggy Stardust And The Spiders From Mars* (1972) was anything other than an artistic advance on the earlier albums. The diverse personae struggling for precedence in his previous work were all subsumed in the doomed figure of Ziggy, Bowie's solution to the paradox of a life both unchangeable and unacceptable, the rock'n' roll star who stood outside the problem and so could solve it. Musically it claimed the middle ground between *The Man Who Sold The World* and *Hunky Dory*, between acid-rock and pop, heavy and accessible. Image-wise it turned Bowie into Ziggy, the bisexual astronaut from another world, both harbinger of doom and prophet of extravagance.

Ziggy Stardust was to be the first of four monolithic concept albums, over all of which hovered this spectre of doom. *Aladdin Sane* (1973) was Bowie's most fully realized album, showcasing all his talents and few of his faults. The lyrics were clear and insightful, rather than spectacularly obscure, and Bowie's musical eclecticism served as a springboard rather than as an end in itself. Above all, Mick Ronson was finally let off the leash, conjuring out of his guitar the necessary blind power to set beside Bowie's driving vocals.

Aladdin Sane viewed the disintegration of world society from the vantage point of an American tour; *Pin-Ups* demonstrated the process by dressing up the hopes of mid-Sixties British music in a 1975 guise. Thus, for example, the Kinks' 'Where Have All The Good Times Gone' was given a resonance beyond mere nostalgia. *Diamond Dogs* (1974) was the culmination of this phase; a musical re-working of Orwell's *1984*, that sorely missed the departed Ronson's guitar. Despite its limitations it presented Bowie's vision at its most acute, tying together the themes of the previous years. Ziggy's spaceman-rock hero-saviour mutates into the doomed figure of Orwell's Winston Smith.

The bisexual astronaut tours of 1972–73 became the Bowie Armageddon extravaganza of 1974, with the star in powder-blue Oxford bags singing of the end of it all beneath vast theatrical props of the urban desert.

Since then Bowie has changed course, using the Philadelphia soul sound for *Young Americans* (1975) which contained two American hits, the title song and 'Fame'. These singles flopped in Britain where re-releases of 'Life On Mars' (from *Hunky Dory*) and 'Space Oddity' were big hits. By 1975, too, he had turned his attention to acting, starring in Nicholas Roeg's *The Man Who Fell To Earth*, after which he returned to both the British and American charts with 'Golden Years' and *Station To Station*.

David Bowie remains one of the very few rock performers of the Seventies to have convincingly cut across age and genre boundaries, to have produced music both danceable and possessed of genuine vision.

Joe Boyd is an American producer who made his name in the late Sixties and early Seventies when his management/production company Witchseason became synonymous with the beginnings of British folk/rock. The stable of artists included Fairport Convention, Fotheringay, John Martyn, Nick Drake, Incredible String Band and Dr Strangely Strange. Boyd was responsible for producing several key albums around 1970, notably John and Beverley Martin's *Stormbringer*. He took the duo to the States to renew contact with East Coast musicians like Levon Helm, John Simon and Paul Harris.

In 1971 he returned to the States for good to head Warner Bros film division in Burbank, leaving a void that was never filled. Fairport Convention, in particular, suffered with Boyd no longer producing after *Full House*. Nowadays he picks and chooses his projects when time permits but still favours working with folk-based musicians. Boyd produced Maria Muldaur's best-selling albums as well as working more recently with her former husband Geoff. He remains one of the most creative back room men in rock today.

Bread was a Los Angeles soft-rock harmony group which racked up six gold albums in a career lasting less than four years from 1969 when it was founded by three session men – David Gates from Tulsa, Oklahoma, James Griffin from Memphis, Tennessee, and Robb Royer. Gates had previously produced an album by Pleasure Faire, a group which included Royer and for which Griffin had written songs. All were multi-instrumentalists and prolific songwriters in that professional manner which at its best can marry the emotional power of rock with the smoothness of mainstream balladry. After an unsuccessful but critically acclaimed first album for Elektra, the hits started coming: 'Make It With You' (1970), 'If' (later recycled by TV cop Telly Savalas), 'Baby I'm-A Want You' (1971), 'The Guitar Man' (1972) and others mostly featured Gates' high, pure and countryish tenor.

After using Jim Gordon on drums for the first album, Mike Botts from Sacramento, California, joined as permanent percussionist. Between the third and fourth albums (*Manna*, 1971 and *Baby I'm A Want You*, 1972), Royer left to be replaced by veteran session keyboards man Larry Knechtel. Following one more album (*Guitar Man*, 1972), the group dissolved following disagreements between Griffin and Gates, both of whom became solo artists.

Brewer and Shipley are a close harmony duo best known for their 1971 song 'One Toke Over The Line', which was eventually banned from the airwaves because of its drug connotations. Teaming up as songwriters in the late Sixties, Mike Brewer (born in Oklahoma in 1944) and Tom Shipley (born in Ohio in 1942) cut an uneventful album for A&M before moving to Kama Sutra and San Francisco producer Nick Gravenites. *Weeds* (1970) and *Tarkio* (1971) were fine examples of Bay Area soft rock with backings by Nicky Hopkins, Jerry Garcia, Mark Nataflin and Red Rhodes.

Based in rural Missouri, Brewer and Shipley cut two more albums for Kama Sutra – *Shake Off The Demon* (1971) and *Rural Space* (1972) – before moving to Capitol in 1974.

Brinsley Schwarz were Nick Lowe, bass; Bob Andrews, keyboards; Billy Rankin, drums; Ian Gomm, guitar and

Brinsley himself, guitar and sax. The nucleus of the group came from Kippington Lodge, an unsuccessful harmony group that was signed to EMI's Parlophone label in the mid-Sixties by Mark Wirtz. In 1970, on the verge of collapse, they signed a management contract as Brinsley Schwarz with Famepushers who signed them to British Liberty/UA with the biggest piece of hype in rock's recent history: they flew the British press to witness the group's debut at New York's Fillmore East. The hype failed – though, ironically, the album that accompanied it, *Brinsley Schwarz* (Liberty, 1970) which was an uneasy mixture of 'heavy' blues and Crosby, Stills and Nash type harmonies, turned out to be their biggest seller.

However, after a promising second album, the aptly titled *Despite It All* (1970), they came back with two magnificent albums, *Silver Pistol* (UA, 1971) and *Nervous On The Road* (1972). The change stemmed from the band's assimilation of influences seemingly as diverse as the Band and New Orleans R&B, Nick Lowe's development as a songwriter and singer, the addition of Ian Gomm on guitar which thickened their sound and the group's renewed pleasure in playing (tightly and disciplined) together that accompanied their pioneering discovery of the pub circuit then opening up in London. But, though those and subsequent albums – *Please Don't Ever Change* (1973) and *The New Favourites Of . . .* (1974) – were critically well received, they didn't sell.

In 1975, tired of the endless touring, either as the support act to groups far worse than they, or as the 'stars' of the pub circuit, the Brinsleys broke up. All the members are pursuing independent projects.

Johnny Bristol. When Johnny's Barry White-influenced 'Hang On In There Baby' (MGM) soared up the British and American charts in 1974, it was the culmination of a 14-year career. Bristol's first release in 1961 was as part of duo Johnny and Jackey (Beavers) for Tri-Phi Records. That song was the original version of 'Someday We'll Be Together', a 1969 chart-topper for the Supremes. After the duo's demise, Bristol worked at Motown, writing and producing for the

Spinners. With Harvey Fuqua, he came up with a string of hits including Marvin Gaye and Tammi Terrell's 'Ain't No Mountain High Enough' (1967) and Stevie Wonder's 'Yester-Me, Yester-You, Yesterday' (1969). But Bristol's greatest success was undoubtedly Jr Walker and the All-Stars, who scored a massive chain of hits with Bristol's help. In 1973, Bristol left Motown and joined Columbia as house producer. His first album as an artist, *Hang On In There Baby*, went gold in 1974.

British Folk-Rock. Despite occasional experiments with traditional jazz bands and dabblings in the skiffle boom, the leaders of the folk-revival, such as Ewan MacColl and A. L. Lloyd, kept their distance from the pop world. The result was that, by the mid-Sixties, hundreds of folk clubs thrived in Britain, forming a parallel musical culture to the dance-halls and clubs of the beat group scene.

In many clubs a cheerful eclecticism prevailed. British traditional songs existed side by side with ragtime guitarists, jug bands and Woody Guthrie imitators. The most important development, though, was the emergence of the contemporary songwriter, often modelling himself on Bob Dylan or Tom Paxton. The first to break through into rock music proper was Donovan whose naïve protest songs appeared in the charts in 1965. But, like others who came after, Ralph McTell, Roy Harper, Incredible String Band, he had little to do with folk songs as such. It was simply that the clubs, with their intense audiences and tolerant atmosphere, offered the only place for the new songwriters to perform.

As a musical genre 'folk rock' can be defined as the mingling of traditional or traditionally influenced material with rock instrumentation. Among its earliest exponents were the Irish group Sweeney's Men and Fairport Convention, who added British folk songs to their repertoire of West Coast music when ex-folk singer Sandy Denny joined in 1968. Their 1969 album, *Liege And Lief*, was Britain's first full-scale folk-rock work.

Steeleye Span, formed in the same year, took a more programmatic stance. Their philosophy was that the only way to make traditional songs relevant to present-day audiences lay in placing them in a rock context. A more purist attitude was taken by former Fairport and Steeleye bassist Ashley Hutchings whose Albion Country Band and Etchingham Steam Band, plus his productions for his wife Shirley Collins (notably *No Roses*, 1971) stuck more closely to traditional melodies and rhythms.

More eclectic were Fairport Convention and Pentangle, based around the 'folk-baroque' guitar playing of Bert Jansch and John Renbourn, while another former club guitarist, John Martyn, had by the mid-Seventies developed a style using electronics and owing much to Indian and East European folk music as well as jazz. A different strategy was taken by Mr Fox, formed by Bob and Carole Pegg in 1971, which performed electric songs written in a traditional vein.

By the early Seventies, much of the energy of folk-rock came from Irish, Scottish and Breton bands, notably Horslips, Alan Stivell, Planxty and the JSD Band, while Lindisfarne and its successor Jack The Lad, from Newcastle, mixed local folk songs with original material.

British Radio. When the Tories won the General Election of 1970 they promptly halved the BBC's local radio allowance, but despite their commitment to the notion of commercial radio, it was not until October, 1973 that Londoners were able to tune in to a commercial music station, Capital Radio.

The BBC, in misjudged anticipation, had narrowed the gap between their two light music programmes with the result that some middle-of-the-road records got on both the playlists of Radios 1 and 2. The BBC had, however, already extended Radio 1's transmission time by providing two hours of weekday broadcasts from 10 to 12 p.m. in a format that allowed selection of records on grounds other than mere commercial potential by disc jockeys like John Peel and Charlie Gillett whose *Honky Tonk* programme on Radio London was perhaps the best example of rock carefully programmed as a minority interest. This policy survived until a tightening of the corporation's budget at the start of 1975.

To the consternation of fans of commercial radio and rock music, but to the undoubted delight of the BBC, Capital initially took little advantage of the potentially fruitful areas left untended by the BBC and followed Radio 1's pattern for bland daytime listening rather than creating a new one. Claims of longer, more adventurous playlists were obscured by phone-ins, competitions and magazine features aimed at the media's inevitable 'housewives'. Rock was confined to evenings and weekends.

Other commercial stations opened during the mid-Seventies in Glasgow, Manchester, Birmingham, Sheffield, Newcastle and other urban areas, some more or less like Capital – feeling the pressure from the vital advertisers to play safe during peak audience hours. But Glasgow's Clyde, in particular, developed a local identity, placing special emphasis on Scottish pop, and within a year Capital had adopted a rather more interesting identity, mainly through the quality of some of its disc jockeys, notably Roger Scott. The station was forced to trim costs on some of its more elaborate plans to provide twenty-four-hour entertainment.

Elkie Brooks was born in Manchester on Feb. 25, 1945. She began singing at 15 as 'Manchester's answer to Brenda Lee', later joining Eric Delaney's dance band and working with Humphrey Lyttelton as a jazz singer. After a spell as a session and back-up singer, she joined up with guitarist Pete Gage (born Aug. 31, 1947), formerly the arranger with Geno Washington's Ram Jam Band, in Dada, an experimental progressive 12-piece jazz/rock band which cut one album for Atlantic in 1971.

Dada was the prototype for Vinegar Joe, which emerged in the following year to critical acclaim. A hard-driving soul-inflected band, it was again led by Gage and the vocals were shared by Elkie Brooks and Robert Palmer (born Jan. 19, 1949). Brooks' energetic Tina Turner-style stage presence caused a stir, but the group's records – *Vinegar Joe* (Island, 1972), *Rock 'n' Roll Gypsies* (1972) and *Six Star General* (1973) – didn't make the charts. They disbanded in 1974, with Palmer and Brooks both set on solo careers. Palmer has since produced two albums for Island and Brooks just one – *Rich Man's Woman* (A&M, 1975).

The Edgar Broughton Band was formed in the aftermath of the underground in early 1969. The group comprised Robert Edgar Broughton (vocals, guitar, born Oct. 24, 1947 in Warwick), his brother Alex (drums, born May 20, 1950), Art Grant (bass, May 14, 1950) and Victor Unitt (guitar, July 5, 1946). A constant presence at benefits up and down the country, the group rose to prominence as much for their anarchic politics and espousal of 'free music' as for their playing. Broughton's anthemic 'Out Demons Out' was a crowd-pleaser at every free festival. Signed to Harvest in 1969, they recorded several uneven albums, including *Sing Brothers Sing* (1970), *Edgar Broughton Band* (1971) and *Oora* (1973), before a series of management problems temporarily brought a halt to their recording and performing career.

Jackson Browne was born in Germany in 1950, his family moving to Los Angeles when he was three. In 1967 he travelled to New York where he performed on the club-circuit for a year, establishing a reputation as a songwriter. Returning to LA, he waited three years before releasing an album, although his songs had already been recorded by Tom Rush ('These Days'), Nico, and the Nitty Gritty Dirt Band ('Jamaica Say You Will'). His first two Asylum albums, *Saturate Before Using* and *For Everyman* (1974), saw the burgeoning of a formidable talent, increasingly imaginative music alongside a vision ever more acute. His themes – the ambiguity of love as salvation and as prison, the struggle in the cities and the peace of the countryside, the hopes of a better world and the fears of apocalypse – have been handled with both insight and a poetic economy, forged into a world-view as integrated for the times as any since Dylan. His music has been much improved by the skills of friend David Lindley on lead guitar and violin, used to such effect on the third (and most successful) album, *Late For The Sky* (1974), a loose concept album that convincingly fuses the personal and social aspects of life in America in the mid-Seventies.

Jack Bruce, born in Glasgow on May 14, 1943, began his career playing acoustic bass in Jim McHarg's Scotsville Jazzband and the city's dancehalls before coming to London where he joined Blues Incorporated in 1962. He quit Alexis Korner's band with altoist-organist Graham Bond and drummer Ginger Baker in February, 1963, and played with the Graham Bond Organization until late 1965 when he left for a short stint with John Mayall's Bluesbreakers, followed by six months with Manfred Mann, before the formation of Cream. His dazzling improvised duets with Eric Clapton raised bass guitar playing to a new level of artistry, and he developed considerably both as a singer and – in partnership with Pete Brown – as a songwriter.

After the break-up of Cream, Bruce pursued a solo career using various combinations of 'friends' who included Larry Coryell, Art Themen, Mike Mandel, Mitch Mitchell, John McLaughlin, Tony Williams, Chris Spedding, John Marshall, Graham Bond, Dick Heckstall-Smith and Jon Hiseman, to record a series of albums – *Songs For A Tailor* (Polydor, 1970), *Things We Like* (1971), *Harmony Row* (1971) – and for occasional live performances, where he successfully ignored demands for Cream oldies. He took part in Carla Bley's jazz suite *Escalator Over The Hill*, but dropped his sights when he joined ex-Mountain members Leslie West and Corky Laing in the sub-Cream group West, Bruce and Laing in 1972, which lasted until the following year.

After the release of *Out Of The Storm* (RSO, 1974), he formed a short-lived new band with ex-Rolling Stone Mick Taylor, Ronnie Leahy, Carla Bley (keyboards), and Bruce Gary (drums).

Roy Buchanan, born in Ozark, Arkansas on Sept. 23, 1939, was propelled into the ranks of guitar superheroes through a Polydor contract in 1971. Poor support bands failed to blunt an incomparable technique perfected over two decades of picking with some of the finest rock'n'roll combos around. Influenced by black (Blind Boy Fuller, Johnny Watson) and white (Scotty Moore, Roy Nicholls) musicians alike, he played in local groups until joining Dale Hawkins in 1958. The breaks on Hawkins' 'My Babe' and the folksy accompaniment to 'Grandma's House' (Checker) were years ahead of their time. He also recorded with Gerry Hawkins, Bob Luman, the Hawks, Freddie Cannon and Bobby Gregg and cut solo sides for Swan and Bomarc before retiring to Washington D.C. in 1962.

Ten years later he was promoted as the new guitar saviour, a role for which his introspective personality was particularly ill-suited. Versatility was a keynote of all four Polydor albums, with slow and steamy versions of 'Sweet Dreams' and 'After Hours' being among the finer cuts.

J. J. Cale, born in Tulsa in 1939, began playing rock'n'roll with a local group, J. J. Cale and the Valentines, in the mid-Fifties, before following Leon Russell to Los Angeles. There he recorded a psychedelic album and began writing. Back in Tulsa, Carl Radle sent a tape of Cale's to Russell who signed him to his Shelter label. His first album, *Naturally* (1972), included two American Top Forty hits, 'Crazy Mama' and the much-recorded 'After Midnight'. Featuring the playing of Tim Drummond (drums), Carl Radle (bass), Norbert Putnam (bass), David Briggs (keyboards), Weldon Myrick (steel guitar) and Mac Gayden (slide guitar) amongst others, the album was notable for the relaxed yet insistent rhythms around Cale's guitar, his soft growling of the words of his songs and Audie Ashworth's sympathetic production. He has recorded further albums in the same mould for Shelter: *Really* (1972), which produced another Hot Hundred hit, 'Lies', and *Okie* (1974).

John Cale, born in Garnant, South Wales, in 1942, studied viola and keyboards at Goldsmiths College, London. A music scholarship transported him to the United States, where he worked with *avant-garde* composer La Monte Young, and then formed the Velvet Underground with Lou

Reed. Cale left the group after the release of their second album and worked as a producer with Iggy and the Stooges, and Nico. While employed as a staff producer, initially with Columbia and then with Warner Bros, he began to record albums of his own songs. *Paris 1919* (Warner Bros, 1973) attracted critical acclaim for its combination of musical elegance with literate, surrealistic lyrics. In 1974 he moved back to Britain, signed with Island Records, and recorded *Fear*, a more abrasive album featuring a metallic, urban sound and images of carefully considered paranoia. As a solo performer, Cale has exhibited a talent for unpredictable stage antics. He has continued to work as a producer, supervising Patti Smith's debut album.

Can was formed in summer 1968 by classically and jazz-trained musicians who believed that rock was the idiom of greatest potential at that time. They started off making film soundtracks in their rented castle outside Cologne, and after a struggle secured a record contract with United Artists. Their albums, from *Monster Movie* (1970) to *Soon Over Babaluma* (1975), have done justice to both rock and the musical education of Can's members. They have been the most consistently experimental of the well-known German groups, producing albums as varied as the stark *Ege Bamyasi* (1972) and the smooth-textured *Future Days* (1974). At that point the line-up included Irmin Schmidt, piano (born May 29, 1937); Holgar Czukay, bass guitar (March 24, 1938); Michael Karoli, guitar (April 29, 1948); Jackie Liebesit, drums (May 26, 1938) and Damo Suzuki, vocals (Jan. 16, 1950).

Jim Capaldi, born in Evesham on August 2, 1944, first found professional fame with Birmingham-based band Deep Feeling before moving down to Aston Tirrold as drummer for Traffic. He immediately achieved an uncanny relationship with Winwood, the spirit of whose music he perfectly matched by his lyrics. His solo songwriting efforts can be seen as early as *Mr Fantasy* ('The Dealer') but it wasn't until 1972 that he released his first solo album, the excellent *Oh*

How We Danced (Island), recorded in Muscle Shoals and featuring the resident musicians there with various members of Traffic including Steve Winwood and Dave Mason. Several Traffic tours later he released the ecologically oriented *Whale Meat Again* (1974) and had a surprise Top Twenty hit with a reissue of 'Evie' from his first album. In 1975 he had further hits with a revival of 'Love Hurts' and the album *Short Cut – Draw Blood.*

Caravan, one of the longest-lasting of British underground bands, achieved unexpected success in America in 1975 where their seventh album, *Cunning Stunts*, was a minor hit. Founded in 1968, the group came out of the Wilde Flowers, a Canterbury band which also supplied personnel to the original Soft Machine.

Caravan's first line-up – Pye Hastings (guitar, vocals), David Sinclair (keyboards), Richard Sinclair (bass, vocals) and Richard Coughlan (drums) – made one album for MGM and two for Decca's Deram label between 1968 and 1970. All involved wistful, eccentric songs and gentle *avant-garde* playing. The Sinclairs left to join Matching Mole and Hatfield And The North, two of the proliferating London *avant-garde* bands. Various replacements were tried (including Steve Miller of Delivery) but it was only when David Sinclair rejoined Hastings, Coughlan, Geoff Richardson (viola) and John Perry (bass, vocals) that Caravan's music began to reach out to new audiences.

Carl Carlton was born in Detroit in 1953 and while still a child was recorded by the local Lando company. In 1968 Carl was signed by Don Robey's Duke Records of Houston and on his initial Backbeat release, 'Competition Ain't Nothin' ', was dubbed 'the fourteen-year-old genius'. He was hardly that, but his stomping Stevie Wonder soundalike became a hit and subsequent soul hits '46 Drums – 1 Guitar' (1968), 'Don't Walk Away' (1969) and 'Drop By My Place' (1970) slowly moved away from vintage Motown imitations to Memphis stylings – they were produced by Willie Mitchell. When Duke/Backbeat was bought out by ABC in 1972,

Carl moved to Los Angeles and after eighteen months of disappointments re-emerged with a successful revival of Robert Knight's 'Everlasting Love'.

The Carpenters are Richard (keyboards, vocals) born on Oct. 15, 1946 and Karen (drums, vocals), March 2, 1950, in New Haven, Connecticut. Moving to Southern California, they formed a six-member group called Spectrum, whose emphasis on soft harmonies and orchestration heralded their later work as a duo. Herb Alpert heard a tape of the group, and signed the brother and sister to his A&M label in 1970. Since then, the Carpenters have made an unbroken stream of hit singles and albums, featuring Karen's pure lead singing. As well as Richard's own compositions with John Bettis ('Goodbye To Love' – 1972, 'Top Of The World – 1973) the hits have included songs by Lennon and McCartney ('Ticket To Ride – 1970), Bonnie Bramlett and Leon Russell ('Superstar' – 1971), Brian Holland ('Please Mr Postman' – 1974) and Hank Williams ('Jambalaya' – 1974). The last two songs plus the Carpenter/Bettis original 'Yesterday Once More' came from a concept album, *Now And Then* (1974), which immaculately cashed in on the nostalgia trend of the time.

Johnny Cash is the only country singer since Jim Reeves to achieve international stardom. His reputation is built upon his instantly recognizable (if limited) voice, his ability to write communicative songs and a 'natural' presence on stage and on film. Additionally, the range of his interests and friendships – prisoners, Indians, railroads, Christianity, Bob Dylan – has won him a following among both liberals and Middle Americans.

Born J. R. Cash in Kingsland, Arkansas, on Feb. 26, 1932, he spent his early life farming, selling vacuum cleaners, serving in the Air Force, and writing poetry. In 1954, he formed a country band in Memphis. In 1955, his first record, 'Cry! Cry! Cry!', made the country Top Ten on the Sun label. Soon Cash was to develop a unique echoing, sparse, melancholy sound that led to hits such as 'Folsom Prison Blues' and 'I Walk The Line'. In 1958 he gained a producer in Jack Clement who took him into the Top Twenty of the Hot Hundred, with 'Ballad Of A Teenage Queen' and 'Guess Things Happen That Way', a manager in Bob Neal who got him into movies, and a new record company in Columbia. Columbia recorded Cash in much the same way as Sun, making the most of his distinctive voice, and hits have been forthcoming ever since, including 'Dont Take Your Guns To Town' (1959), 'Ring Of Fire' (1963), 'Folsom Prison Blues' (1968), 'A Boy Named Sue' (1969), 'What Is Truth' (1970) and 'Sunday Morning Coming Down' (1971). He has also had forty or so country hits.

Cash's audience broadened considerably in 1968 when he recorded an album 'live' in Folsom Prison and gained a national TV series and an international reputation. At this time he recorded 'Girl From The North Country', with Bob Dylan, and began to encourage young singer/songwriters such as Kris Kristofferson and Glen Sutton. He had already issued several concept/conscience albums, like the *Ballads Of The True West, Bitter Tears*, and *Ride This Train*, and was in demand for TV documentaries.

During the Seventies, he continued to expand his activities, visiting and writing and singing about Jerusalem and Vietnam and recording a 'family' album – he is married to singer June Carter of the famous country music family. As an actor he starred opposite Kirk Douglas in *A Gunfight*, having starred in Hollywood 'B' features a decade earlier, and he narrowly failed to outwit Columbo on television.

Johnny Cash has become a larger-than-life figure, whose importance goes beyond country music, or even rock, but that importance should nevertheless be underlined. For country music, he became an international ambassador and undoubtedly he greatly helped to popularize the sound without projecting a stereotyped image as others have done. For rock, his early hits opened the way for an injection of country sounds by others, and his recording with Dylan influenced the thoughts of many country artists and promoters about the viability of country-rock.

David Cassidy (born in New York City, his official birth date is April 12, 1950) was already a teen idol when he was booked to appear with his stepmother Shirley Jones in the TV series *The Partridge Family.* The shows consolidated his appeal to schoolgirls, and soon he, Jones and a group of session musicians were making smash hits as 'the Partridge Family' ('I Think I Love You' went to the top of the American charts in 1970). Cassidy's solo career was, for a brief period, phenomenal. By 1972 he was the hottest property in pop, and his international tours were sellouts despite the bland simplicity of songs like 'How Can I Be Sure' (1972) and 'The Puppy Song' (1973). His complaints that he wanted to be taken seriously as a singer (with the 1975 concept album *I Write The Songs*) coincided with many of his fans deserting him in favour of the younger Donny Osmond, but enough people accepted the new image to put two singles from the album in the British Top Twenty.

Chairman of the Board is one of the most intriguing groups in the whole black music mainstream. Formed in 1969 by ex-Motown producers Holland-Dozier-Holland as one of the initial acts for their Invictus label, it consisted of General Norman Johnson, the wheezing voiced ex-lead singer of the Showmen, Eddie Curtis, Harrison Kennedy and Danny Woods. With every singer on occasion singing lead and also possessing an ability to play a variety of instruments, the group none the less worked mainly as a showcase for the extraordinary vocal and songwriting talents of General Johnson on hits like 'Give Me Just A Little More Time' (a million-seller in 1970) and the Top Twenty 'Pay The Piper' (1970). By 1972 the group had become a trio (Curtis leaving) and each group member also cut solo albums. With Johnson spending a good deal of his time writing and producing (with Greg Perry) for others, Chairman of the Board's successes became more infrequent, partly because of the gradual winding down of Invictus. But their ability to move from Motown-influenced good time soul like 'Give Me' to the searing black rock of *The Skin I'm In* has emphasized their flexibility and resilience.

Bryan 'Chas' Chandler. Even before the Animals' final American tour, which preceded their break-up in September 1966, Chandler (born Dec. 18, 1941), the group's bass player, had decided to move into record production, and it was during that tour that he 'discovered' Jimi Hendrix playing in the Café Wha in Greenwich Village, New York. He brought Hendrix to England, found a bass player, Noel Redding, and drummer, John 'Mitch' Mitchell, and guided Hendrix's career until the end of 1968 when Chandler ended their association. He went on to confirm his ability as a talent scout, manager and record producer when he transformed an unknown Midland group, Ambrose Slade, into the chart-topping Slade, whose success in the early Seventies drew comparisons with the Beatles. As in Hendrix's case, Chandler's contribution was to plot a distinctive musical direction, create an instantly recognizable sound, and mould a strong visual identity. In 1974 he turned to film production with *Flame*, a vehicle for Slade intended to give them a harder image and broaden their audience.

Harry Chapin was born on Dec. 7, 1942. Before embarking on a recording career in 1972, he flew aeroplanes, became expert at pool, received an Academy Award nomination for directing a silent film about boxing, and wrote songs for the celebrated shark film, *Blue Water, White Death*. He was also temporarily part of the Brothers and Sisters, whose members included Carly and Lucy Simon, as well as Harry and his brother Tom.

As a writer, Chapin tends towards narrative songs, e.g. *Short Stories* (Elektra, 1973) and 'W.O.L.D.', an American Top Ten hit in 1974. He has been far more successful in America than in Britain, with, for example, the 1975 No. 1 'Cat's In The Cradle'.

Bobby Charles hails from the Southern State of Louisiana where he was born Robert Charles Guidry in 1938. He grew up with an ear to the local black radio stations and also to the music of the French-speaking Arcadian peoples of Louisiana, absorbing a synthesis of raw, earthy R&B and accordion-dominated cajun music. From these influences he composed such rock'n'roll classics as Fats Domino's 'Walking To New Orleans', Bill Haley's 'See You Later Alligator' and Clarence 'Frogman' Henry's 'But I Do', sometimes under the name of Robert Guidry. His own solo career began around 1955 in Chicago with the Chess record company, working in both a recording and A&R capacity. Then, after a brief three-year period, he was back down South with New Orleans-based Imperial Records, and in 1967 was signed to Paula, a subsidiary of Stan Lewis's independent Jewel Records of Shreveport, Louisiana.

In 1972, Bobby made his album debut on Bearsville with *Bobby Charles.* An excellent collection of new songs like 'Small Town Talk', 'Tennessee Blues' and 'Street People', the album was critically acclaimed, most notably for the relaxed superb back-up support from The Band plus Amos Garrett and Dr John. Since then he has been inactive, save for brief appearances on both Better Days albums featuring Paul Butterfield.

Cheech and Chong came to the fore in the early Seventies with the first comedy act rooted entirely in the hippie and drug culture. Less savage in their satirizing of the world of the stoned freak than National Lampoon, they found a large audience among those whose habits they used as their subject-matter.

Richard Cheech (born in Chicago in 1946) and Tommy Chong (Edmonton, Canada, 1941) had rock band backgrounds before meeting up as part of the City Works comedy group in Vancouver. In 1971 they were signed as a duo to Lou Adler's Ode label, releasing *Cheech and Chong* (1971) and *Big Bambu* (1972). On their later albums the jokes seemed to be stretched thin, although they remain very much a part of the Los Angeles rock scene.

Chicago are both the most successful and the most criticized jazz-rock group of the Seventies. They were formed in 1968 as Chicago Transit Authority by Robert Lamm (keyboards, vocals, born Oct. 13, 1944), Terry Kath (guitar, vocals, born

Jan. 31, 1946), Jim Pankow (trombone, born Aug. 20, 1947), Walter Parazaider (saxes, clarinet, born March 14, 1945), Lee Loughnane (trumpet, flugelhorn, born Oct. 21, 1946), Peter Cetera (bass, vocals, born Sept. 13, 1944) and Dan Seraphine (drums, born Aug. 28, 1948).

The first Columbia album, *Chicago Transit Authority*, released in 1969, followed hard on the heels of the pioneering brass-rock arrangements of Blood, Sweat And Tears. Produced by the group's manager and mentor, James William Guercio, it bobbed in and out of the charts for the next six years, becoming one of the biggest-selling records ever. Pankow's horn arrangements were strong and melodic, if not exactly innovative by contemporary jazz standards. Combined with Lamm's lukewarm quasi-political lyrics, they mirrored the mood of the end of the decade, ensuring vast sales for the succeeding albums. These were simply numbered *Chicago I–VIII* and appeared regularly one a year, with the exception of the fourth, a live album, *At Carnegie Hall*, which appeared in 1971, the same year as *Chicago III*.

The unvarying approach of the group and its virtually unchanged line-up (Brazilian percussionist Laudir Oliviera joined in 1974) have frequently reduced critics to apoplexy. By the mid-Seventies, the Chicago sound seemed positively middle-of-the-road compared with the newer waves of jazz-rock fusions.

The Chieftains looked set to follow the Dubliners to international success by the mid-Seventies. Unlike their predecessors, however, they offered a version of Irish traditional music unleavened by stage humour or show business values. Deriving from the Irish music revival inspired by Sean O'Riada, the group, led by uillean piper Paddy Moloney, gave instrumental concerts of skilfully arranged folk tunes with extensive improvisation.

Four albums were cut for the small Irish label, Claddagh, between 1962 and 1974, before the Chieftains were signed to Island by manager Jo Lustig. *Chieftains 5* was released on that label in 1975, and Island re-released the earlier records the following year. As well as Moloney, the group included

Sean Potts (tin whistle), Michael Tubridy (flute, concertina), Martin Fay (fiddle), Peader Mercier (bodhran – hand drum), Derek Bell (harp) and Sean Keane (fiddle). In 1975 they provided music for the soundtrack of Stanley Kubrick's *Barry Lyndon.*

The Chi-Lites. Dominated by Eugene Record, the extraordinary singer/songwriter/producer and creator of one of the most sensuously romantic soul sounds, the Chi-Lites hail from Chicago. Formed in 1960, they consisted of Marshall Thompson, Robert Lester, Creadel Jones and Eugene Record. Originally using names like the Chanteurs and the Hi-Lites they changed to the Chi-Lites and recorded locally for James Shelton Jr before gaining their first national hit in 1969 with 'Give It Away', on Brunswick. It was the start of a phenomenal hit run including the shuddering slab of black rock '(For God's Sake) Give More Power To The People' (1971), the unashamedly sentimental 'Have You Seen Her' (Top Five in 1971) – a reissued hit in Britain in 1975 – 'Oh Girl', an American No. 1 in 1972, the soaringly produced 'Coldest Days Of My Life' (1972) and the charmingly lilting 'Homely Girl' (1973). Eugene and his fellow Chi-Lites have brought a unique blend of rich, billowing sophistication to the black music mainstream.

Eric Clapton was born in Ripley, Surrey, on March 30, 1945, and joined his first group, the Roosters, at Tom McGuinness' invitation early in 1963. When the group folded in August he and McGuinness went to Casey Jones' backing group, the Engineers, but Clapton quit within two months to replace Tony Topham as lead guitarist with the Yardbirds, who had recently taken over the Rolling Stones' residency at Richmond's Crawdaddy club. It was with the Yardbirds that Clapton first encountered adulation as a guitar hero, but his development as a player was limited by the Yardbirds' ambitions, and their decision to record the pop-oriented 'For Your Love' (British Columbia) prompted him to leave in March, 1965.

John Mayall at once asked him to join his Bluesbreakers,

but Clapton stayed only for a short time before departing with a makeshift group, the Glands, on an abortive world tour which wound up in Greece, from where some weeks later Clapton travelled home to rejoin Mayall. During this second period with the Bluesbreakers between November, 1965 and June, 1966 (when he formed Cream with Jack Bruce and Ginger Baker) Clapton's status amongst the growing army of British blues fans grew to the point of deification. The guitar hero, meanwhile, demonstrated his outstanding talent on *Bluesbreakers* (Decca, 1966).

The format and musical ambitions of Cream inspired Clapton to progress far beyond the role of blues copyist into areas of improvisation previously ignored in rock. After the trio split up at the end of 1968, he teamed up with Stevie Winwood, Ginger Baker and Rick Grech in Blind Faith, a 'supergroup' that was unable to live up to the public's expectations or survive commercial pressures.

In search of anonymity and a release from the intense demands of both fans and businessmen, Clapton joined Delaney and Bonnie Bramlett's backing group and recorded a solo album, *Eric Clapton* (Polydor, 1970), with them, produced by Delaney. He eventually took three of the Bramletts' 'friends' – Bobby Whitlock (keyboards), Carl Radle (bass), Jim Gordon (drums) – to form Derek and the Dominos in May, 1970, adding Duane Allman on the recording sessions for the magnificent *Layla* (Polydor, 1970).

After a live album, Derek and the Dominos broke up in May, 1971, and apart from his performance at George Harrison's Bangla Desh concert three months later, an unannounced appearance with Leon Russell that December, and his own concert in January, 1973 with Pete Townshend, Ron Wood, Stevie Winwood, Rick Grech, Jim Capaldi, Jim Karstein, and Reebop, recorded as *Eric Clapton's Rainbow Concert* (RSO, 1973), he virtually retired amidst increasing speculation about his health and future until his emergence in 1974 with a new group – George Terry (guitar), Dick Sims (keyboards), Carl Radle (bass), Jamie Oldaker (drums), Yvonne Elliman (vocals) – and a newfound serenity in his music. His evident distaste for the role of guitar idol having forced his development as both singer and songwriter, *461 Ocean Boulevard* (RSO, 1974), which featured his biggest single hit of the Seventies, Bob Marley's 'I Shot The Sheriff', and *There's One In Every Crowd* (RSO, 1975), contained his most balanced work to date, though the live album *E. C. Was Here* (1975) was a disappointment.

Gene Clark was born in Missouri on Nov. 17, 1941. A member of the New Christy Minstrels in the early Sixties, he founded the Byrds with Jim McGuinn and David Crosby in 1964. His plaintive voice and distinctive love songs were prominent features of the Byrds' first two albums, before he left in April, 1966, because of his fear of flying, and perhaps also as a result of his diminishing control over the group's direction.

He then made an album with the Gosdin Brothers and two with Doug Dillard, the first of which, *The Fantastic Expedition Of Dillard And Clark* (A&M, 1969), was a beautifully constructed example of the country-rock fusion that would dominate west coast rock in the early Seventies. He has since made several solo albums of simple folk/country rock, with sparse instrumentation behind a succession of outstanding songs: *Gene Clark/White Light* (A&M, 1971), *Roadmaster* (1973) and *No Other* (Asylum, 1974). The characteristic Clark lyric uses simple words in complex ways to explore Sixties themes in a Seventies context, still with the same plaintive, mournful voice.

Jimmy Cliff, born in Jamaica in 1948 as James Chambers, 'reggae's first superstar', began his career in the early Sixties, recording for a number of producers, notably Leslie Kong ('Hurricane Hattie', 'Miss Jamaica'). On a government-sponsored tour of America with Byron Lee and the Dragonaires, he met Chris Blackwell of Island Records. Settling in Britain, having signed with Blackwell, Cliff developed a strong club following, but had little success disc-wise until 1968 when he won the Brazilian Song Festival, with a self-penned song, 'Waterfall'. A year later he scored worldwide with the catchy reggae song 'Wonderful World, Beautiful People' and had European success with its follow-up 'Vietnam'. In the interim, two albums, *Hard Road To Travel* (1967) and *Jimmy Cliff* (1969) had demonstrated the artist's talent, particularly on painful, emotive songs like 'Sitting In Limbo' and 'Many Rivers To Cross'. Another hit, in 1970, with Cat Stevens' plaintive 'Wild World', spotlighted his versatility, but lost him much of his ethnic following.

Ironically, it was as an actor, in the lead role in *The Harder They Come* (the soundtrack of which was released by Island 1972), that Jimmy Cliff gained his greatest success and earned the 'superstar' tag. Musically, he tended increasingly to pop, with the Muscle Shoals recorded *Another Cycle*, and the uneven EMI sets *Unlimited* (1973), *House Of Exile* (1974) and *Brave Warrior* (1975), and with hit songs for the Pioneers ('Let Your Yeah Be Yeah') and Desmond Dekker ('You Can Get It If You Really Want'). One of the best stage performers of his generation, Cliff seems constantly on the verge of great success while never quite fulfilling his obvious potential.

Climax Blues Band – Colin Cooper, Peter Haycock, Arthur Wood, Derek Holt, Richard Jones, George Newsome (Jones dropped after first album, Newsome replaced by John Cuffley in 1973) – were originally called the Climax Chicago Blues Band. They began in 1968 as part of the British Blues revival, playing in a fairly traditional postwar blues style, but recording mostly original songs for Harvest. A 1972 tour introduced them to American audiences, who liked the group so much that within a year they were headlining and a live album recorded in New York became a top seller and made them FM radio favourites. Their albums since then, notably *Rich Man* (1972) and *Sense of Direction* (1974), produced by Richard Gottehrer, have refined the group's tightness, economy and fullness of sound.

Leonard Cohen, born on Sept. 21, 1934 in Montreal, Canada, studied English Literature at McGill and Columbia Universities. He first made an impression with his 1966 novel, *Beautiful Losers,* which contained an attractive mixture of eroticism, spiritual longings, slapstick, and existential despair. He repeated this mixture on his first two albums, *The Songs Of Leonard Cohen* (Columbia, 1967) and *Songs From A Room* (1969) which were enormously successful. Cohen's droning voice, his minimal backing, his attitude of humorous desperation towards existence and sexual relationships, made him a major figure in the 'bedsitter' singer/songwriter league. His songs, particularly 'Suzanne' and 'Sisters Of Mercy', became acknowledged classics, and Cohen rose to his commercial success by turning his concerts into experiences of communal catharsis (as documented on 'Please Don't Pass Me By' on *Live Songs*, 1973). The later *New Skin For The Old Ceremony* (1974) displays an undiminished gift for subtle imagery and striking political/sexual metaphors.

Colosseum was an attempt to develop the fruitful interplay between jazz, blues and rock characteristic of Sixties London R&B bands like those of Graham Bond and John Mayall. Drummer Jon Hiseman (born in Blackheath, London on June 21, 1944) had worked with both groups, as had horn player Dick Heckstall-Smith (born in Ludlow, on Sept. 26, 1934).

They were the nucleus of the group which was formed in 1968. Other members were Dave Greenslade (keyboards, vibes), Jim Roche (guitar) and Tony Reeves (bass). Roche was later replaced by first James Litherland, then Dave Clempson. Mark Clark replaced Reeves. Colosseum's records were dominated by Hiseman's penchant for extended pieces, on *Those Who Are About To Die Salute You* (Fontana, 1969) and notably *Valentyne Suite* (Vertigo, 1969). In 1970 singer Chris Farlowe joined the group for the last studio album, *Daughter Of Time*.

A year later, the band broke up, leaving a live album released on Bronze. Hiseman formed Tempest with guitarist Ollie Halsall in 1972, while both Heckstall-Smith (briefly) and Greenslade formed their own bands, the latter, with an unusual double keyboards line-up with Dave Lawson, making three albums on Warner Bros. In 1975, Hiseman formed

Colosseum II with Gary Moore (guitar), Don Airey (keyboards), Neil Murray (bass) and Mike Starrs (vocals).

Commander Cody And His Lost Planet Airmen. While studying at Michigan University in Ann Arbor, George Frayne (piano) formed a variety of bands (including the Amblers, the Fantastic Surfing Beavers and Lorenzo Lightfoot) with John Tichy (guitar), before amalgamating with the R&B band of Billy C. Farlow to form Commander Cody And His Lost Planet Airmen in 1967.

The line-up of the much-changing group eventually settled down to Frayne (Commander Cody), Tichy, Farlow, Lance Dickerson (drums), Andy Stein (fiddle, sax), Bill Kirchen (lead guitar), Buffalo Bruce Barlow (bass) and the West Virginia Creeper (steel guitar) when the band emigrated to Berkeley in 1969, where they soon acquired the reputation of being the best bar band in town. Signed to ABC-Paramount in 1971, they recorded their most successful and influential album *Lost In The Ozone*, which included the infamous 'Seeds And Stems' and saw the band mixing rockabilly and traditional country music. The Commander's novelty song – there's one on every album – a version of Johnny Bond's 'Hot Rod Lincoln', gave them a Top Ten hit in 1972. Subsequent albums for ABC, including *Hot Licks, Cold Steel And Truckers' Favourites* (1972) and *Country Casanova* (1973), which included their only other major hit, another Cody novelty song, 'Smoke! Smoke! Smoke! (That Cigarette)', revealed a growing fondness for trucking songs and Western Swing, but were not as powerful as the first. In 1974 they switched to Warner Bros, releasing two better-produced but unexciting albums in 1975. In 1976, after completing a live album, a massive shift in personnel occurred. The future of the band was in doubt.

Ry Cooder, born on March 15, 1947 in Los Angeles, first came to the fore as a Los Angeles session musican in the late Sixties, although back in 1965 he had been a member of the legendary Rising Suns with Taj Mahal and Jesse Lee Kincade, and then of Captain Beefheart's first Magic Band – it is his slide guitar on *Safe As Milk*.

Despite growing up on the West Coast, Cooder absorbed every aspect of southern folk music and his reputation grew through appearances at the Ash Grove in Los Angeles and his work as a session musician.

On *Ry Cooder* (Reprise, 1970) he showed exciting innovations in the use of the bottleneck technique but it was *Into The Purple Valley* (1972) that established him as a guitarist and interpreter of the American folk heritage. Subsequent albums, *Boomer's Story* (1972) and *Paradise And Lunch* (1974) were also well received.

Cooder remains a unique guitarist in his treatment of folk standards from the depression period and if his style owes anything to one musician then it is the Bahaman guitarist Joseph Spence whom Cooder idolizes.

Rita Coolidge was born in Nashville, Tennessee on May 1, 1944. Schooled in country and gospel music with her sister Priscilla (who married and recorded with Booker T. for A&M), she came to prominence as a backing singer on the Mad Dogs And Englishmen tour in 1970, having previously worked with Delaney and Bonnie.

Signed to A&M as a solo artist the following year, she went to make a series of albums alone and with Kris Kristofferson, whom she married in 1973. The most outstanding were *The Lady's Not For Sale* (1972) and *Fall Into Spring* (1974), both produced by David Anderle. Her main quality as a singer is purity of tone, and her best records combine that with a well-chosen group of songs by leading contemporary writers, usually in the country-rock area.

Chick Corea's musical activity is wide-ranging. He has worked as pianist and resident composer with Stan Getz on e.g. *Sweet Rain* (Verve, 1967) and (inevitably) Miles Davis, co-led the rather forbidding free-improvisation group, Circle, and finally settled on the small band format of Return To Forever. The group's music is immediately attractive because of Corea's melodic flair – e.g. *Return To For-*

ever (ECM, 1972) and *Light As A Feather* (Polydor, 1974). His tunes are superficially simple, but have enough tricky twists and turns to keep the ears alert.

The Cornelius Brothers and Sister Rose – produced one of the most insidiously memorable American hits of 1971 with the churning 'Treat Her Like A Lady'. Creatively, if not commercially, it was the zenith for the Miami-based group. Born in Fort Lauderdale, Florida, Eddie, Carter and Rose Cornelius began singing in a family gospel quintet, the Split Tones, before 'crossing over' and signing with a tiny Miami independent, Platinum Records. Producer Bob Archibald recorded Eddie Cornelius' droning, pulsating 'Lady'. It became a local hit and the master and the group's contract were snapped up by United Artists. Just after the record had gone gold the group were in a car crash and eleven months elapsed before a follow-up was released – 'Too Late To Turn Back Now', another Top Five record in 1972. The group went on to hit with 'Don't Ever Be Lonely' (1972), 'Big Time Lover' (1973) and several more but their over-produced, limp pop soul featuring Eddie's flat, rather unmusical voice had palled by 1974.

Larry Coryell was born in Galveston, Texas on April 2, 1943. A guitarist who made his first impact with the Gary Burton Quartet in 1967–68, Coryell is an immaculate player with a seemingly inexhaustible supply of ideas and technique. Despite spells with Charles Lloyd and Gary Burton he has not yet really found a context in which his gifts can appear to their greatest effect. By far his best album is *Spaces* (Vanguard, 1971), where he is partnered by Billy Cobham, Chick Corea and Miroslav Vitous.

Count Ossie, an authentic rastafarian drummer, led various bands through the Sixties – his Afro Combo backing the Folks Bros on 'Oh Carolina'; Mello Cat Count Ossie and his Warrickas with 'Another Moses'; Count Ossie Band, 'Nyiah Bongo'; Im and Count Ossie, 'So Long Rastafari Calling' – before forming the Mystic Revelation of Rastafari, including

'Im' Cedric Brooks (tenor sax), Brother Sam Clayton (poet), his own son Time (fundae drum) and a dozen further musicians in 1970. The Mystics' legacy has been institutionalized through state visits to Africa and Guyana, appearances at the African Cultural Centre in Jamaica and culminated in the 1973 release of their three-album set – *Grounation.* Featuring poems, songs, narrations, serenades with a sustained bongo-accompanied chant of traditional folk tunes (cf. the thirty-minute title track), *Grounation* remains the definitive display of rasta music (in which reggae is rooted) recorded to date.

Jim Croce was born in Philadelphia on Jan. 10, 1943 and came to prominence in 1972 with his Top Ten hit 'You Don't Mess Around With Jim' (ABC). With his guitarist Marty Muehleisen, Croce had previously made albums for Columbia and Capitol without success.

'Jim' was simple, melodic and acoustic, while the album of the same title was set in the world of bars and car-washes. Other hits (including 'Operator' – 1972, 'Bad Bad Leroy Brown', 'I Got A Name' – 1973, and 'I Have To Say I Love You In A Song' – 1974) and two more albums, produced by Cashman and West, followed: *Life And Times* (1972) and *I Got A Name* (1973), the latter recorded a few months before Croce's death in an air-crash on Sept. 20, 1973. It cut short a developing career based on a refreshingly straightforward merging of folk and pop songwriting which led to immense posthumous sales of his singles and albums in America.

David Crosby, born on Aug. 14, 1941 into a Los Angeles movie family, served his musical apprenticeship as a folk singer on the West Coast club and coffee house circuit. A founder-member of the Jet Set – later the Byrds – his rhythm guitar, harmony voice, and songwriting abilities were a mainstay of the group through their first four albums.

In 1967, he was sacked after losing a struggle for the group's leadership. The large cash settlement bought him a yacht before joining Steve Stills and Graham Nash in Crosby, Stills and Nash. Through that group's (later

CSN&Y) part-time existence he sang harmony for many friends, notably the Jefferson Starship and Jackson Browne, and produced a first solo album, *If I Could Only Remember My Name* (1971), which featured the softer side of Crosby's dialectic trip between the politics of anger and the oceanic life-style. It was followed by a weaker joint album with Graham Nash. His main importance, though, lies in his position between the studio professionalism of LA and the spontaneous extravagance of the San Franciscan scene, which he eventually tied together as the catalyst of CSN&Y.

Crosby, Stills, Nash and Young was formed in late 1968, 'one night round at Joni's place', by refugees from the Byrds, the Buffalo Springfield, and the Hollies. They made one album as a trio, *Crosby, Stills And Nash* (Atlantic, 1969), with Dallas Taylor helping out on drums, which featured Stills' desperate love songs, Nash's gentler celebrations of 'peace and love' consciousness, and Crosby's mixture of romanticism and angry politics – all smoothed into a soft electric/acoustic music topped off by dazzling virtuoso harmony singing. To go out on the road, and to add a darker ingredient, they added a second Springfield refugee in mid-1969, Neil Young. They played their second gig at Woodstock in August, and made one studio album, *Déjà Vu*, early in 1970. The sound was tougher, more electric than CSN's, counterpointing Nash's soft admonitions to 'teach your children' with Young's wails of pain, Crosby's politics with Stills' intense self-preoccupation. The overall effect was an album – and a group – that offered a multi-faceted view of American youth in the year of Kent State. The level of musicianship displayed on the album was reflected in their stage shows through late 1969 and 1970. The concerts contained an acoustic half in which the four of them sang solo and together, and an electric half of rock'n'roll in which the hired rhythm section and Crosby's rhythm guitar laid down the base for Stills and Young to engage in ferocious electric guitar duelling.

What separated CSN&Y from the rank and file was their conquest of both the Los Angeles and the San Francisco approaches to rock. In the studio, they were as perfectionist as the Byrds had been; on stage, they were every bit as real, as separate personalities singing for each other as much as for the audience, in the manner of Jefferson Airplane. They sparked an infectious joy in the making of music. Some of it was captured on the live *Four-Way Street* album (1971), particularly in devastating performances of Crosby's 'Long Time Gone' requiem to Robert Kennedy and Young's 'Southern Man'.

At the end of 1970 they went their separate ways, partly to pursue directions that couldn't be pursued in the always loose structure of the group, partly because of more personal differences. Crosby and Nash would continue to extol nature and love, Stills to explore his desperation in countrified rock, Young to mirror the doubts and anguish of a dissolving dream. In 1974 they reunited for an American tour, after attempts in previous years had failed. The tour ended at Wembley Stadium in London, with a display of the old magic in a time and situation that barely escaped a hint of irony. The music was superb, but CSN&Y were always about more than music, and the Woodstock dream had been shoved aside by events beyond their control.

Mike D'Abo was born in Betchworth, Surrey on March 1, 1944. He attended Harrow School where he joined the Band Of Angels. 'Invitation' in 1966 was their closest to a hit single. That year D'Abo replaced Paul Jones in Manfred Mann, starting his career as their group's singer with Dylan's 'Just Like A Woman'.

While singing with Manfred Mann he was composing and producing records for others like Rod Stewart, Chris Farlowe and the Fortunes. He wrote 'Build Me Up Buttercup', a hit for the Foundations and the oft-recorded 'Handbags And Gladrags' before making his acting debut in *Gulliver's Travels*, a new-style pantomime to which he contributed the music. In 1969 he sang the part of Herod on the original album of *Jesus Christ Superstar* and in 1970 recorded an album for UNI, *D'Abo*. In 1972 he teamed up with a young record producer, Chris Demetrieu, the first fruits of which was an impressive solo album *Down At Rachel's Place* (A&M). Today he mixes recording, acting and writing both songs and scores for films and the theatre.

Roger Daltrey, the Who's singer, was born in 1945 in Hammersmith, London, and has developed, over ten years, a convincingly unmannered voice and a powerful and distinctive stage presence. His successful first solo album, *Daltrey* (Track, 1973), featuring songs by Leo Sayer and Dave Courtney and produced by Courtney and Adam Faith in his home studio at Burwash, Sussex, included the hit single, 'Giving It All Away'. Following his appearance in the title role of Ken Russell's film version of the Who's *Tommy* in 1974, he was cast as the composer Franz Liszt in Russell's *Lisztomania.* A second solo album, *Ride A Rock Horse*, was released in 1975.

Mac Davis was born in Lubbock, Texas in 1941 and moved to Atlanta, Georgia in his teens. In the late Fifties he began writing ('Mau Mau Mary') and formed his own rock'n'roll group. He quit performing in 1961 to become the regional manager for Vee Jay Records until 1965 when he moved over to Liberty and then transferred to Hollywood as head of Liberty's Metric Music, a position which allowed him to present his own songs to a wider range of singers much more easily – e.g. 'You're Good To Me' (Lou Rawls), 'Within My Memory' (Glen Campbell) and 'A Little Less Conversation' (Presley). In 1969 Presley gave Davis his first Top Ten songs with his versions of 'In The Ghetto' and 'Don't Cry Daddy'. Other hits Davis has written include: 'Daddy's Little Man', 'Friend, Lover, Woman, Wife' (O. C. Smith, 1969), 'Watching Scotty Grow' and 'Something's Burning' (Top Twenty hits for Bobby Goldsboro and Kenny Rodgers respectively in 1970). In 1970 he signed with Columbia, had a No. 1 record in 1972 with 'Baby Don't Get Hooked On Me' that began a string of successful singles ('Stop And Smell The Roses', 1974) and albums (*I Believe In Music*, 1972 and *Mac Davis*, 1973), each a commercial mixture of sentimentality, melodrama and sensuality.

Miles Davis – who first recorded on Nov. 25, 1945 – was born in Alton, Illinois on May 25, 1926. The junior member of altoist Charlie Parker's band, Miles displayed in his choice of apprentice-master, as in so many other things, instinctive good judgement. Over the next quarter-century he brought about a number of decisive and radical changes in jazz, both technical and stylistic. In 1949 he introduced a completely new orchestral conception to the music and brought belated recognition to arranger Gil Evans as one of jazz's most original composers. In the mid-Fifties there was the classic quintet with tenor saxist John Coltrane; towards the end of the decade came his bold introduction of modal improvisation, and the Sixties saw his first moves into the field of rock music. It was only the latest of a series of examples of his genius for grasping a musical problem and proposing its solution in a single imaginative leap.

His album *Miles In The Sky* (Columbia, 1967) gave the first indication of his interest in rock forms and the numbers on it, particularly 'Big Stuff', contained the seeds of all his later explorations into the idiom. The fragmentary, attenuated theme and sidelong approach to the beat provide a perfect sketch for the records which followed. On these he dropped the Quintet format in favour of larger, irregular line-ups and began to abandon tight chorus-structure in favour of free-flowing meditation on a single harmonic and rhythmic mood. Typical of this period is *Live Evil* (1972), with its brilliant use of the bass clarinet which wanders from front-line to rhythm section in a most haunting and disturbing way. As the form became looser, the results became less predictable. Live appearances varied wildly in quality while the albums, particularly *In Concert* and *At The Fillmore* (1971), were rather forbidding slabs of go-for-broke improvisation. This loosening of form may, by now, have passed the point of balance and toppled into incoherence. Since his extension of electronics to include his own trumpet sound, the notes themselves have become almost meaningless and all significance is invested in rhythmic tension and tonal distortion. This cannot be entirely satisfactory, especially since Miles has, for 25 or 30 years, been a 'notes' man *par ex-*

cellence. It is certainly true, however, that the interface between jazz and rock exists in its present form through the influence of Miles Davis. Ex-Davis players like Herbie Hancock, Joe Zawinul, Billy Cobham, Chick Corea and Keith Jarrett are not only leading figures; they can be considered as a stylistically identifiable 'school', and the characteristics of their style and procedure derive quite clearly from their experience with his bands from 1968–72.

Tyrone Davis is a Chicago-based singer whose extraordinarily hypnotic 'Can I Change My Mind' (Dakar, 1968) is considered a classic of soul. Born in Greenville, Mississippi in 1938, Davis worked as 'Tyrone The Wonder Boy'. He employed a rasping, gasping vocal style on recordings for Tangerine (including an early version of 'Can I Change My Mind') and 20th Century Fox with little success. Signing with Carl Davis' Dakar Records, Tyrone cut his immortal 'Change' (though as a flip side) which months later hit the Top Ten in December, 1968. Subsequent hits have included the lilting 'Turn Back The Hands Of Time' in 1970, 'You Keep Me Holding On' in 1971 and the 'concept-production' 'I Had It All The Time' in 1973. Although limited in the kind of mid-tempo material he invariably chooses, Davis' mixture of smooth crooning and raw-edged emoting, vaguely similar to Bobby Bland, is one of the most riveting black music voices.

Dawn comprises Tony Orlando (born April 3, 1944, in New York), Joyce Vincent (born Dec. 14, 1946 in Detroit) and Thelma Hopkins (born Oct. 28, 1948 in Louisville, Kentucky). Both women had worked as back-up singers on various Motown sessions. In the early Sixties, Orlando had been a successful singer in the Ben E. King mould. He entered the music business, rising to general manager of Columbia Records' April Blackwood publishing division by 1970. In that year he was approached by Hank Medress, a former member of the Tokens turned producer for Bell Records, with a song he asked Orlando to record. The result was 'Candida', an almost clinically perfect pop record that mirrored the then emerging MOR strand in American pop and which reached both the British and American Top Twenty on Bell. The follow-up, 'Knock Three Times', was a transatlantic No. 1 in 1971, the year that Orlando left publishing to concentrate on recording and performing once more. Further hits followed, including 'What Are You Doing Sunday?' (1971), 'Tie A Yellow Ribbon Round The Old Oak Tree' (the group's biggest hit), and 'Say, Has Anybody Seen My Sweet Gipsy Rose' (1973), and the group began successfully touring the American cabaret circuit.

Kiki Dee, born Pauline Matthews in Bradford, Yorkshire, in 1947, spent most of the Sixties decorating the outskirts of pop but, even when she became the first British girl to record for Tamla-Motown in 1970, she made little headway. In 1973 old friend Elton John signed her to his Rocket label and this resulted in her first hit, 'Amoureuse'. The following year 'I've Got the Music In Me' introduced her new image and accompanied by the Kiki Dee Band (Bias Boshell, Phil Curtis, Jo Partridge and Roger Pope) she began to make an impression as a live performer. The band broke up in 1975 when Pope joined the augmented Elton John Band.

The DeFranco Family, comprising Benny, Nino, Marisa, Merlina, and young lead singer Tony, were the biggest teenybop sensations of 1974, a year in which David Cassidy, the Osmonds, and the Jackson Five all dropped off sharply in the subteen sweepstakes. Tony wasn't as cute or as talented as Donny Osmond, but a great song ('Heartbeat, It's A Lovebeat') with supercharged production gave the DeFranco Family the biggest hit single of the year (over two-and-a-half million sold), helped along by a full-scale effort on the part of Laufer Publications (*Tiger Beat, Fave!*) who also managed the group and marketed their fan club products.

Delaney and Bonnie acted as a focus for many of the best musicians of the early Seventies with their successful American and European tours. Delaney Bramlett was born in Pontotoc County, Mississippi on July 1, 1939 and, moving to the West Coast, joined the famous Shindogs, the house band for Jack Good's *Shindig* television show.

There he met and married Bonnie Lynn (born in Acton, Illinois on Nov. 8, 1944). Their first album was made for Stax in 1968, with Don Nix producing, and the next year they put together Delaney and Bonnie and Friends to tour with Blind Faith. The resulting album, *Accept No Substitute* (Elektra, 1969) involved such then unknown players as Carl Radle (bass), Jim Keltner (drums), Bobby Whitlock (guitar), Jim Price (trumpet), Bobby Keys (sax) and singer Rita Coolidge. So infectious was the band's brand of white soul that Eric Clapton joined them for the subsequent tour, which produced *On Tour With Eric Clapton* (Atco, 1970).

Next, virtually the entire band deserted the Bramletts for the Leon Russell / Joe Cocker extravaganza, Mad Dogs And Englishmen. This coincided with the breakup of the couple's relationship, with a divorce following in 1972. Each released a solo album through Columbia, and in 1975 Bonnie signed with Capricorn.

The Delfonics. William Hart (born Jan. 17, 1945, in Washington), his brother Wilbert (born Oct. 19, 1947, in Philadelphia), Randy Cain (born May 2, 1945, in Philadelphia) and Ritchie Daniels formed the 4 Guys in Philadelphia in 1964. Cain left to study in 1965, returning in 1967 when Ritchie was conscripted, and the trio became the Delfonics at manager Stan Watson's instigation. Discs on Fling and Moon Shot flopped, so Watson formed his own Philly Groove label for the group, and the debut 'La La Means I Love You' was an immediate Top Five hit in 1968. Subsequent releases (including 'Break Your Promise', 'Ready Or Not Here I Come', 1968, and 'Didn't I (Blow Your Mind This Time)') were also substantial hits, though in 1971 Cain quit the group to be replaced by Major Harris, from Richmond, Virginia, who in late 1973 in turn was replaced by Chicagoan Bruce Peterson. The wistful, melodic sweet-soul trio are now signed to Curtom Records.

The Dells. In 1953, Marvin Junior (first tenor), Verne Allison (tenor), Mickey McGill (baritone), Lucius McGill (tenor), Johnny Funches (lead) and Chuck Barksdale (bass) formed a vocal group at high school in Harvey, Illinois, and recorded without success, for Checker as the El Rays. Lucius quit in 1954 and the group signed with Vee Jay as the Dells, recording prolifically through the next six years. Funches left in 1958 after a serious car crash – replaced by ex-Flamingo Johnny Carter – and in 1962, the group returned to Chess where '(Bossa Nova) Bird' (Argo) became their first (minor) national hit. 1964 saw them back on Vee Jay, whose demise in 1966 led to their return to Chess, where they have since remained, enjoying more than twenty hits of varying proportions, including Top Ten entries 'Stay In My Corner' (1968) and a re-recording of their 1956 R&B hit, 'Oh What A Night' (1969). The medley 'Love Is Blue/I Can Sing A Rainbow' (1969) is the group's only British Top Twenty hit to date.

Sandy Denny has pursued an erratic career as a singer and songwriter since she left Fairport Convention at the end of 1969. She had emerged on the British folk scene a few years earlier and after a series of performances at the Troubadour and Les Cousins in London, she joined the Strawbs briefly in 1968, recording one album with them.

As a lead singer with Fairport Convention, Denny (born Jan. 6, 1941) was instrumental in introducing traditional folk songs into the group's repertoire, as well as her own material, notably 'Who Knows Where The Time Goes', later recorded by Judy Collins and other singers. Leaving Fairport, she formed Fotheringay with her future husband Trevor Lucas and American guitarist Jerry Donaghue. The band was short-lived and Denny went on to record three solo albums of her own songs for Island: *The North Star Grassman And The Raven* (1971), *Sandy* (1972) and *Like An Old Fashioned Waltz* (1974).

In 1974, she rejoined Fairport Convention, which now included Lucas and Donaghue. After an uncertain beginning, she had, by 1975 and *Rising For The Moon*, established herself as a fully integrated member of the band. She was continuing to record as a solo artist in parallel with her work with Fairport.

John Denver was born in Rosell, New Mexico in 1943 and started off as a folk artist in Los Angeles in the early Sixties. He joined the Chad Mitchell Trio in 1965 and stayed for four years before signing a solo contract with RCA in 1969. He has made numerous solo albums and is currently one of the top-selling artists worldwide. Denver's early songs were second generation folk protest, centring on the evils of social injustice and war. Since going solo, he has increasingly spoken out in song for ecological awareness. His best songs, like 'Take Me Home Country Roads' and 'Rocky Mountain High' (both Top Ten hits), combine an evocation of natural wonder with lyrics that stress the fragility of such feelings in the contemporary world. The sense of space in his songs is conveyed by powerful acoustic guitars behind his nasal, but clear, singing voice. His other, and most popular, theme is romance, explored in that uncertain ground between realism and sentimentality in songs like 'Leaving On A Jet Plane', a hit for Peter, Paul and Mary, and 'Annie's Song'.

Lynsey de Paul. Born in 1951, she is Britain's most successful woman singer-songwriter. Trained as a child in classical music she later changed to art. Graduating from Hornsey Art College she began designing record sleeves, and soon after, writing songs. One of her first efforts, 'Storm In A Teacup', was a Top Twenty success for the Fortunes on Capitol. In July, 1972, she recorded her first single, 'Sugar Me', a Top Five success throughout Britain and Europe; since then she has written eleven Top Twenty records, either by herself or in collaboration with Barry Blue. In 1974 she became the first woman to win the Ivor Novello Award for Best Ballad with 'Won't Somebody Dance With Me' and in 1975 she won a further Ivor Novello Award for the TV theme 'No Honestly'. Other TV themes include *Pilger* and *The Golden Shot*. Her future would seem to lie in songwriting rather than performing where her high girlish voice sounds over-coy after a few listenings.

Derek and The Dominos. Originally formed by Eric Clapton in order to play a charity concert in London in June, 1970 with members of Delaney and Bonnie's band – Bobby Whitlock (organ), Carl Radle (bass), Jim Gordon (drums), and ex-Traffic guitarist Dave Mason – the group's name reflected the post-Cream Clapton's desire for anonymity. He kept the group together – minus Mason – for a low-key British tour later that year which was interrupted for recording sessions in Miami that produced the brilliant double album, *Layla* (Polydor, 1972), featuring Duane Allman on slide guitar. It was a song-cycle incorporating originals by Clapton and Whitlock as well as classics like Chuck Willis' 'It's Too Late'. *Layla* showed Clapton to be not just a guitarist, but a writer and singer of range and power. It was said later to have been inspired by his relationship with Patti Harrison.

After recording a live album, not released until 1973, the group broke up in May 1971 reportedly after disagreements during the sessions for a projected second album.

Rick Derringer (real name Zehringer) was a member of the McCoys whose 'Hang On Sloopy' (Bang, 1965) was a No. 1 hit. With his brother Randy, he was later brought in by manager Steve Paul to form the nucleus of Johnny Winter's backing band. Rick Derringer also produced the next four albums by Winter.

During Johnny Winter's long lay-off to undergo treatment for narcotics addiction, Rick Derringer became lead guitarist for the Edgar Winter Group. His best-known number, 'Rock And Roll Hoochie Koo', appeared on albums by both Winter brothers, as well as his own first solo record, *All American Boy* (Epic, 1974), a technically proficient set of heavy metal rock.

The Detroit Emeralds are a pleasant but unexceptional soft-soul trio – Abe and Ivy Tillmon (born in Little Rock, Arkansas in 1943 and 1941 respectively), James Mitchell (born in

Perry, Florida in 1941) – who first recorded in 1968 for Detroit label Ric-Tic. One minor hit, 'Showtime' (1968), and two flops later they signed to Westbound and produced themselves at Willie Mitchell's in Memphis on a series of steady rolling hits, typified by 'Do Me Right', 'You Want It, You Got It' (1971), and 'Feel The Need In Me' (a British hit in 1972). In 1974 Abe Tillmon split from his partners to continue on Westbound with new men as A. C. Tillmon and The Detroit Emeralds, while the others recruited Carl Johnson and became Now on the Fee label.

Neil Diamond, like Carole King, has been successful as a singer and composer in both the Sixties and Seventies. He was born in New York on Jan. 24, 1945 and peddled his songs in the song-factory of the Brill Building until his potential was recognized by Jeff Barry and Ellie Greenwich, who took him to Bert Berns' newly established Bang label in 1965.

His first single for the label, 'Solitary Man', was a minor hit, but he followed with a series of five Top Twenty records, beginning with 'Cherry Cherry' in 1966. Diamond's compositions were also recorded by the Monkees ('I'm A Believer'), Elvis Presley and Deep Purple ('Kentucky Woman') and Lulu ('The Boat That I Row').

To this point, Diamond's songs were well-crafted Brill Building commercial pop. In 1968, artistic ambitions took him to Uni where 'Brooklyn Roads', his first single, was a self-consciously autobiographical piece. Over the next few years, his work included calculated pop ('Cracklin' Rosie'), experimental sequences ('African Trilogy', described as a folk-ballet, on *Tap Root Manuscript*, 1970) and a handful of classic songs, notably 'I Am . . . I Said' (1971) and 'Stones' (1971).

As his success grew, his artistic horizons (critics called them pretensions) kept pace. In 1973, he signed to Columbia for a vast advance, releasing his songs for the soundtrack of *Jonathan Livingston Seagull* as his first album for them. It justified critical scepticism about his judgement, though *Serenade* (1974) did something to redress the balance.

The Dillards – originally Doug (born March 6, 1937) and Rodney Dillard (May 18, 1942), Dean Webb (March 28, 1937) and Mitch Jayne (May 7, 1930), were richly imbued with the inbred and isolated traditions of the Ozark Mountains in the southern states of America. Their music was high-powered bluegrass with a strong emphasis on comedy, notably on their second album *Live Almost* in 1964. Doug played banjo, Rodney, guitar – both sharing work on fiddle and dobro – Dean Webb played mandolin and Mitch Jayne, once a local disc jockey, played bass and handled all the introductions and routines. Later they added a young but accomplished fiddle player, Byron Berline, for occasional gigs and sessions, most notably their more old-timey album *Pickin' And Fiddlin'* (1965).

The group arrived in LA in 1963 and were signed by the (then) essentially folk-blues label Elektra. A shared management brought them into early contact with the Byrds. The new electric sound turned Doug Dillard's head and he left, unhappy about the group's direction. By 1968 he had teamed up with ex-Byrd Gene Clark to form the short-lived but highly influential Dillard and Clark.

The Dillards, with Herb Pederson replacing Doug, trod initially well and tastefully between country and rock on two albums, *Wheatstraw Suite* (1968) and *Copperfields* (1969). Pederson left a year later and was replaced by Billy Ray Latham. At this point the group strayed further from its original path, featuring electric instruments with greater regularity on albums like *Roots And Branches* (Liberty, 1972) and *Tribute To The American Duck* (1973).

Dr Hook And The Medicine Show comprises Ray Sawyer (vocals, guitar, born Feb. 1, 1937 in Alabama), Dennis Locorriere (vocals, guitar, born June 13, 1949 in New Jersey), William Francis (keyboards, born Jan. 16, 1942 in California), Richard Elswit (guitar, born July 6, 1945 in New York), George Cummings (guitar, steel guitar, born July 28, 1938), Jance Garfat (bass, born March 3, 1944 in California), and John David (drums, born Aug. 8, 1942 in New Jersey), replaced by John Wolters. Originally known as the Chocolate Papers, the group was formed in the late Sixties in New Jersey. Manager Ron Haffkine put them in touch with Playboy cartoonist, songwriter and singer Shel Silverstein, who was writing the score for the film *Who Is Harry Kellerman And Why Is He Saying Those Terrible Things About Me?* and asked them to perform it. As a result the group got a contract with Columbia in 1971.

In 1972 they had their first British and American Top Ten hit with Silverstein's plaintive 'Sylvia's Mother'. 'The Cover Of "Rolling Stone"' followed 'Sylvia' into the American Top Ten but was banned in Britain by the BBC for advertising. They recorded three albums for Columbia, *Dr Hook And The Medicine Show, Sloppy Seconds* (1972) and *Belly Up* (1973), before leaving the company for Capitol. They are best known as the performers of Silverstein's comic songs – though Silverstein has recorded a collection of them himself, *Freakin' At The Freakers' Ball* (Columbia, 1972), and also writes in a more serious vein for artists like Bobby Bare. *Bankrupt* (1975), however, saw the group expanding their range through versions of songs like 'Only Sixteen' which revealed their strong Southern roots, as well as maintaining their reputation as rock's most accomplished humorists.

Dr John. A survivor of the darker sides of the music business, and vehement champion of New Orleans music and musicians, he was born Malcolm (Mac) Rebennack in that city in 1941, and first recorded in 1958 as session guitarist for R&B labels Ace, Ebb, Ric, Ron, and Specialty, while writing and arranging for several artists on these labels – notably Jerry Byrne ('Lights Out', 'Carry On'). He also toured behind local rock stars like Byrne and Frankie Ford, and recorded one single himself – a fiery instrumental called 'Storm Warning' (Rex). After he was shot in the hand in 1961 he played bass in a dixieland band before learning organ and resuming session work for Harold Battiste's AFO organization. Transferring to Los Angeles he continued working with Battiste and other producer/arrangers (René Hall, J. W. Alexander, H. B. Barnum, Gene

Page) until his disenchantment with West Coast ideas forced him to form his own bands – Drits and Dravy (with Ronnie Barron), The Zu Zu Band (with Jessie Hill), Morgus and The Three Ghouls – and sessions with The New Orleans Musicians Association in Los Angeles. In 1968 he emerged as voodoo man, Dr John Creaux The Night Tripper, with the startling *Gris-Gris* (Atlantic), a collection of hypnotic chants and mystic symbolism, including the eerie 'I Walk On Gilded Splinters', that was far more impressive than bemused critics would allow. Following releases in the same general style were less well conceived, although *Babylon* (1969) had some memorable cuts (particularly 'Twilight Zone'), and some of *Remedies* (1970) anticipated his return to basic New Orleans rhythm and blues – as celebrated on his fifth album *Gumbo* (1972). A masterly tribute to The Crescent City's contribution to popular music, it established Dr John as a creditable artist without frills or gimmicks and paved the way for his excellent *In The Right Place* (1973) and *Desitively Bonnaroo* (1974) albums – both produced by fellow New Orleans veteran, Allen Toussaint.

The Doobie Brothers were formed in 1970 when John Hartman (drums) moved from West Virginia to the San José, California area intending to re-form Moby Grape with Skip Spence. He was introduced by Spence to Tom Johnston (guitar) and with Dave Shogren (bass) they formed a band called Pud. In the course of playing the San Francisco Bay Area they met Pat Simmons (guitar) and one night over a 'doobie' (California slang for a joint) changed their name to the Doobie Brothers.

They were signed to Warner Bros Records by A&R man Ted Templeman on the strength of a demo tape, Templeman then making his producing debut with the band. Their initial success was in mid-1972 with the Top Twenty hit 'Listen To The Music'. By this time they had added second drummer Michael Hossack and replaced Shogren with Tiran Porter. From this time they had a string of hits based on the infectious rhythm and phrasing of 'Music'. In 1974 Hossack left to join Bonaroo; he was replaced by Keith

Knudsen. Also that year they were joined by guitarist Jeff 'Skunk' Baxter, late of Steely Dan.

Nick Drake, a British singer-songwriter, first came into the public eye in 1969 as support act for concerts promoted by Joe Boyd's company Witchseason. His first album *Five Leaves Left* (Island, 1969) didn't receive the same exposure as albums by his Witchseason colleagues – but that's how Drake wanted it. He never spoke on stage, rarely looked at the audience and never gave interviews. A complete enigma, his small but fanatical following grew with the release of his best album *Bryter Layer* (1970) but by this time live appearances had ceased altogether. In 1972 he turned up at Island Records' office with the master tape of *Pink Moon* and disappeared as mysteriously as he had arrived.

Many saw a tragic presentiment in his lyrics, and after a deep depression Drake died in his sleep at the end of 1974. He left behind four songs from an unfinished album he had begun with producer John Wood.

Pete Drake is one of the first – and best – steel guitar players of the modern era. Born in Augusta, Georgia, on Oct. 8, 1933, the brother of another country figure, Jack Drake, he was a product of the mid-Fifties when the modern shaped, electric, jazz-influenced steel guitars were being perfected. Playing on radio WLWA in Atlanta, he worked too for Wilma Lee and Stoney Cooper and came with them to WSM in Nashville in 1959. Developing further the style of his favourite 'steelie', Jerry Byrd, he became one of the busiest session players throughout the Sixties, enhancing the sound of artists from Marty Robbins and Don Gibson on down. He also played on Bob Dylan's *John Wesley Harding*, *Nashville Skyline* and *Self Portrait* albums.

Recording as a solo artist for Smash, Starday and Stop, he had one popular hit in 1964 with 'Forever', on Smash. From there he branched out to take up production work for, among many others, Ringo Starr. He part-owns Stop Records and a studio in Nashville, Pete's Place.

Gus Dudgeon, one of the most commercially successful British record producers of the Sixties and Seventies, is best known for his clean, dramatic work on Elton John's records. Born on Sept. 30, 1942, he began as the tape engineer on Joe Brown's 'Picture Of You' in 1962. A Decca engineer on sessions with John Mayall's Bluesbreakers, Marianne Faithfull, the Zombies, Small Faces and others, he switched to production for a live Zoot Money album. Ralph McTell, the Strawbs, David Bowie's 'Space Oddity' single, Joan Armatrading, the Bonzo Dog Band, Audience, and John Kongos followed before the classic, second Elton John album in 1970. He is a director of Rocket Records for whom he has produced Kiki Dee among others.

The Eagles were formed in August, 1971, since when their immaculate combination of neat harmonies and countrified rock music has made them the premier Los Angeles rock band. All four members were experienced musicians. Randy Meisner (bass, born March 8, 1945) had played with Rick Nelson, Poco and Linda Ronstadt, who had also employed Glenn Frey (guitar, born Nov. 6, 1946) and Don Henley (drums, born July 22, 1946). Bernie Leadon (guitar, born July 19, 1945) was a former Flying Burrito Brother.

The first album, *Eagles* (1972), included Jackson Browne's 'Take It Easy', an American Top Twenty hit. *Desperado* (Asylum, 1973), recorded in Britain and produced by Glyn Johns, remains their best album to date. It pursued the theme of the gunslinger/outlaw as rock star with flair. It was followed by *On The Border* (1974) and *One Of These Nights* (1975), which included hit singles with the title track and 'Lyin' Eyes'.

Earth Quake, formed in 1966, were one of San Francisco's first groups. But like the Flamin' Groovies, they stayed away from the psychedelic scene, preferring English pop and oldies. They built a following in Berkeley through a series of free concerts, and in 1970 the group (John Doukas, Robbie Dunbar, Stan Miller, Steve Nelson) signed with A&M. Two albums were recorded, and their singles ('Tickler', 'I Get

The Sweetest Feeling') were regional hits, but a lack of promotional effort kept them from going further, and Earth Quake left A&M. They continued performing regularly in Berkeley, and in 1973 a single ('Mr Security') was issued on their own label, Berserkley. This was followed by 'Friday On My Mind' in mid-1974, which received heavy airplay locally and was eventually picked up nationally by Jonathan King's UK label. They released a live album in 1975 and began recording several other artists, such as the Modern Lovers, another critically acclaimed band whose career had been badly mismanaged.

Earth, Wind and Fire, more than any other black band, fulfilled the promise offered by a jazz-funk fusion. Formed by singer/drummer Maurice White in Chicago in the mid-Sixties (and recording for Capitol as the Salty Peppers) the band were eventually picked up by Warners in 1971 after Sly and the Family Stone had made it obvious that 'progressive black music' was a commercial proposition. Their first single, 'Love Is Life', was a minor hit but their two Warners albums failed despite massive promotional campaigns. The bulk of the band split and Maurice and brother Verdine formed a new group with Phillip Baily, Jessica Cleaves, Roland Battista, Larry Dunn, Ronald Wayne Laws and Ralph Johnson. Pulling free from jazz elements into wickedly electric rhythms, the group's reputation began to build with the Columbia 1972 album *Last Days Of Time* which was followed with hit discs like 'Open Our Eyes', 'Head To The Sky' and 'That's The Way Of The World'.

Dave Edmunds, born 1946 in Cardiff, Wales, spent eight years playing guitar in various local bands, until he formed a group with bassist John Williams and drummer Bob Jones called Love Sculpture, whose repertoire consisted of early rock standards and lightning-speed guitar adaptations of classical themes – one of which, 'Sabre Dance', was a Top Ten hit single on Parlophone in 1968. It was the group's only hit, however, and after they disbanded Edmunds signed with Gordon Mills' management agency, then retired to Wales with Kingsley Ward to build his own recording studio, Rockfield.

Rockfield soon became one of the most active studios in Britain, with a distinctive 'sound' that couldn't be matched elsewhere. He spent months experimenting, until he could produce exact replicas of his favourite records, from early Sun rockabillies to the most elaborate Phil Spector masterpieces. The first product of his applied talents was 'I Hear You Knockin'', an electrifying tribute to his Fifties idols that was a worldwide smash on MAM towards the end of 1970, reaching No. 1 in Britain and No. 8 in America.

Among his productions have been records by the Flamin' Groovies, Deke Leonard, Brinsley Schwarz, Ducks Deluxe, Shakin' Stevens and the Sunsets and Del Shannon. In 1972 and 1973, Edmunds released two singles on the Rockfield label glorifying the Phil Spector sound, 'Baby I Love You' and 'Born To Be With You', which were Top Ten hits in Britain. In 1974 he appeared in the David Essex film *Stardust*, incidentally creating all the music supposedly done by the Beatles-like group in the film. In 1975 he released a long-awaited second album *Subtle As A Flying Mallet.*

Electric Light Orchestra was originally conceived by Carl Wayne and Roy Wood as a classically oriented offshoot of the Move. ELO (initially Roy Wood, Jeff Lynne, Bev Bevan) made one critically acclaimed album in 1972, then split apart, with Wood and ex-Move bassist Rick Price forming Wizzard, and Lynne and Bevan adding Richard Tandy (keyboards), Mike De Albuquerque (bass), Mike Edwards, Colin Walker (cellos) and Wilf Gibson (violin), the last three from the London Symphony Orchestra (Walker and Gibson were replaced in 1974 by Hugh McDowell and Mike Kaminski). This group scored almost immediately with 'Roll Over Beethoven', a single cleverly combining themes from Chuck Berry and Beethoven. In three subsequent albums, ELO has refined and developed their concept of using classical instruments and motifs in a rock format, with occasional hit singles ('Showdown', 'Can't Get It Out Of My Head') and a heavy American touring schedule. *Eldorado*, a rock symphony, became their first gold album in 1975. By this time, the band had changed labels from Harvest to Warner Bros. 1976 saw them move to Jet and find further American success with 'Evil Woman'.

Mama Cass Elliot, born on Sept. 9, 1941 in Alexandria, Virginia, began her career in New York singing with the Big Three, via whom she met Denny Doherty and then John and Michelle Phillips. The four sang together as the Mamas and Papas between 1966 and 1968, and for a short period in 1971. Following the first break-up of the group Cass employed her strong and distinctive voice on more pop-oriented music, for TV shows and cut a number of solo albums, notably, *Dream A Little Dream* (Dunhill, 1968) and *Make Your Own Kind Of Music* (1969). In 1970 she worked briefly with ex-Traffic member Dave Mason, returning to the rock music she had abandoned, but following the failure of the Mamas and Papas' comeback she went back once more to the TV/cabaret scene. She died of heart failure in London in July, 1974.

EMI Records. In both Britain and America (where it is the major shareholder of Capitol) EMI rose and fell with the Beatles. The Beatles provided the company with a secure foundation to the mid-Sixties: in Britain its music profits rose by 80% in 1964. However, in America, despite the success of its British groups, the Beach Boys and its country division, a series of bad management decisions at Capitol restricted the company's growth and it was only after Baskhar Menon, from EMI India, was appointed president that the company, with the help of groups like Grand Funk Railroad, returned to the black.

In the wake of the underground, EMI set up its own 'progressive' label, Harvest, but even with the success of groups like Pink Floyd, the company's major assets were still the Beatles and the fact that it distributed and/or manufactured nearly half of the records sold in Britain. Accordingly, EMI's fortunes also fluctuated with the rise and fall of the market and changes in its licensee rights. This latter point became especially important in the late Sixties and early Seventies when American companies were more concerned than ever to integrate their international operations and open their own British offices, to sign new acts as much as to oversee the selling of their own product. For example, MCA moved in and ABC and Elektra/Asylum out of EMI House in 1974–75.

However, by the mid-Seventies, under the direction of Gerry Oord from Bovima Records in Holland, who kept all the individual Beatles bar George Harrison, set up the EMI label on which Queen were phenomenally successful, kept the rights to important American companies like Motown and Fantasy, and signed a successful production deal with Mickie Most (RAK Records), EMI had re-affirmed its place as the British market leader and its position as the world's largest record company.

David Essex was born in London on July 23, 1947. After an undistinguished career as a pop singer dating back to the mid-Sixties, Essex achieved his first success in the London stage version of *Godspell.* The part of Jim McLain in the film *That'll Be The Day* (1973) proved to be prophetic, as Essex himself went on to become a rock star with a string of hit singles on CBS ingeniously produced by Jeff Wayne with the artist himself as composer. Among them were 'Rock On' (1973, a big American hit), 'Lamplight' (1973), 'Gonna Make You A Star' (1974), 'Stardust' (1975), 'Hold Me Close' (1975) and 'If I Could' (1975). His singing ranged from a staccato, heavily echoing style on the earliest discs to a more coy English-accented voice developed out of the Anthony Newley/ Bowie manner.

European Pop. Despite British membership of the Common Market, European influence on the country's pop charts remains slight and unpredictable. Heintje, a 14-year-old Dutch boy, may well have garnered over thirty gold discs in Germany, but his name wasn't worth a light in Britain. Nor was that of Italy's Adriano Celentano or Raphael, the toast of Spain. Recently the only Europeans who have made a place for themselves in British hearts have been Sacha Distel, Nana Mouskouri and the phenomenal bandleader James Last, reputed to have sold more records than the Beatles, and the worldwide middle-of-the-road market leader. Not far behind are Demis Roussos, former lead singer with Aphrodite's Child, and French crooner Charles Aznavour whose 'She' was a big hit in 1974.

Of the continental singles that have made the grade in Britain since 1969, none has had more success than 'Je T'aime . . . Moi Non Plus', Jane Birkin and Serge Gainsbourg's set of orchestrated bedroom noises. Of the less sensational items, Holland's Shocking Blue, the first Continental group to top the American charts, were popular for a while but fizzled out after one hit, 'Venus' (1970). The same year Germany's Rattles family won British approval and made it to No. 6 with 'The Witch' while Spain's Miguel Rios scored with 'A Song Of Joy' from Beethoven's Ninth Symphony. The man who arranged the latter, Waldo de los Rios, then had a hit in his own right when he stuck a rhythm section behind Mozart's 40th Symphony.

Since then, however, it has been rock bands like Germany's Can and Tangerine Dream that have drawn attention at the expense of Europe's pop stars. With the exception of the Eurovision Song Contest winners, the only European entries to the British charts since 1971 have been two by Holland's Focus and 'Vado Via' by the Italian Drupi (Gian Piero Anelli) in 1973; 'Radar Love' by Holland's Golden Earring in 1974; and 'Autobahn' by Germany's Kraftwerk in 1975. As far as Eurovision is concerned, it would seem that British record buyers are becoming increasingly anxious to demonstrate their condemnation of the British entries by buying up large quantities of the opposition, e.g. Dana (1970), Severine (1971), Vicky Leandros (1972), Anne-Marie David (1973), Abba, Gigliola Cinquetti and Mouth and McNeal (1974) and Teach-In (1975).

European Rock. Before 1967 rock on the European mainland was dominated by its Anglo-American origins. The European product was seen to be derivative and inferior. As far as mainstream rock is concerned this has remained essentially true, but since 1967 European groups have done more than their fair share of expanding the frontiers of rock music.

The reasons for this are varied. Youth markets for popular music did not develop on the continent to the same degree, and the sweeping changes of the mid-Sixties did not receive the mass-culturization that they did in Britain and America. Rather they remained the concern of the student strata, not least those pursuing a formal education in music. The boundary between popular culture and art was not narrowed in the same way; the boundaries of expression remained artistic rather than commercial. The lack of a large market for rock, and particularly live (danceable) rock, reinforced the process, leaving European rock as a playground for experimentation by highly trained musicians: in form, instrumentation, studio techniques, and electronics.

The influences on the various groups have naturally been wide. Many have stressed their debt to twentieth-century classical composers, like Satie, Messiaen, Varese, and Stravinsky. The influence of American jazz has been equally marked, with musicians like Miles Davis, John Coltrane, and Charlie Parker often cited. The rock influences have largely been those similarly emphasizing improvisational techniques: West Coast acid-rock (Jefferson Airplane and Grateful Dead), and the London Underground scene (Pink Floyd and the Soft Machine), and Cream.

Such a range of influences makes generalization about European rock an obvious problem, and it is only in the contrast with the main body of Anglo-American rock and its retreat towards the roots of country and rock'n'roll, that the clearly futuristic thrust of most European bands can be seen. This thrust, though, has been expressed in very different ways. A group like Tangerine Dream, from Berlin, is clearly operating on the technological frontiers of rock, fascinated by pure sound and its possibilities, whereas Amon Duul II has been more concerned to make music around futuristic themes, evoking the unknown through the use of conventional instrumentation. The Dutch band Focus share with the former a devotion to music as an end in itself, and with the latter the rock notion of music as a physical assault on the senses.

Two well-known French-based groups illustrate opposite poles. Gong, led by ex-Soft David Allen, play simple songs employing jazz techniques and electronic wizardry. Their themes revolve around a mythical planet populated by gentle hippies. Magma, on the other hand, have integrated heavy rhythms and operatic singing into a Wagnerian trilogy of galactic war marches.

Overall the commitment to advancing musical frontiers that has characterized the best European bands has seen their wide influences integrated into a number of radically different musics that bodes well for the future of rock as an arena for the musical imagination.

The Faces were a coalition of three leaderless Small Faces, Ronnie Lane, bass (born in London on April 1, 1946), Ian McLagan, keyboards (May 12, 1946), and Kenny Jones, drums (Sept. 8, 1948), and two refugees from the Jeff Beck Group, Rod Stewart (Jan. 10, 1945) and guitarist Ron Wood (1947), whom Beck had temporarily converted to bass. The group worked hard on the road for two years after their formation in 1969 before establishing themselves in Britain by reason of their ebullient live performances and Stewart's solo hit, 'Maggie May' (Mercury, 1971), though they were accepted sooner in America where Stewart enjoyed a lingering reputation from his days with Beck. The band's boozy, easygoing approach tended to work less well in the recording studio and the group's albums, consistently overshadowed by Stewart's solo efforts, moved from the patchily successful *First Step* (Warner Bros, 1970), *Long Player* (1971), and *A Nod's As Good As A Wink To A Blind Horse* (1972), to the disappointing *Ooh La La* (1973) and then – apart from a live album in 1974 – apparent stalemate, as Lane left in mid-1973 to be replaced by Tetsu Yamauchi and Wood and Jones made solo recordings. However, they remain one of the most exciting live groups in the world. Ron Wood's tour with the Stones in 1975 and the group's relative inactivity because of Stewart's British 'tax problems' undermined the group's cohesion.

Family. In the late Sixties and early Seventies Leicester band Family were one of the most talked about British bands without ever breaking into the top league. Originally they set out as Jim King and the Farinas but changed their name and soon made two fine albums, *Music In A Doll's House* (Reprise, 1968) and *Family Entertainment* (1969). The frenetic approach of their cadaverous lead singer Roger Chapman (born April 8, 1944) set a new trend in vocal styles although the band's performances were often erratic and their personnel was never constant for long, only Chapman, Charlie Whitney (June 24, 1944) and Rob Townsend (July 7, 1947) remaining throughout the band's career.

Rick Grech left to join Blind Faith and Jim King returned to Leicester. With Poli Palmer (born May 25, 1943) and John Weider (April 21, 1947), Family recorded two further albums before John Wetton replaced John Weider. *Fearless* (1971) and *Bandstand* (1972) did something to restore the band's flagging credibility but with the departure of Wetton and Palmer, Family could scarcely accommodate further personnel changes. With Tony Ashton and Jim Cregan they recorded *It's Only A Movie* (1973) for the short-lived Raft label, but later that year Chapman and Whitney decided to wind up Family. The band went out in a blaze of glory with a memorable farewell tour and Chapman and Whitney formed Streetwalkers, who have subsequently enjoyed limited success.

Freddy Fender was strictly a regional artist for twenty years until in 1975 the hitherto mysterious cornerstone of Texas rock'n'roll became a Chicano national hero with two Top Five smashes on ABC, 'Before The Next Teardrop Falls' and 'Wasted Days And Wasted Nights'.

Born into an exclusively Mexican environment in San Benito in 1936 as Baldemar Huerta, he picked up on blues and country music while accompanying his migrant farm-worker parents on trips to the Mid-West. In 1959, he recorded numerous swamp blues for Duncan, including 'Wasted Days And Wasted Nights', which quickly scaled the San Antonio charts. However, in May, 1960, Fender – as he now called himself – was arrested for marijuana possession and spent the next three years in prison. During this period R&B collectors' items appeared on Imperial, Argo, Talent Scout (as Scotty Wayne) and Goldband. On his release, Fender returned to the beer and tamale Chicano dance circuit, cut (then unfashionable) R&B for Norco and then retired in 1969. However, publicity from Doug Sahm, a longtime admirer of Fender, led to fresh recordings – on Starflite and Crazy Cajun – for Huey Meaux whose innovative production, which mixed pedal steel, harpsichord and accordion, was the perfect vehicle for Fender's soul-inflected, Tex-Mex, country vocals.

Michael Fennelly was born in 1948 in New Jersey, and after leading several amateur bands in that area, moved to Los Angeles in 1965. For the next four years, his career was heavily influenced by Curt Boetcher, who led a succession of critically acclaimed and commercially disastrous groups such as Sagittarius and the Millennium, of which Fennelly was a part. In early 1970, Fennelly discovered a group called Stonehenge, whom he joined and renamed Crabby Appleton. After one hit ('Go Back', Elektra, 1970) and two albums on Elektra, the group disbanded, and Fennelly embarked on a solo career with *Lane Changer* (Columbia) in late 1973. He now plays occasional sessions, but is at present without a record contract.

Bryan Ferry was born in Washington, County Durham on Sept. 26, 1945. An ex-Newcastle Arts student and the guiding light of Roxy Music, Ferry has also since late 1973 pursued a solo career, producing by 1975 two albums of his own for Island Records whilst remaining at the helm of the group. He has said that his music for the group represents the serious side of his work, but in fact the tone of both is very similar.

Unusually, it is the group that records his own songs, while the solo albums (*These Foolish Things*, 1973, *Another Time Another Place*, 1974) carry his interpretations of a wide range of popular music, from Bob Dylan ('A Hard Rain's Gonna Fall') to the Platters ('Smoke Gets In Your Eyes') – both British Top Ten hits. All feature his polished arrangements and dryly exaggerated enunciation to create that particular mood of romantic nostalgia that is only too aware of its own falsity. Ferry himself stares out of his record covers in tuxedo and bow-tie, his expression halfway between amusement and a malicious irony.

First Choice were discovered by Philadelphia disc jockey Georgie Woods in 1972 when, as the Debronettes, the three soul sisters were brought to MFSB guitarist/producer Norman Harris. Their first release, 'This Is The House Where Love Died' (on Wand Records) failed but Stan Watson of Philly Groove signed the girls – Rochelle Fleming (born on Feb. 11, 1950 in Philadelphia), Annette Guest (born in Chester, Pennsylvania on Nov. 19, 1954) and Joyce Jones (born July 30, 1949). At once, their 'Armed And Extremely Dangerous' with its arresting production, featuring all the ingredients of the rising Philly Sound, was a huge hit, first in Britain and then in America in 1973. Subsequent hits with 'Smarty Pants' (1973) and 'The Player' (1974) show First Choice to be one of the few black girl groups who owe little or nothing to the Supremes' vocal stylings.

Roberta Flack, born in Asheville, North Carolina on Feb. 2, 1937, was exposed to musical expertise from her earliest days – her mother was a classical pianist, while her father played jazz. She graduated with a BA in music from Howard University, Washington and, after teaching music for a year, began to accompany opera singers. Finally in 1967 she took a job playing and singing jazz at a Washington club. Roberta was spotted by eminent jazz pianist Les McCann, upon whose recommendation she was signed to Atlantic by producer Joel Dorn. Having enjoyed some chart success in duet with Donny Hathaway, Roberta topped the American charts in 1972 with the haunting 'First Time Ever I Saw Your Face'

– also a British Top Twenty hit – taken from her first album, *First Take.* She followed that with another huge international hit in 1973, Charles Fox and Norman Gimbel's 'Killing Me Softly With His Song'. Supposedly inspired by seeing Don McLean, 'Killing Me' made it clear that Flack was rapidly becoming a jazz-tinged MOR singer and leaving 'soul' far behind, a shift which her later work has made even clearer.

Flamin' Groovies, formed in San Francisco, 1966, were originally known as the Chosen Few, then the Lost and Found. Cyril Jordan, George Alexander, Roy Loney, Tim Lynch, and Danny Mihm were the first line-up as the Flamin' Groovies, with Lynch replaced by James Farrell and Loney by Chris Wilson in 1971, and Mihm replaced by David Wright in 1973. Never an accepted part of the San Francisco scene, the Groovies were rock'n'roll purists with a traditional approach, doing Fifties rock, Beatle music and folk-rock in a no-nonsense, anti-progressive style that built them a solid cult following but held back the attention lavished on more fashionable groups.

A self-issued album in 1968 was followed by an album on Epic (*Supersnazz*) the next year. A contract with Kama Sutra resulted in two albums, *Flamingo* (1970) and *Teenage Head* (1971). With the latter, the Flamin' Groovies were hailed as the new Rolling Stones, and it seemed that mass idolatry was just around the corner, but then a two-year stay in England under the auspices of United Artists resulted in only two singles (produced by Dave Edmunds) and a series of misunderstandings that found the group back in San Francisco in 1973. Their cult following was by now immense, and their recordings collectors' items. Enormously popular in Europe, they toured France and were treated as heroes. Back home, the group exercised more caution in dealing with the record industry, releasing only one single (the Edmunds-produced 'You Tore Me Down'), on the independent Bomp Records label, an offshoot of *Who Put the Bomp*, a leading fanzine, resulting in a contract with Sire Records in 1975.

Flash Cadillac and the Continental Kids. 1969 was a year in which many groups did well with parodies of Fifties rock, with Sha Na Na the model for dozens more such as Big Wheelie and the Hubcaps and Vince Vance and the Valiants who became fixtures on all the regional club circuits over the next few years. Flash Cadillac and the Continental Kids – Sam McFadin, Warren Knight, Linn Phillips, Kris Angelo, George Robinson and Ricco Masino – formed in Colorado in 1969, were arguably the only such group to bring any originality to the genre, while also being closest to the true spirit of Fifties rock'n'roll. They moved to California in 1970 and made a strong impression with the press and audiences, then went on to appear in the film *American Graffiti* and from there to a recording contract. Their first album for Epic consisted of fairly well-known classics, but the second (*There's No Face Like Chrome*, 1974) presented a surprising synthesis of Fifties, Sixties and Seventies pop styles, not unlike groups such as Ducks Deluxe in England. A single of Barry Blue's 'Dancin' On A Saturday Night' flirted with the charts, while 'Good Times, Rock And Roll', their first on the Private Stock label, was a smallish hit in early 1975.

Flo and Eddie, originally known as the Phlorescent Leech and Eddie when they joined the Mothers of Invention after the breakup of the Turtles (of which they'd been the founding and leading members) in 1970, Mark Volman (born April 19, 1944) and Howard Kaylan (born June 22, 1945) have since been recognized as among the most adept rock satirists of the Seventies, overshadowing Zappa in the movie *200 Motels* and the European tour from which it evolved, and moving on to record two albums on their own for Reprise. Ironically, though their humour didn't come across fully on these albums, their effortless ability to create brilliant pop was evident in their treatment of such classics as 'Afterglow' and 'Days', rivalling the originals.

A 1972 tour with Alice Cooper was followed by a break from recording during which they did a movie soundtrack (*Cheap*), backed Marc Bolan on many of his hits, began writing for rock magazines and launched a syndicated radio show featuring oldies, popstar interviews, and the duo's own dazzling repartee and lightning-fast quips. 1975 saw a recording contract with Columbia and a series of tours (in which they performed devastating parodies of the entire pop pantheon, including themselves).

King Floyd, an underrated singer from New Orleans, was born on Feb. 13, 1945. He had local hits on Uptown (1964–66) and Pulsar (1967) produced by Harold Battiste, before breaking nationally with the Top Ten hit 'Groove Me' (Chimneyville, 1970). Recorded at Malaco studio in Jackson, Mississippi, and produced by another Crescent City veteran, Wardell Quezergue, it was prematurely acclaimed as the start of a 'Malaco-sound'. Apart from Jean Knight's 'Mr Big Stuff' (1971) the studio has had no more notable successes, but Floyd continues to score minor hits, including the Top Thirty 'Baby Let Me Kiss You' (1971), 'Think About It' (1973), and 'Don't Cry No More' (1974).

The Flying Burrito Brothers was formed in Los Angeles in 1968 by musicians interested in an integration of rock and country music. The original line-up was Gram Parsons (guitar, born in 1946), Chris Hillman (guitar, born Dec. 4, 1942), Sneaky Pete Kleinow (pedal steel), Joe Corneal (drums), and Chris Ethridge (bass) – the first four of whom had played on the Byrds' ground-breaking *Sweetheart Of The Rodeo* (1968). The band never made two albums with the same line-up. Temporary recruits included Bernie Leadon (guitar), Rick Roberts (guitar), Al Perkins (pedal steel), Byron Berline (fiddle), Martin Scougat (triangle).

The original concept was more than a simple fusion of country and rock music. It was also a 'cosmic' American fusion, a bringing together of Sixties lifestyle and consciousness with the full width of the American musical heritage, from uptempo jigs to 'the saddest love songs ever heard'; from biblical righteousness to country breezes. A song like 'Sin City', from their first and finest album *Gilded Palace Of Sin* (A&M, 1969), managed to sound as beautiful as an updated Everly Brothers, whilst retaining the bits of the traditional country theme of uprootedness in the context of the vanished Sixties dream. This vision, though, was largely Gram Parsons', and found its fullest expression in his sadly truncated solo career – he died on Sept. 19, 1973. After his departure from the Burritos in 1970, the group pursued a simpler aim, in which the early bite was sacrificed for a simpler music that still proved too subtle for commercial success. Their albums after *Burrito De Luxe* (1970) – *The Flying Burrito Bros* (1971) and *Last Of The Red Hot Burritos* (1972) – while boasting some fine music, suffered in comparison with the half-realized vision of the early years. The 1974 double album *Close Up The Honky Tonks*, a compilation of the first two albums plus unreleased material, was a fitting epitaph for the group. However, the appeal of the name was so strong that in 1975 Kleinow and Ethridge got together another band of Burritos (including Joel Scott Hill, Gene Parsons and cajun fiddler Gib Guilbeau) and secured a Columbia record contract.

Focus, a Dutch group who came together in 1969 as the back-up musicians to the Amsterdam version of the musical *Hair*, are four formidable musicians – Thijs Van Leer (organ, flute, vocals, born March 31, 1948), Jan Akkerman (guitar, born Dec. 24, 1946), Burt Reiter (bass, Nov. 26, 1946), and Pierre Van Der Linden (drums, Feb. 19, 1946). With the exception of the self-taught Reiter, the group has behind it an extensive array of formal musical education. Since 1969 they have produced a number of albums, notably *Moving Waves* (Blue Horizon, 1971), *Focus 3* (Polydor, 1972) and *Focus At The Rainbow* (1973), featuring their unique style of music, combining elements of rock (Cream, Traffic), modern jazz (Davis, Coltrane, Parker) and classical music from Bach through to Bartok, into a driving instrumental sound topped off by Thijs Van Leer's extraordinary scat-singing and Akkerman's imaginative guitar solos. 'Sylvia' and 'Hocus Pocus' were British Top Twenty hits for the group in 1973. Van Leer and Akkerman have also cut solo albums, for CBS and Harvest respectively. The group's former bass-player, Cyril Havermanns, has also cut an album, on MGM.

John Fogerty. The driving force behind Creedence Clearwater Revival, John Fogerty (born in Berkeley, California on May 28, 1945) pursued a solo recording career after CCR disbanded in 1972. As the Blue Ridge Rangers, he recorded country-and-western and gospel standards – e.g. 'Jambalaya' (a Top Twenty single for him in 1972), 'Hearts Of Stone' and 'Workin' On A Building' on which he played all the instruments and sang all the vocal parts. The result was a classic album *Blue Ridge Rangers* (Fantasy, 1972) on which Fogerty demonstrated his mastery of studio technique and ability to inject new life into old material. Three years later, after a lengthy dispute with his record company, Fogarty re-emerged with another hit single, 'Rockin' All Over The World', and the fine *John Fogerty*, a collection of mostly original songs performed in the Creedence manner.

Peter Frampton, born on April 22, 1950, in Beckenham, Kent, started his musical career with the Herd. Named 'the face of 68' by several British music papers seeking the star of tomorrow, Frampton was quickly disenchanted with teeny-bopper music and formed Humble Pie with the similarly disenchanted Steve Marriott. After two years, he left to pursue his own music – a gentler, more romantic style of rock than the Humble Pie manner. His main strength is his lead guitar playing, and it is this which has dominated his solo albums, lifting an average songwriting ability into music that at times comes close to Eric Clapton's definitive rendition of the romantic guitar on *Layla*. His lyrics centre on romance, displaying – particularly on the second album *Frampton's Camel* (A&M, 1973) – a powerful knack for marrying telling hook lines to imaginative guitar-playing.

Free were given their name and some early encouragement by Alexis Korner. Paul Rodgers, vocals (born on Dec. 12, 1949); Paul Kossoff, guitar (Sept. 14, 1950); Andy Fraser, bass (Aug. 7, 1952); Simon Kirke, drums (Aug. 27, 1949) made up one of many blues-based bands to form in the shadow of Cream and the blues renaissance of 1968. From the start they mixed original compositions with blues standards and their bare-wired style quickly earned them a strong reputation with club audiences, although neither of their first two albums – *Tons Of Sobs* (Island, 1968) and *Free* (Island, 1969) – nor the singles taken from the latter made any impact on the charts. Then 'All Right Now', released in May, 1970, became one of the year's major singles. Let down by the failure of the follow-up, the excellent 'Stealer', and perhaps too young to handle their sudden stardom, the group split up early the following year.

Rodgers and Fraser, Free's songwriters, formed Toby and Peace respectively, while Kossoff and Kirke teamed up with Tetsu Yamauchi (bass) and John 'Rabbit' Bundrick (keyboards). The original line-up re-formed in 1972 for the patchy *Free At Last* and a hit single, 'Little Bit Of Love', but live work was frequently disrupted by Kossoff's drug problems. Fraser left to form Sharks with Chris Spedding and Tetsu and Rabbit rejoined; Kossoff's increasing unreliability led to the bulk of *Heartbreaker* (1973) being recorded without him and he quit altogether at the end of 1972. Wendell Richardson was used on an American tour early the following year, but after Tetsu's departure for the Faces that summer Free folded, Rodgers and Kirke subsequently forming Bad Company with Mick Ralphs (guitar) and Boz Burrell (bass), while Kossoff and Fraser put together their own groups.

Kinky Friedman, a leading performer of the 'new country' music, is both a Texan and a Jew, an unlikely combination emphasized in the name of his road-band, the Texas Jew-Boys. Born on Oct. 31, 1944 in Rio Duckworth, Texas, his first band was called King Arthur and the Carrots. After serving as a frisbee instructor for the Peace Corps Friedman began to develop a highly individual form of country-and-western which mixed raunchy humorous songs and delicate ballads. In the studio he has been backed by the best of Nashville musicians, and the collaboration of such as the

Glaser Brothers, Waylon Jennings, Billy Swan and Willie Nelson stresses the particular area of country music in which Friedman works. After a critically successful first album on Vanguard (*Sold American*, 1973), he moved to ABC for the patchy *Kinky Friedman* (1974).

Friends of Distinction. Not only did the Los Angeles-based Friends of Distinction evolve from the same root as the more famous Fifth Dimension, but their subsequent musical paths seem identical: smooth, sophisticated supper-club music mixed with the spirited sound of soul, overcoming the apparent disparity of styles by sheer professionalism. Like Fifth Dimension, the Friends were formed by ex-members of the Ray Charles Review group, the Vocals. The Friends – Harry Elston (born Nov. 8, 1938), Floyd Butler (June 5, 1941), Jessica Cleaves (Dec. 10, 1948) and Barbara Love (July 24, 1941) – started out in 1968 and, a year after signing with RCA Records, their vocal version of Hugh Masekela's 'Grazin' In The Grass' was a Top Ten hit. They went on to establish themselves both in the Vegas cabaret circuit and the American charts – 'Goin' In Circles' was a ballad hit in 1969 as was 'Love Me Or Let Me Be Lonely' in 1970 – though they faded by 1973 after Charlene Gibson had replaced Love and then left herself, leaving the group a trio. Recent productions by hitmaker John Florez (Hues Corporation) have yet to re-establish them.

Funkadelic is the extraordinary alter ego of vocal group Parliament, masterminded by founder-member George Clinton (born July 22, 1940). Originally formed in the mid-Fifties (The) Parliament(s) floundered until 1967 when the Top Twenty '(I Wanna) Testify' and 'All Your Goodies Are Gone' on the Detroit Revilot label encouraged them to employ a regular back-up band. By 1969 the two groups were interchangeable expressions of Clinton's experimental ideas and while records continued to be issued by Parliament on Invictus (1971–72) and then Casablanca (where they had a hit in 1975 with 'Up For The Down Stroke'), another contract was signed with Westbound for releases by Funkadelic.

At this point the group comprised Clinton, Raymond Davis (born March 29, 1940), Grady Thomas (Jan. 5, 1941), Calvin Simon (May 22, 1942), Clarence Haskins (June 8, 1941), Lucius Ross (Oct. 5, 1948), Bernard Worrell (April 19, 1944), Eddie Hazel (April 10, 1950), William Nelson (Jan. 28, 1951) and Ramon Fullwood (May 23, 1944).

Wild, erratic, but always entertaining, these include hard-driving funk, 'I Got A Thing, You Got A Thing, Everybody's Got A Thing' (1970), 'Standing On The Verge Of Getting It On' (1974); less definable oddities, 'Fish, Chips, and Sweat', 'Jimmy's Got A Little Bit Of Bitch In Him'; and a series of bizarre albums, *Maggot Brain, America Eats Its Young, Cosmic Slop* – all conceived as 'A Parliafunkadelicment Thang'.

Gallagher and Lyle, from Largs in Scotland, won a song-writing contract with Apple in 1968. A couple of songs, including 'International', were recorded by Mary Hopkin. As Apple went into decline, they left to join McGuinness Flint, writing two Top Ten hits for the band; 'When I'm Dead And Gone' (1970) and 'Malt And Barley Blues' (1971).

Benny Gallagher and Graham Lyle eventually signed to A&M as a duo, with Glyn Johns as producer. They have continued as a group, apart from a brief spell with Ronnie Lane's Slim Chance in 1974. Their songs are melodic and thoughtful, with a concern for the history and contemporary situation of their native Scotland, notably on *Seeds* (1973). *The Last Cowboy* (1974) and *Breakaway* (1976) saw them further develop their incisive harmony singing.

Rory Gallagher was born in Ballyshannon, Ireland on March 2, 1949. He played guitar with the Impact showband before forming his first trio to play in Hamburg in 1965. The following year he teamed up with Norman Damery and Eric Kittringham to form Taste. By this time Gallagher was moving away from Chuck Berry-influenced rock'n'roll towards his modern blues style. In 1968 John Wilson (born Dec. 3, 1947) and Richard McCracken (June 26, 1948) joined on drums and bass and Taste signed with Polydor.

Four albums including *On The Boards* (1970) were produced by Tony Colton between 1968 and 1970, when Taste disbanded and Gallagher continued with Wilgar Campbell (drums) and Gerry McAvoy (bass), the others forming Stud. On *Rory Gallagher* (1971) and *Deuce* (1971), he introduced some of his own compositions while retaining his committed blues approach. He remains perhaps the only white guitarist to have maintained the Sixties commitment to blues without seeming either narrow-minded or rigidly purist.

Gamble and Huff – Kenny Gamble and Leon Huff – are producers/writers and the uncrowned kings of the 'Philly Sound'. Their Philadelphia International label has been the most powerful and creative force in Seventies soul music, boasting virtually every topline name in the genre – Harold Melvin and the Blue Notes, the O'Jays, the Three Degrees *et al.* When they met up in 1964, Huff had already established a reputation as a top New York R&B session pianist, working out of Leiber and Stoller's offices on numerous sides. He moved back to his home town of Philadelphia, and had a hit with Patti and the Emblems in 1964 ('Mixed Up Shook Up Girl'). Kenny Gamble had been singing and songwriting since leaving school. Huff played on Candy and the Kisses' 'The 81', one of Gamble's songs, and a partnership was born, Huff replacing Thom Bell in Kenny Gamble's Romeos.

In 1966, the duo formed Excel Records, and recorded the Intruders, scoring a local hit. The company's name was changed to Gamble. Both soul and Hot Hundred hits emerged from the new company by the Intruders. All were written and produced by Gamble and Huff. Although 1968 was a rough year for Philadelphia – with Cameo being forced to fold – Gamble Records continued to have hits and the duo began to work as outside producers for Atlantic (breaking Archie Bell and the Drells) and Mercury (Jerry Butler). In 1970, a hook-up with Leonard Chess was arranged, resulting in the launch of Neptune Records. Despite a brilliant roster of acts – the O'Jays, the Vibrations, the Three Degrees, Bunny Sigler, Billy Paul, etc. and encouraging sales, Neptune folded when Leonard Chess died and his Chess Records were swallowed by the GRT conglomerate. Still getting hits with the Intruders and independent productions (notably Wilson Pickett) they regrouped and in 1971 secured a Columbia Records tie-up and formed Philadelphia International Records. For a year things moved slowly, but once the Ebonys and then Harold Melvin and the Blue Notes broke through to the national charts, Columbia began to pay real attention to Philadelphia International. Million-selling smashes for the O'Jays and Billy Paul brought waves of interest in the 'Philly Sound'. Certainly, since 1972, Gamble and Huff's immaculate fusion of sophisticated orchestrations (supplied by the brilliant MFSB session band and recorded at Philly's Sigma Sound studio) and rich, vibrant soul vocalists have brought immense success – and payola investigations – and more evidence that the diverse threads of black music are now inseparably interwoven into the pop music mainstream.

Jerry Garcia was born in San Francisco on Jan. 8, 1942. After a brief spell in the army in 1959 he teamed up with Robert Hunter to play the coffee house circuit, supplementing meagre earnings by giving guitar lessons, repairing guitars and working in Dana Morgan's music store, all the time absorbing new musical styles. In 1962 he bought a banjo and soon put together a series of string bands, a late variation being Mother McCree's Uptown Jug Champions. Financed by Morgan they became the electric Warlocks, eventually the Grateful Dead. Late in the Sixties Garcia took up pedal steel, finding an outlet for his playing (from spring 1970) with the spin-off band the New Riders of the Purple Sage. He also took up the banjo again, and along with Peter Rowan, guitar, David Grisman, mandolin, John Kahn, bass and Vassar Clements, fiddle, formed a bluegrass band called Old And In The Way. They gigged locally and played bluegrass festivals through the summers of 1973 and 1974, also releasing an album on Round Records.

Garcia is an obsessive musician who just loves to play. This is borne out by the stream of albums he's been involved in. Album work includes three albums with keyboard player Merle Saunders, one with another keyboard man, Howard Wales, *Hooteroll,* sessions for Crosby, Stills, Nash and Young, the Airplane (Garcia plays uncredited on *Surrealistic Pillow*) plus work with other members of the San Francisco family. His two solo albums in 1972 and 1974, both titled *Garcia*, have been generally unimpressive. They reflect the fact that Jerry Garcia's true lifeblood is playing in the band, any band, but especially the Dead, mutually trading ideas and creating fluent guitar runs that, at their best, are quite riveting.

Art Garfunkel has divided his time between music and film-acting since the break-up of his partnership with Paul Simon in 1970. *Angel Clare* (Columbia, 1974) and *Breakaway* (1975, co-produced by Richard Perry) continued the lush arrangements characteristic of the later Simon and Garfunkel, while the vocals retained the high, breathy tone of 'Bridge Over Troubled Waters'. The songs were selected from the work of various writers of the past twenty years, and in 1975 Garfunkel enjoyed international hits with his mawkish version of 'I Only Have Eyes For You', a Fifties doo-wop hit for the Flamingoes, and Gallagher and Lyle's 'Breakaway'.

Simon and Garfunkel reunited briefly for 'My Little Town', which appeared on the second solo album, but the impression remains that Garfunkel's commitment to a musical career is far less than his former partner's.

David Gates, born in Tulsa, Oklahoma on Dec. 11, 1939 left Bread after some conflict with James Griffin, on the subject of whose material should be used on Bread's records. The outcome was that both Gates and Griffin released solo albums around the same part of 1973, with backing musician credits being almost identical. Gates, an ex-rockabilly singer (with discs on East-West and Robbins) and producer, has had the greater success, and made a highly successful British debut in early 1975, hot on the heels of his second solo album, *Never Let Her Go* (Elektra, 1975). His largest hit as a solo artist has been 'Clouds', on which his airy tenor is at its best. His songs have been widely recorded by singers as diverse as Ken Boothe ('Everything I Own'), Telly Savalas ('If') and Gladys Knight ('Part Time Love').

Gloria Gaynor, crowned 'Queen of the Discotheques', has been at the forefront of the New York disco revival. Born in Newark, New Jersey, she had her share of days scuffling on the chittlin' circuit. After a Johnny Nash-produced flop single on Jocida in 1965, she sang with a touring band, the Soul Satisfyers, for two years. In 1973, she began working with manager Jay Ellis (who found her at a Manhattan night club), Tony Bongiovi, whizz kid recording engineer, and Meco Monardo, musical consultant. With the canny crew producing her, Gaynor became just part of an immaculately conceived disco sound, tailor-made for dancing the night away. The hits (for MGM) began: 'Never Can Say Goodbye' (1974), and 'Reach Out I'll Be There' (1975). But it's a depressingly faceless, robot-like soul that Gloria and Bongiovi/Monardo/Ellis have conceived for the disco audiences.

Genesis was formed by a group of songwriting enthusiasts at a public school near London. The original members were Tony Banks (keyboards, born on March 27, 1950), Michael Rutherford (bass, Oct. 2, 1950) and Peter Gabriel (vocals, May 13, 1950). Signed to Decca by Jonathan King, they made an uninspiring album (*From Genesis To Revelation*, 1969) with John Mayhew on drums and guitarist Anthony Philips.

The arrival of Phil Collins (drums, born Jan. 31, 1951) and Steve Hackett (guitar, Feb. 12, 1950) for *Trespass* (Charisma, 1970) strengthened the band, while Gabriel was beginning to explore the theatrical dimensions of their act. Genesis gained a wider following with *Nursery Cryme* (1971) and *Foxtrot* (1972), where the music matched the melodrama of live performances.

They were by now especially popular in Europe, where the sophisticated shock-rock of *Selling England By The Pound* (1973) and the ambitious song-cycle *The Lamb Lies Down On Broadway* (1974) were successful. In 1975, Peter Gabriel left the group, leaving Genesis to hunt for a replacement and ponder over their future.

Gentle Giant. The Glasgow-born brothers, Ray (born Dec. 8, 1949) and Derek (Feb. 2, 1947) and Phil Shulman (Aug. 27, 1937) formed Simon Dupree and the Big Sound, who had a British Top Ten hit with 'Kites' in 1967. In 1969, frustrated with the cabaret nature of the group, they planned Gentle Giant. They teamed up with Kerry Minnear (April 2, 1948), newly graduated from the Royal Academy of Music, a multi-instrumentalist, lead guitarist Gary Green (Nov. 20, 1950), with John Weathers, an experienced Welsh musician once with the Eyes Of Blue and the Grease Band, on drums. The brothers themselves play a wide range of instruments: Ray, bass, guitar, violin, drums and piano; Derek, lead vocals, bass, alto; Phil, tenor sax and trumpet.

Gentle Giant slipped into a multi-instrumental experimental niche. Their fourth release, *Octopus* (Vertigo), was a surprise hit in America in 1973. Phil Shulman left in 1973, since when Giant have released three albums; the rushed-sounding *In A Glasshouse* (WWA), the freer, more spontaneous *Power And The Glory* (1974), and *Free Hand* (1975) – all offering plenty of light and shade from delicate acoustic playing to climactic heavy riff building often featuring well-arranged vocal interweaving.

Gary Glitter, born Paul Gadd in Banbury, Oxfordshire, on May 8, 1940, pursued a singing career as Paul Raven which survived through the Sixties on stamina rather than success, although he did appear on the original *Jesus Christ Superstar* album, before changing his record company – to Bell Records – in 1971, and his name. In 1972, the 'B' side of his first single in his new identity 'Rock And Roll Part 2' became an enormous and unexpected hit after 'sleeping' for several months in both Britain and America. The consistent success of the string of singles – though only in Britain – that followed over the next years 'Do You Wanna Touch Me', 'I'm The Leader Of The Gang' (1973), 'Always Yours' (1974) etc., prompted him to develop his persona into an extravagant parody. He wrote all his songs with his producer Mike Leander and by 1974 had joined pop's showbiz *élite* and launched his backing group, the Glitter Band, on their own career.

Steve Goodman. Born on July 25, 1948 in Chicago, this diminutive songwriter took British audiences by storm with appearances at the Lincoln Festival and Cambridge Folk Festival in 1972 and 1973. In America however, he has continued to live in the shadow of John Prine, who was discovered in Chicago simultaneously by Paul Anka, and Kris Kristofferson. He recorded two fine albums for Buddah but failed to receive any great national exposure despite writing 'The City Of New Orleans', a Top Twenty hit for Arlo Guthrie in 1972. In an attempt to re-launch his career Steve Goodman left Buddah for Elektra-Asylum, but his first album for the new company (*Jessie's Jig And Other Favourites*, 1975) was disappointing and failed to project his writing ability and extrovert personality.

Grand Funk Railroad, originally the brainchild of pop Svengali Terry Knight, were formed from the remnants of Terry Knight and the Pack and other Flint, Michigan bands. The group – Mark Farner (guitar, vocals, born Sept. 29, 1948), Mel Schacher (bass, born April 3, 1951), Don Brewer (drums, born Sept. 3, 1948) – asked Knight for help after an initial failure managing themselves. He signed them to Capitol Records and engineered an unpaid appearance at the 1969 Atlanta Pop Festival where they stole the show. They quickly became a growing attraction, but the press and radio showed universal revulsion for their unrelenting, earsplitting, rhythmic attack. Knight turned this to the band's advantage, making them a generational emblem for their largely teenage audience. By December, 1970, with albums like *Grand Funk* and *Closer To Home*, Grand Funk were the hottest group in America, without benefit of reviews, features, or much radio play. In late 1971, the band severed relations with Knight in a flurry of million-dollar suits and countersuits. The band added Craig Frost on keyboards and in 1973, the suits settled, Todd Rundgren produced *We're An American Band*, the title song becoming their first Top Twenty hit. Over the next year, with singles like 'Locomotion', they consolidated their now broader-based popularity and began establishing their reputation outside of America. They have ten platinum albums.

Dobie Gray, born in Brookshire, Texas in 1943, first appeared on the Hot Hundred Charts in 1963 with 'Look At Me' (Cor Dak), recorded after he had travelled to Los Angeles in search of a recording contract. He had his first big hit with the insistent dance record, 'The In Crowd' (Charger) in 1965, which he co-wrote. A follow-up, 'See You At The Go Go', made the lower reaches of the Hot Hundred later that year but it was eight years before Gray had another major hit with the Mentor Williams composition/production, 'Drift Away' (MCA, 1973), an anthem to the power of rock to soothe as well as excite. In between, Gray cut demo discs (which is how he met Paul Williams and through him his brother Mentor), worked with the group Pollution, acted in Rip Torn's New York production of *The Beard* and appeared in *Hair*. Under Mentor Williams' direction Gray recorded three albums for MCA, *Drift Away*, *Loving Arms* (1973) and *Hey Dixie* (1974), all fine examples of progressive Southern music, before moving to Capricorn where, with Troy Seals producing, he released *New Ray Of Sunshine* (1975).

R. B. Greaves. Of Indian descent, Ronald Bertrand Greaves was born in Georgetown, Guyana but moved to California as a child. He spent several years singing country music until 1963 when he toured Britain as an R&B singer under the name of Sonny Child. On his return to America, he faded from the scene, until he was signed to Atco, the label on which 'Take A Letter, Maria' made No. 2 in the Hot Hundred in 1969. After a smaller hit with 'Always Something There To Remind Me', he moved away from Latin-based soul into a rock repertoire, recording 'Fire And Rain', 'A Whiter Shade Of Pale' and 'Paperback Writer' in 1970.

Greaves had no more hits on Atco and records for Sunflower (1972) and MGM (1973) similarly fell still-born from the presses.

Rick Grech. Lured from Family – of which he was a founder member – in May, 1969, to join Eric Clapton, Steve Winwood and Ginger Baker as bass guitarist and violinist in the short-lived Blind Faith, Grech, born in Bordeaux, France, on Nov. 1, 1945, went on to play with Ginger Baker's Airforce in 1970, Traffic (1970–71), and the Crickets (1972–74). He was reunited with Clapton in January, 1973, for Clapton's Rainbow Concert and *The Last Five Years*, a compilation album of his compositions – e.g. 'Hey Mr Policeman', 'Kiss The Children' and 'Rock'n'Roll Star' – recorded by Family, Blind Faith, Airforce, Traffic, Rosetta Hightower, and Gram Parsons with whom Grech co-produced *GP* (Warner Bros, 1973) was released later that year on RSO.

Al Green was born on April 13, 1946 in Forest City, Alabama and raised in Grand Rapids, Michigan, where he sang with the Creations before his first recording 'Back Up Train' (Hot Line) gave him a Top Fifty hit in 1967. This beautiful soul ballad was followed unsuccessfully by similar releases, and he had slipped back into obscurity by 1969 when he was signed by Willie Mitchell, producer and vice-president of Hi Records, Memphis. After trying deep soul ('One Woman'), adapted pop ('I Wanna Hold Your Hand'), and a bit of thump-and-strut ('Right Now, Right Now'), they finally cracked the charts with a bluesy interpretation of the Temptations' 'Can't Get Next To You' (1970). A similar treatment of 'Drivin' Wheel' was not so well received, but Green's own song 'Tired Of Being Alone' (1971) gave him the hit – and the formula – that has made him one of the major black stars of the Seventies. Green employs all the vocal gymnastics of a typical gospel-influenced soul singer, yet stays so restrained that often he's barely audible; Mitchell's band sets up insidious rhythms without ever driving the songs to any sort of dramatic conclusion. The effect of tightly reined emotions has been heard in a dozen smash hits (including 'Let's Stay

Together', a No. 1 in 1971, 'I'm Still In Love With You', 'You Ought To Be With Me', 1972; 'Livin' For You', 1973; 'Sha-La-La', 1974; and 'Oh Me, Oh My', 1975), but after four years the Green style is in need of rejuvenation.

Norman Greenbaum, born Nov. 20, 1942, in Malden, Massachusetts, became an occasional folk singer while at Boston University. He moved to LA where he put together Dr West's Medicine Show And Junk Band (inspired by Boston's Jim Kweskin Jug Band). The group – Bonnie Wallach, vocals, guitar; Jack Carrington, washtub, bass, guitar, banjo; and Evan Engber, percussion – plus Greenbaum, anachronistic though they were in 1966, had a surprise Top Fifty hit with 'The Eggplant That Ate Chicago' (Go Go), but hardly found their style flourishing in the changing climate of the mid-Sixties. Ironically, after the single hit, they toured extensively to odd reactions among audiences, who saw in their weird appearance (painted faces and light shows) all the nastier manifestations of California psychedelia.

In 1967 the group split up. A fortuitous meeting with Eric Jacobson in 1968 resulted in Greenbaum's first solo album *Spirit In The Sky* (Reprise). The title track, culled as a single, gave Greenbaum another surprise hit, a million-seller worldwide, with its compelling fuzz-tone riff. Greenbaum again failed to follow this up and consolidate his success, releasing the weaker 'Canned Ham' and patchy second album *Back Home* (1970). He has been in semi-retirement since, mixing music (he released a third solo album for Warners, *Petaluma*, in 1972) and goat breeding in Petaluma, California.

Richard Greene, a fiddler *extraordinaire*, comes from Los Angeles and was first influenced by bluegrass music. He formed the Dry City Scat Band in the early Sixties, which was admired for nice harmonies and deft instrumental work and can be heard on Elektra's *String Band Project*. Greene then spent some time in Nashville with Bill Monroe's Bluegrass Boys before heading for Boston and the Jim Kweskin Jug Band. Later he discovered electric music and joined the

Blues Project, which contained the nucleus for Seatrain, Greene's best-known group. They recorded in England for Capitol under the supervision of George Martin. However, Greene quit the band in 1972, just before they signed with Warner Bros. In late 1973, he recorded *Muleskinner*, a Warners album featuring Clarence White and others, and also completed a solo album for the company, which was never released because of economic cut-backs. He now works as a session musician with artists like Maria Muldaur and Emmylou Harris.

Greyhound, a Jamaican reggae group resident in Britain, scored a trio of reggae hits in the early Seventies on Trojan with 'Black And White' (Top Ten in 1971), 'Moon River' (Top Twenty in 1972) and 'I Am What I Am', all commercial, trivial tunes replete with strings. Earlier they had been Freddie Notes and the Rudies, a rock-steady band who had made the interesting period album *Unity*, before their lead singer returned to Jamaica. Popular in ballrooms, Greyhound never really established themselves as any real reggae force, despite their hits, and split up in the Seventies to re-form as the seven-piece Dhanzak.

Stefan Grossman, born in New York on April 16, 1945, first made his mark as far back as 1965–66 as part of those amorphous New York City dinosaurs, the Even Dozen Jug Band and the Fugs. He was an avid student of the blues, worshipping the old east coast ragtime pickers and in particular the Rev. Gary Davis. He spent many hours learning first hand from Davis and by the time the country blues revival took place in Britain around 1968, Grossman had crossed the Atlantic to show the way.

His popularity in Europe grew and he settled down to live in Rome, recording a number of instructional albums for Transatlantic. Hotly tipped to join forces with Paul Simon after the split with Garfunkel, in the end all that happened was that the duo cut a single track on Simon's first solo album. He continues to compile tablature books and albums on all styles of blues guitar playing and in 1972–73 launched his own Kicking Mule label in an effort to focus attention on the large school of unknown folk/blues instrumentalists throughout Europe and North America.

The Groundhogs were in the forefront of the purist British R&B groups during the early Sixties. Named after a John Lee Hooker song, they were Tony McPhee (guitar, vocals, born on March 22, 1944), Pete Cruikshank (bass, born July 2, 1945), Ken Pustelnik (drums) and Steve Rye (harmonica).

After three standard blues albums for United Artists, Rye quit and the remaining trio joined the ranks of the progressive bands. With *Thank Christ For The Bomb* (1970) and *Split* (1971), McPhee took to electronics and social comment. He went on to record a guitar/synthesizer solo album as well as two further Groundhogs records (*Who Will Save The World*, 1972 and *Hogwash*, 1973) before finally winding up the trio at the end of 1974. In 1976, McPhee re-formed the group with new sidemen.

Gryphon. Although Amazing Blondel had tried before, Gryphon were the first band to achieve popularity by adapting medieval tunes and instruments (such as the crumhorn and glockenspiel) for a rock context. The group, formed in 1971 as Spell Thorn, comes from London and the home counties and comprises Brian Gulland (born 1951), Richard Harvey (1953), Graeme Taylor (1954) and David Oberle (1953). They have lately been joined by Malcolm Bennett. It was not until 1973 that their arrangements of minstrel airs, Beatle music and 'Chattanooga Choo Choo' caught on, and since then the band has played a much wider field (lecture tours, incidental music for Peter Hall's *Tempest*, etc.) than most rock musicians. By 1975, they had eschewed all connection with medieval music, becoming a skilful if less original mainstream rock band.

Jim Guercio, a student of classical composition at university in Chicago, supplemented his money by playing guitar in bars. On a Mid-West tour with a Dick Clark Caravan Show – as a member of the backing group – he met J. Holvay who handed him a song called 'Kind Of A Drag' which Guercio recorded with a local Chicago outfit, the Buckinghams, in 1966. Two years later, Guercio had become one of four guitarists with the Mothers of Invention in LA, then at their most outrageous. At the same time he was planning a brass rock group. Al Kooper pipped him to the post with Blood, Sweat And Tears but Guercio had the satisfaction of producing their second, most successful album, *Blood, Sweat And Tears* (Columbia, 1969) after Kooper had left. It was Guercio's own group, Chicago Transit Authority, that coveted the brass rock niche thereafter. Their debut album *CTA* (Columbia) released in April 1969 was an enormous critical and commercial success. Critical acclaim became scarcer, however, as Guercio sustained Chicago's impressive work rate – three two-record sets in under two years, all packaged with posters, lyrics sheets and colour photographs, culminating in a dubious four-record set recorded live at Carnegie Hall in 1971. A torrent of critics screamed overkill but Guercio, still in his twenties, ploughed on relentless.

Chicago became part of James William Guercio Enterprises along with his Caribou studios in Colorado, where Elton John, among others, has recorded. He's had less dramatic success and even failures like the Chicago group, Illinois Speed Press, and his period as manager of Firesign Theatre. The film *Elektra Glide In Blue* (1972), produced, directed and scored by Guercio, marked a new diversification in his interests. In 1975 he took control of the Beach Boys' affairs and appeared with them on live dates.

The Guess Who were Burton Cummings (lead vocals, keyboards), Randy Bachman (guitar, vocals), Jim Kale (bass) and Gary Peterson (drums). Bachman was replaced in summer 1970 by Greg Leskiw and Kurt Winter (guitars), Leskiw and Kale were replaced by Don McDougal (guitar) and Bill Wallace (bass, vocals) in 1972. Winter and McDougal were replaced by Dominic Troiano (guitar and vocals) in 1974.

The Winnipeg group Chad Allen and the Expressions became the Guess Who in 1965 after Allen left and scored a minor hit, 'Shakin' All Over'. Their run of million-sellers began in 1969 with 'These Eyes', 'Laughing' and 'No Time' mostly written by Bachman, who left while his 'American Woman' was No. 1 to re-join Chad Allen in Brave Belt which later evolved into Bachman Turner Overdrive. Jack Richardson has produced all their eleven albums of which the foremost are *The Best Of The Guess Who, Volumes I And II*. The arrival of ex-Hawk and James Gang member Troiano may shift the balance of the band as *Flavours* (1975) suggests.

Arlo Guthrie had, by the mid-Seventies, overcome the twin handicaps of living in his father's shadow and the 'arch-hippie' tag which followed his appearance in Arthur Penn's movie, *Alice's Restaurant*. Albums like *Hobo's Lullabye* (Reprise, 1972) and *Last Of The Brooklyn Cowboys* (1973) established his personal synthesis of folk and country traditions with contemporary themes.

Born in New York on July 10, 1947, his earliest success came in 1967, the year of his father, Woody's, death. The epic ballad 'Alice's Restaurant' spawned an album and the film, and was followed by five more Reprise albums before the live double with Pete Seeger in 1975. In 1973 he had a Top Twenty hit with Steve Goodman's 'City Of New Orleans', a song which summed up Guthrie's own clear-eyed stance towards the American past, while 'Presidential Rag', dealing with Watergate, was a vigorous piece of social comment in the best family manner.

Merle Haggard. Probably still best remembered outside the country market for 'Okie From Muskogee', a song seemingly defending small-town American virtues, which topped the country charts for several weeks in 1969 and also made the lower reaches of the Hot Hundred, Haggard's most successful record was 'If We Make It Thru December', a Top Twenty pop hit in 1973 that described the pain of urban unemployment.

Haggard is a country superstar; the best-known product of the strong Californian country scene centred on the town of Bakersfield. Nearby Hollywood and Los Angeles have always been foremost recording centres and country music has long been established in California since half the population came from the rural South anyway. Haggard's family came from Oklahoma, and Merle was born in Bakersfield on April 6, 1937.

During the early Sixties the most renowned singers in the area were Billy Mize, Wynn Stewart and Buck Owens, until 1963 when Fuzzy Owens began to record Merle Haggard, a rough, tough product of the oilfields, and lately out of San Quentin prison, on his Tally label. By 1965 Haggard had scored three country hits including the Top Ten hit '(All My Friends Are Gonna Be) Strangers'. A move to Capitol brought a No. 1 hit, 'I Am A Lonesome Fugitive', and in 1968 'Mama Tried', which embodied an idealized Haggard life story; but idealized in an unusual manner – for Haggard is the bad boy who's going to go straight, but not deny his past experiences. By now, Haggard had not only married Buck Owens' ex-wife, Bonnie, but also was challenging Owens' reputation as the Nashville-West superstar. Songs like 'Working Man Blues', 'Daddy Frank' and 'Okie From Muskogee' had a sense of purpose and a simple brilliance wrapped in an interestingly formulated instrumental sound, featuring session guitarist James Burton or his own back-up man, Roy Nichols. Haggard also recorded tribute albums to country stars Jimmie Rodgers and Bob Wills, and a double album of gospel songs.

Haggard has a following that is not solely country and not confined to America. He does not travel in the same circles as the west-coast country-rock musicians but his songs often reach the same audience as the Burrito Brothers or Country Gazette and have also been converted by countless mainstream country and popular ballad singers to their own needs, often financial. Songs like 'Swinging Doors', 'Today I Started Loving You Again' and 'Branded Man' are standards outside the country field.

Tom T. Hall, born in Olive Hill, Kentucky on May 25, 1936, worked in factories, stores, the US Army and as a radio DJ until he set his sights on becoming a songwriter in the Nashville of the Sixties. 'I Washed My Face In The Morning Dew', and two redneck war songs, 'Hello Vietnam' (a country No. 1 in 1964) and 'What Are We Fighting For', endeared him to the Southern country establishment. Then he wrote 'Harper Valley P.T.A.' an international hit for Jeannie C. Riley in 1968 and his success was assured.

By now a singer as well, he started writing songs directly from his own experiences – his nickname is 'The Storyteller' – and, hostile to the MOR direction country music was taking, with Willie Nelson was a forerunner of the 'new' Nashville rebel singer/songwriter fraternity.

'The Year That Clayton Delaney Died' ushered in an era of hits for Hall on Mercury. Songs like 'Ballad Of Forty Dollars', 'Ravishing Ruby', 'America The Ugly' and 'Trip To Hyden' are in the best traditions of the understated realism country music is capable of.

Albert Hammond, born in London in 1944, was brought up in Gibraltar, and became a highly successful Spanish language artist before he was 21. He moved to England, where his initial success was in writing songs for artists like Leapy Lee ('Little Arrows') and the Pipkins ('Gimme Dat Ding') in collaboration with Mike Hazlewood. In the early Seventies, Hammond moved to Los Angeles, and registered strongly in 1972 with 'It Never Rains In Southern California' – which was written in Fulham, West London. After three successful Columbia solo albums in America, Hammond gained an additional songwriting partner – Hal David, who previously worked with Burt Bacharach.

Herbie Hancock first became widely known as a pianist for his work with the classic Miles Davis Quintet of the mid-Sixties, although his career had got off to a flying start some years earlier with the hit composition, 'Watermelon Man'.

After participating in Miles' early excursions into rock, Hancock left to lead his own band. His music is a beautifully poised amalgam of the jazz and rock idioms, with highly controlled dynamics and exquisite ensemble voicing. As a composer he admits a debt to Gil Evans which is evident in his grasp of instrumental colour and the fine precision with which he controls the band's sound.

Herbie Hancock has composed soundtrack music for the films *Blow Up* (Antonioni, 1967) and *Death Wish* (Michael Winner, 1974), while the best of his post-Miles albums are *Speak Like A Child* (Blue Note, 1969), *Mwandishi* (Warner Bros, 1971), *Head Hunters* (Columbia, 1974) and *Thrust* (Columbia, 1974).

Roy Harper was born on June 12, 1941 in Manchester, joining the Royal Air Force at 15. His career included spells in mental hospital and prison before his highly personal songs made him a cult figure on the London folk scene in 1965. The next year he made his first album (*The Sophisticated Beggar*) for Strike.

Other albums for CBS and Liberty followed, before Harper signed a long-term contract with Harvest in 1970. The resulting albums were a faithful reflection of Harper's erratic live performances, in which he would often harangue audiences for long periods of time. On the credit side, he is highly respected by such rock luminaries as Jimmy Page, who has played with him live and on record, and is capable of producing songs of genuine strength such as the 1975 single 'When An Old Cricketer Leaves The Crease' from *H.Q.*

George Harrison. As a Beatle he grew from guitarist and harmony singer into a writer and singer in his own right, eventually becoming a third creative force alongside John Lennon and Paul McCartney. It was primarily his interest in Eastern religion, and the subsequent (temporary) involvement of Lennon, that pushed the Beatles, and helped to push popular music in general, into a cultural stance heavily indebted to Eastern modes of thought. His songs on Beatle albums from *Revolver* onwards were usually explorations of common romantic themes through Hinduistic perspective, centring on the possibilities of egoless love.

This philosophy has illumined the four solo albums he has

made since the Beatles' demise. The first, *All Things Must Pass* (Apple, 1970) – made after two experimental albums, *Wonderwall* (1968) and *Electronic Sounds* (1969) – in particular represents a further development of the music bequeathed by the Sixties, and ranks as one of the classic albums of the Seventies.

Much of the credit for this must go to the production of Harrison and Phil Spector, which, with an infinite attention to detail in the creation of a massive, multi-layered sound, manages to make the most of Harrison's strengths and minimise his weaknesses. The thinness of his singing voice becomes a strength set against the imagination of the music; the guitars of himself, Eric Clapton, and Dave Mason ring clearly regardless of the complexity of instrumentation. All combine to give the songs an emotional strength both compelling and uplifting, seen most notably on 'My Sweet Lord', the international hit that launched the album. On this and his second album, *Living In The Material World* (1973), Harrison has continued the role much rock performed in the Sixties, that of proselytization. He is still, like fellow-Beatle Lennon, a believer: in the wrongs of the present and the vision of another way. Similarly the Seventies' obsession with relationships has been treated as thoughtfully in Harrison's songs as any others.

His belief in rock music's duty to a wider world received its most obvious expression in the Concert For Bangla Desh, organized in 1972 to make money for the relieving of the plight of that country. George got Ringo Starr and Eric Clapton, among others, to play with him, and even coaxed Bob Dylan on stage to sing a few of the old protest songs. *Rolling Stone* called the concert 'a brief and incandescent revival of all that was best about the Sixties'.

Since then Harrison has kept out of the public eye, except for the over-publicized separation from his wife. The third album, *Dark Horse*, received less than critical acclaim, as did his tour of the States in 1974. He seems to have lost the power of the first two solo albums, although *Extra Texture (Read All About It)* (Capitol, 1975) saw a return to form. In 1974, he launched his own label, Dark Horse, with Splinter, a singer/songwriting duo whose 'Costafin Town' was a turntable hit in Britain.

John Hartford, born Dec. 30, 1947 learnt his craft first as a fiddle player at square dances, then playing rock guitar in East St Louis and West Memphis honky tonks. This background of extremes has left its mark and is evident on some of Hartford's far-ranging, erratic work. He arrived in Nashville in 1965, quickly forged a reputation as a session picker (guitar, banjo and fiddle) and earned a certain notoriety as the local hippie. This changed when Glen Campbell recorded his 'Gentle On My Mind', a minor country hit for Hartford in 1967. Campbell's recording was a spectacular hit, setting him on the road to superstardom and country music in the direction of the sweet and lush countrypolitan sound which Hartford himself despised.

Hartford moved from Nashville to LA, the natural home of countrypolitan, where he cut his sixth solo album, *John Hartford* (RCA, 1969). A supporter and advocate of country rock in its beginnings, Hartford plays fiddle and banjo on the Byrds' classic pioneering country rock album, *Sweetheart Of The Rodeo. Aereo-Plain* (Warner Bros, 1971) – which includes his own 'They're Tearing Down The Grand Ole Opry' – similarly demonstrated his ongoing commitment to traditional country styles.

Alex Harvey's was one of the most unusual success stories in British rock during the Seventies. An R&B and beat group leader in the previous decade, he re-emerged with his Sensational Alex Harvey Band and a mixture of rabble-rousing stage antics and studiedly outrageous songs.

Born in Glasgow on Feb. 5, 1935, he led the Alex Harvey Soul Band on guitar and vocals from 1958 to 1966, playing much of the time in Hamburg and recording occasionally, notably *Big Soul Band* (Polydor, 1964). Dissolving the group, he joined the pit band for the London production of *Hair*, where he stayed for five years. In 1972 he teamed up with the Scottish group Tear Gas to form his current band which includes Zal Cleminson (guitar, born May 4, 1949), Chris

Glen (bass, born Nov. 6, 1950), Hugh McKenna (piano, Nov. 28, 1949) and Ted McKenna (drums, March 10, 1950).

Signing to Vertigo, they gradually built up an enthusiastic live following through Harvey's oddball songs and dramatic delivery. By the end of 1975, after five albums, the SAHB had their first hit single with a revival of Tom Jones' 1968 record, 'Delilah'.

Donny Hathaway was born in Chicago on Jan. 10, 1945, and grew up in St Louis, getting his musical grounding in the gospel field – his grandmother was a noted performer of sacred music. He gained a scholarship to Howard University, Washington, where he studied piano and music teaching before majoring in musical theory. While in Washington he played and sang in church before joining a 'cocktail' jazz trio, then met Curtis Mayfield who invited him to Chicago as a producer for his Curtom label for which he also recorded with June Conquest as June and Donnie. Pressure of work forced him to quit Curtom, and Donny signed with Chess as staff musician/producer, though also dabbling freelance with Uni, Kapp and Stax before establishing his own independent production company. He met up with King Curtis, who introduced him to Atlantic Records, where he signed as performer, writer and producer, and has enjoyed chart success both on his own – e.g. 'The Ghetto' (1970) and 'I Love You More Than You'll Ever Know' (1972) – and with Roberta Flack – most successfully with 'Where Is The Love', a Top Five record in America in 1972.

The Edwin Hawkins Singers. Edwin Hawkins was born in August, 1943, in Oakland, California. While studying at the University of California, Berkeley, in 1967 he became choir director at a Berkeley church where he formed the North California State Youth Choir with leading soloists from other San Francisco-area choirs. They recorded an album to sell in aid of choir funds, and went to represent North California at a youth convention in Cleveland, Ohio, selling their album there. In 1969, an Oakland DJ began playing 'Oh Happy Day' from the album, featuring soloist Dorothy

Coombs Morrison (born in Longview, Texas in 1945), and Pavilion Records signed the choir as the Edwin Hawkins Singers. The song became a surprise American and British Top Ten hit in 1969. However, such success was never repeated, though Dorothy Morrison went on to enjoy a limited secular solo career.

Hawkwind were originally Group X, emerging from London's Ladbroke Grove, the nearest thing in Britain to a hippie ghetto in 1970. They still manage to maintain that stoned ambience. X became Hawkwind Zoo, then plain Hawkwind when their manager Doug Smith signed them to United Artists. Formed by Dave Brock (guitar, vocals) the original line-up included Huw Lloyd Langton (guitar), Terry Ollis (drums), Nick (later Nik) Turner (saxophone), Dave Anderson (bass) and Dikmik (electronics).

The band became known as regulars on the free festival circuit and the first album (*Hawkwind*, 1970) was unimpressive. But the following year, poet and writer Bob Calvert joined the ensemble and inspired Hawkwind's 'space-rock' persona on *In Search Of Space* (1971), and their surprise hit single 'Silver Machine' (1972).

Various personnel changes occurred as Hawkwind consolidated a large, youthful following on both sides of the Atlantic. Langton, Ollis and Anderson left, with Lemmy (bass), Simon King (drums) and Del Detmar (electronics) joining. The statucsque Stacia eventually became a permanent fixture as a dancer, while in 1974 Dikmik and Calvert departed, the latter to follow a solo career. The next year Lemmy formed Motorhead, a hard rock band whose lack of prowess was reminiscent of the early Hawkwind.

Further tours and albums (e.g. *Space Ritual*, 1973) saw Hawkwind continuing in their time-warp, their anachronistic image and pulp sci-fi material appealing to teenage audiences unfamiliar with flower-power and all its trappings.

Isaac Hayes, born on August 6, 1938 in Covington, Tennessee, learned to play piano and saxophone in his teens. He sang in local clubs and cut his first discs in 1962 for tiny labels. They were mainly Brook Benton imitations. A long-standing friendship with David Porter led him to join Stax Records as a writer/producer. The Hayes/Porter working partnership led to gold records for Sam and Dave ('Hold On I'm Coming' and 'Soul Man') and proved to be one of the key factors in the emergence of the Memphis Sound.

When the Gulf and Western Corporation bought Stax in 1968, the label was asked for 30 albums, so Hayes cut an album himself – *Hot Buttered Soul*. Unlike its predecessor (the jazz-styled *Presenting Isaac Hayes*), it was complex, sophisticated, sensuous and highly controlled, a watershed between the old, raunchy Stax sounds, and the later 'sophistisoul' releases. *Hot Buttered Soul* was an immediate success and subsequent albums featuring extended raps, huge orchestrations and pungent rhythm tracks quickly made Hayes into a superstar, culminating in *Black Moses*. When asked to write the score for the film *Shaft*, Hayes created a double set that some consider his masterpiece, and established his name internationally.

However, despite his *Wattstax* movie appearance, subsequent albums on Stax (including two tepid film scores) failed to sell like Hayes' earlier discs (or those of a new sophistisoul star, Barry White). Hayes finally left Stax in 1974 after a publicized royalties wrangle. Early in 1975 he signed with ABC Records and the success of his *Chocolate Chip* album indicated that the bald-headed, chain-vested prophet of Middle American soul could rediscover his immense audience.

Dick Heckstall-Smith was born on Sept. 26, 1934. At school he led a traditional jazz band and played clarinet and soprano saxophone. After taking up tenor saxophone in Sandy Brown's jazz band and doing a stint with a rock'n'roll group at Butlin's holiday camps, he worked freelance until 1962 when he joined Blues Incorporated. From there he moved to Graham Bond's breakaway Organization and then on to John Mayall's Bluesbreakers, eventually forming Colosseum with Mayall's drummer, Jon Hiseman. When Colosseum broke up in 1971, he returned to freelance work, though for a while he led his own group. Heckstall-Smith made two solo albums on Bronze, *A Story Ended* (1972) and *Manchild* (1973).

Dan Hicks And His Hot Licks. A member of the Charlatans, the first San Francisco group – originally, George Hunter (vocals) who was later to become a renowned poster artist, Mike Vilhelm (guitar), Mike Ferguson (piano) and Sam Linde (drums) – Hicks, from Santa Rosa, New Mexico, left the group in 1968 to form Dan Hicks And His Hot Licks. That group originally comprised John Girton (guitar), Sid Page (violin, mandolin), Maryann Price (vocals, cornet), Jaime Leopold (bass) and Naomi Eisenberg (vocals, violin). They recorded a series of interesting albums for Blue Thumb, *Where's The Money* (1970), *Stricking It Rich* (1972) and *Last Train To Hicksville* (1973), all gentle mixtures of folk, blues, Forties jazz and Western Swing. However, the band was beset by personnel problems and in 1973, with *Hicksville* climbing up the American album charts, Hicks folded the group.

Chris Hillman, born on Dec. 4, 1942 in Los Angeles and raised in San Diego County, became one of the best bluegrass mandolin players on the West Coast, fronting his own group, the Hillmen, before joining the nascent Byrds as bassist in 1964. He played a fairly passive role in the group's first three years as McGuinn, Crosby and Clark sparred for the leadership, but with the latter pair's departures his songwriting and jazz-influenced bass-playing became a major feature of their music on *Younger Than Yesterday* and *The Notorious Byrd Brothers.* He brought Gram Parsons into the group and between them they led the Byrds into electrified country, before both departed to form the Flying Burrito Brothers and further define the new genre of country rock. Hillman subsequently played with Stephen Stills' Manassas and then formed the Souther-Hillman-Furay Band with J. D. Souther and Richie Furay. The latter group, though playing solid LA country rock, have not approached the innovatory power of the groups with which Hillman has previously been associated.

Eddie Holman, born in Norfolk, Virginia, in 1946, is an extraordinary balladeer with a piercing variety of falsetto top notes. He first penetrated the charts with 'This Can't Be True' (Parkway, 1965). Four years later, after a series of records including the lovely 'I'm Not Gonna Give Up', Holman was back in the charts with an equally stratospheric rendering of an old Ruby and the Romantics hit, 'Hey There Lonely Girl' (and several other ABC releases, including 'Since I Don't Have You', 1969) which was unexpectedly revived in Britain with great success in 1974. His later sides on Silver Blue were not so well received.

Winston 'Niney the Observer' Holness was born in 1941 in Jamaica, where he is acknowledged as the island's leading 'rebel' producer. In the late Sixties, alongside Bunnie Lee, he helped produce artists of the calibre of Slim Smith and Pat Kelly, culminating in his own 'Blood And Fire' (1970) – a reggae classic. Further Niney hits were 'International Pum', 'Message To The Ungodly' and 'Observer Station', while he doubled as producer for Max Romeo ('Rasta Bandwagon', 'The Coming Of Jah') and Ken Boothe ('Silver Words'). His biggest success, since 'Westbound Train' in 1973, has been producing teenage reggae idol Dennis Brown. The pair have scored consistently with roots tunes like 'No More Will I Roam', 'Cassandra' and the LP *Just Dennis.* Other Niney albums include the acclaimed dub set *Dubbing With The Observer*, and *Live At The Turntable* featuring Big Youth and Delroy Wilson.

John Holt, born in Kingston, Jamaica in 1946, began his career in 1960 via the talent-contest circuit. He was lead vocalist with the Paragons from 1965 during which time the group enjoyed many successes, including 'Wear You To The Ball' and 'Love At Last'. He started his solo career in 1968, with a series of smooth, sentimental songs, notably 'Stick By Me' and 'Help Me Make It Through The Night' – a 1975

British hit. The most consistently popular singer in Jamaica, steady sales of *Sings For 'I', 1,000 Volts Of Holt* and *Pledging My Love* confirm his place as reggae's leading album artist.

Honey Cone comprises Carolyn Willis (born in Los Angeles in 1946), Edna Wright (born in Los Angeles in 1944) and Shellie Clark (born in Brooklyn, New York in 1943). All had previously worked as session singers or been in various groups before they were put together as a backing group for an Andy Williams television show in 1969: Carolyn Willis toured with Bob B. Soxx and the Blue Jeans, Edna Wright sang behind records by the Righteous Brothers and Johnny Rivers before joining the Raelettes, and Shellie Clark was an Ikette. They were signed by Holland, Dozier and Holland, who had left Motown to form their own Hot Wax label. Under their direction Honey Cone had a couple of small chart hits and then a No. 1 with the powerful 'Want Ads' in 1971, which began a string of bluesy hits ('Stick Up', 'One Monkey Don't Stop No Show', 1971, and 'The Day I Found Myself', 1972). Later releases were not so successful and in 1973 the group disbanded.

Hookfoot were originally session musicians for various artists on the DJM label, including Elton John. Formed in 1971, the band comprised Caleb Quaye (guitar, keyboards), Ian Duck (guitar, harmonica), Dave Glover (bass) and Roger Pope (drums). After their first album (*Hookfoot*, DJM, 1971), the band adjourned to the country town of Andover to prepare material for the mellower *Good Times A-Comin'* (1972).

When *Communication* (1973) and *Roaring* (1974) (for which Fred Gandy had replaced Glover) were also unsuccessful commercially, the band split up. Quaye moved to America to continue session-work, and with Pope played in Elton John's augmented band.

Nicky Hopkins was perhaps the most important session pianist in British rock during the late Sixties and early Seventies. As a child he had taken piano lessons, then turned to rock'n'roll by joining Screaming Lord Sutch's Savages at the start of the Sixties. The band then joined pioneer British R&B mouth-harp player Cyril Davies, recording 'Country Line Special' (Pye, 1963), on which Hopkins played a remarkable electric piano break.

Sessions with many British beat stalwarts followed, culminating in the Rolling Stones' *Their Satanic Majesties Request* album. In 1968 he joined the Jeff Beck Group, touring and recording with them for a year. Moving to California in 1969, Hopkins joined Quicksilver Messenger Service for two albums. He continued playing on sessions, appearing on every Rolling Stones album since 1967, as well as the *Jamming With Edward* record. He released a solo album on CBS (*The Tin Man Was A Dreamer*) in 1973.

Keith Hudson, born in Jamaica in 1946, entered the music industry in 1967 as promoter/producer of artists like John Holt, Delroy Wilson and Ken Boothe – he produced the latter's Jamaican No. 1 'Old Fashioned Way'. An experimental, 'rebel' producer, he was the first to record U Roy and Dennis Alcapone, and was responsible for Big Youth's biggest seller 'Ace 90' (1972). By 1975, recording himself, he had released *Entering The Dragon* and the acclaimed 'message' albums, *Torch Of Freedom* and *Flesh Of My Skin*. Firmly established in reggae circles, despite a weak singing voice, Keith Hudson seems poised for even wider success.

Hudson Ford. Richard Hudson and John Ford, both born in London in 1948, played in Elmer Gantry's Velvet Opera before joining the Strawbs in 1969 (at the same time as Rick Wakeman). They wrote some of the band's best-known numbers, including 'Part Of The Union', a British Top Three single in 1973, but musical differences led them to quit after the Strawbs' second American tour in 1973. Their first single together, the highly attractive 'Pick Up The Pieces' (on A&M), was tailor-made chart material but the following year 'Burn Baby Burn', 'Floating In The Wind' and 'Free Spirit' were disappointingly ordinary.

Humble Pie. Formed in 1969 in the then fashionable 'supergroup' manner by Peter Frampton, guitar, vocals (born on April 22, 1950 in Beckenham, Kent) from the Herd; Steve Marriott, guitar, vocals (born on Jan. 30, 1947 in London) from the Small Faces; Greg Ridley, bass, vocals (Oct. 23, 1947) from Spooky Tooth, and Jerry Shirley, drums (Feb. 4, 1952), Humble Pie wavered between the straightforward rock style of their first single, 'Natural Born Bugie' (Immediate, 1969), and the lightweight tastes of Frampton until, during a period of extensive American work, Marriott rediscovered his former confidence and began to dominate the group, as *Live At The Fillmore* (A&M, 1971) demonstrated. Frampton quit and was replaced by guitarist Dave 'Clem' Clempson (born Sept. 5, 1949) from Colosseum as the music grew steadily heavier, apart from a brief flirtation into soul with the addition of a vocal trio, the Blackberries (Clydie King, Venetta Fields, and Billie Barnum). The band, always at its best on stage, where Marriott's audience control and showmanship remained superb, broke up in 1974. Marriott formed Steve Marriott's All Stars out of its ashes in 1975.

Marsha Hunt, born in 1947, left Berkeley University, California, to come to England and was one of several unknowns who emerged from the chorus of the first London production of *Hair* (1969). Her first solo single, Dr John's 'I Walk On Gilded Splinters', and stage presence were rousing, but her earthy brand of Afro-rock had limited support, and she turned to straight acting (as Marsha Hunte). Returning to rock in 1973, she went out on the road with a five-man band, Marsha Hunt's 22, and later in the year became a chat show *commère*, enlivening early, experimental days of London's Capital Radio.

Luther Ingram, best-known for his original million-selling version of the dramatic soul ballad 'If Loving You Is Wrong (I Don't Want To Be Right)' (Koko, 1972), enjoyed four years of increasing popularity culminating in a highly acclaimed appearance in the film *Wattstax*, before falling victim to ill-fated business deals. Born in Jackson, Tennessee, he had recorded unsuccessfully in New York for Smash (where he cut the original version of 'I Spy For The FBI', produced by Leiber and Stoller), Decca (1964), Hib (1967), and Koko, until Stax assumed distribution of the latter company in 1968. His dozen hits also included the beautiful 'Ain't That Loving You (For More Reasons Than One)' (1970).

The Intruders. The present line-up of the Philly soul group is the same as in 1961 when they first sang on the North Philadelphia streets: Sam 'Little Sonny' Brown, Eugene Daughtry, Phil Terry and Robert Edwards. The group's first real break came in 1964, when they teamed up with a young pianist/producer, Leon Huff, who together with Leroy Lovette produced a disc with the group. When Huff formed Excel Records in 1965 with Kenny Gamble the Intruders were signed and cut a local hit. Within a year Excel (renamed Gamble) had put the Intruders' '(We'll Be) United' in the national soul charts and hits like 'Cowboys To Girls' (their first million-seller) followed in 1968.

In the Seventies with Gamble/Huff's CBS-backed Philly Sound ascendant, the Intruders' success continued with 'I'll Always Love My Mama', 'Rainy Days And Mondays', and 'Win, Place Or Show (She's A Winner)', possibly their greatest recording. Featuring the expressive lead of Little Sonny, the Intruders' sound is still one of the most distinctive in black music.

Island Records. Formed by Chris Blackwell in 1962 to distribute Jamaican record labels (including his own) in Britain, Island slowly expanded its repertoire, first licensing the New York Sue R&B label and then plunging headlong into 'progressive' rock when it signed Traffic in 1967. Formed following the break-up of the Spencer Davis Group which Blackwell had managed but placed with Philips because Island was too specialist a label for the group, Traffic provided Island with its first hit single, 'Paper Sun', and album, *Mr Fantasy*, in 1967, and created the image of a progressive label that Island was to henceforth carefully nurture. The signing of groups like Fairport Convention and Free confirmed this image and by 1970, when WEA offered Blackwell six million dollars for the company, Island was the most successful independent record company in Britain.

Since the mid-Sixties, Island had assigned its Jamaican product to Trojan Records and in 1972 it sold its interest in Trojan to B&C Records, only retaining progressive reggae acts such as Bob Marley and the Wailers and Toots and the Maytals, a move anticipated by the financing of *The Harder They Come*, the film that more than anything else paved reggae's way to becoming a part of the rock mainstream rather than purely a specialist music.

By the mid-Seventies, Island had maintained its position in the progressive rock market-place with the successful signing of acts like Cat Stevens, the Chieftains, Roxy Music and Bad Company, as well as signing a licensing deal with Fania which gave it the cream of 'Salsa' music, and making tentative steps into the pop field with the signing of Sparks. At the same time, it made distribution deals with smaller companies like Rocket, Chrysalis and Virgin, set up its own pressing plant, and formed an American company which by 1976 had signed Joe South and provided Island with its first British Top Twenty hit, War's 'Low Rider'.

The Isley Brothers – Rudolph (born on April 1, 1939), Ronald (May 21, 1941) and O'Kelly (Dec. 25, 1937) survived twenty years of musical changes, scoring definitive hits in each era along the way, to emerge as one of the most innovative black groups of the Seventies. Raised in Cincinnati, Ohio, the brothers moved to New York in 1957 where they recorded mediocre doo-wop/rock'n'roll sides for Teenage, and George Goldner's Cindy, Mark X, and Gone labels before signing with RCA. Produced by Hugo and Luigi, their driving gospel style enlivened a weak selection of pop material, but was best displayed by 'Shout' (1959), an exciting adaptation of the climax to their wild stage act which has since become a rock classic. They next worked with writer/producers Leiber and Stoller (Atlantic, 1961–62) and Bert Berns (Wand, 1962–63; UA, 1963–64) who tried unsuccessfully to fit their raw sound into a commercial package, although it was Berns who gave them 'Twist And Shout' (1962), a one-take, end-of-session dance riff that became their first Top Twenty pop hit, later immortalized by the Beatles. Forming their own production company, T-Neck, in 1964–65 they cut several memorable sides (including the rousing 'Testify' and dramatic ballad 'The Last Girl') featuring their young guitarist, Jimi Hendrix, before joining Tamla the following year.

After hitting with some typically slick corporation product (the Top Twenty 'This Old Heart Of Mine' and 'I Guess I'll Always Love You', for example, in 1966) the trio were relegated to second-rate material and quit to revive T-Neck in 1969. From their first release, the million-selling 'It's Your Thing', they projected a new heavy image and soon began using two younger brothers (Ernie, on guitar, and Marvin, on bass) and Chris Jasper (keyboards) to create 'progressive' hits that anticipated modern trends in black music and brought them to the attention of wider audiences. By the early Seventies they were interpreting songs by Steve Stills (the Top Twenty hit 'Love The One You're With', 1971) and Dylan ('Lay Lady Lay', 1971) and including Hendrix's traumatic 'Machine Gun' in their act. In 1973, they crystallized all their influences and ideas in the highly acclaimed *3+3* album, which included the million-selling 'That Lady'. Subsequent releases in a similar style (*Live It Up*, *The Heat Is On*) have kept them in the forefront of black music.

Terry Jacks, though chiefly known for his 1974 hit 'Seasons in the Sun' (a Jacques Brel song translated by Rod McKuen and originally arranged by Jacks for the Beach Boys, who recorded but never released it), has a wide and varied history stretching back to the early days of Canadian rock. Born in Winnipeg and raised in Vancouver, he led the Chessmen, one of Canada's most popular groups of the early-mid Sixties. In 1969 he married Susan Pesklevits, and together they recorded as the Poppy Family. Their records, which Terry wrote, arranged and produced, sold over four million, their biggest hits including 'Which Way You Goin', Billy?' and 'Where

Evil Grows' (London, 1970). Although they now record separately, he still writes and produces for Susan, as well as operating his own record label, Goldfish Records, on which he has had several large Canadian hits, including 'Concrete Sea'.

Millie Jackson is arguably the greatest of the many impressive black girl singers to emerge in the Seventies. Her raw emotive style has inhibited mass acceptance, but within 18 months of her first hit, 'Ask Me What You Want' (1972), she was voted Top R&B Vocalist alongside Aretha Franklin. Born in Thompson, Georgia in 1944, she moved to New York in the Sixties where she played local clubs and recorded unsuccessfully for MGM before signing to Spring in 1971. From her first release – the devastating portrayal of ghetto life, 'Child Of God' – she has hardly cut a bad track and seems equally at ease on uptempo dance tunes ('Ask Me What You Want', 'My Man A Sweet Man' – 1972), sensuous love songs ('It Hurts So Good' from the film *Cleopatra Jones* – 1973), or down-on-the-knees wailers ('If Loving You Is Wrong' – 1975). This last track was drawn from her beautiful concept album *Caught Up* which also provided the hit single 'I'm Through Trying To Prove My Love To You' and was one of the most highly acclaimed black music albums of 1975. *Still Caught Up* consolidated her reputation.

The Jackson 5 are popular music's ultimate anomaly. Promoted and packaged as teenybop whimsy at the same time as the Osmonds and the Partridge Family, the Jackson 5's music differed considerably. The Jacksons were black and their music, despite some pandering to a youthful audience, still retained links with the continually evolving soul music mainstream.

Born and raised in Gary, Indiana, Michael (born Aug. 29, 1958), Jermaine (Dec. 11, 1954), Jackie (May 4, 1951), Marlon (March 12, 1957) and Tito Jackson (Oct. 15, 1953) were the sons of Joe Robinson, a musician/singer and one-time member of the Falcons. The Jackson 5 began playing local hops around Indiana, eventually recording two obscure discs (for Steeltown Records). When 'discovered' by superstar Diana Ross they were immediately whisked away by the Motown Record Corporation and given one of the most extensive groomings ever. Staff writers, producers and musicians (including a couple of the Crusaders) worked for weeks on some of the most pungently rhythmic tracks the Detroit company had ever laid down and when 'I Want You Back' was released in 1969 its success was immediate. More gold discs quickly followed: 'ABC', 'The Love You Save' and 'I'll Be There', all American chart toppers in 1970. Lead singer Michael was sometimes asked to use his high quavering soprano on maudlin, rather slushy ballads rather than the highly charged dance numbers with which the group excelled, but considering the size and relative immaturity of their mass audience the Jacksons' discs were often staggeringly good. A slump did occur however when Michael began to record solo albums (*Got To Be There* and *Ben*) and when the group were asked to parody their original effervescent style ('Little Bitty Pretty One'). Motown, still ringing the changes, were able to launch Jermaine Jackson as a fairly successful solo act and as late as 1974 the group had a million-seller with 'Dancing Machine'.

But the group's failure to develop as songwriters, to move sufficiently in new musical directions (though the riveting electro-funk of 'Dancing Machine' was an intriguing possibility) and especially to shake off their decidedly *passé* image, have caused a decline from the stupendous successes of old, though the change from Motown to Epic Records (with Jermaine electing to stay put) may see the group recover.

The James Gang was formed in 1967 by Jim Fox in Cleveland, Ohio. When guitarist Glenn Schwartz left in April, 1969, to join Pacific Gas and Electric, Joe Walsh joined Tom Kriss and Fox, and in November, 1969 they released their first album, *Yer Album* (ABC). Kriss soon left to be replaced by Dale Peters and over the next 18 months the band produced its best work – thinking man's hard rock, intelligently and sensitively performed – that resulted in three gold albums: *Rides Again* (1970), *Thirds* (1971) and *Live In Con-*

cert (1971). As the central force behind the band, Walsh left a vast hole when he quit in November, 1971 – a hole that neither guitarist Dominic Troiano nor singer Roy Kenner could fill. The band dissolved in summer 1974, but Peters and Fox resurfaced six months later with Bubba Keith and Richard Shack to release their *New Born* album on Atlantic.

Jazz Rock. During the Second World War jazz began to separate itself from black entertainment music in general. Nevertheless, throughout the immediate post-war period it would have been impossible to draw a confident line between current jazz style and, say, the idiom of R&B or jump blues. Records by Wynonie Harris, Sonny Thompson or Tiny Bradshaw contain passages, particularly tenor saxophone solos, which could easily have been played at a Jazz At The Philharmonic concert, while the jazz playing of Illinois Jaquet or Charlie Ventura would fit perfectly into any R&B band. A common basis in the blues rendered this a perfectly natural state of affairs, and in the work of Gene Ammons, Stanley Turrentine and many organ-combos this jazz/R&B fusion has continued almost unaltered to the present day.

The arrival of rock'n'roll brought a mass white audience for the first time to black popular music, which coincided with a movement in jazz towards greater complexity and a view of the musician as artist rather than entertainer. Jazz, in consequence, vanished from popular music almost overnight.

In the middle Sixties this process went into reverse. Jazz had, by now, assumed a more explicit and extrovert manner, while rock music was entering an experimental phase. In both America and Britain a generation of musicians appeared which took advantage of this situation and refused to make a sharp distinction between the two idioms. Gary Burton's quartet, for instance, played in a style almost exactly midway between jazz and rock and their example encouraged a host of others, as did that of Miles Davis during the early Seventies. In Britain several groups came into being composed of young players with a jazz background who moved, as if by instinct, into the rock world. Among them were Soft Machine, Nucleus and Colosseum, whose members had served their apprenticeship with bands as diverse as the New Jazz Orchestra, John Mayall's groups and the Graham Bond Organization.

It is impossible to overestimate the effect of this cross-fertilization upon the development of rock. Improvisation, the stock-in-trade of jazz, was brought to a music which hitherto had concentrated on finished, definitive performance. Cream, perhaps the most influential progressive rock band, was two-thirds composed of players whose musical imagination had developed in a jazz context and their emphasis on long, exploratory solos derived directly from the jazz tradition.

Of much less importance is the practice, often described as 'jazz rock', of simply adding brass and reed sections to rock bands. The pioneers in this field, Blood, Sweat And Tears, produced some interesting music on their first two albums, but soon degenerated into mannerism and displays of mere virtuosity, as did Chicago and other groups who followed.

The relationship between jazz and rock is a complex one and no two groups work in exactly the same way. The only generalization that can be made is that the jazz tradition has reasserted itself as a vigorous current in popular music.

Waylon Jennings had a bit part in a 1966 movie, *Nashville Rebel*, and has since done much to earn that title. Born on June 15, 1937 in Littlefield, Texas, he played bass with Buddy Holly in 1959 and 'Jole Blon', his first record on Brunswick was produced by Holly. He moved to a folk-country style, recording for Trend, J.D.'s (leased to Vocalion), Ramco and A&M. In 1965, Jennings became involved in mainstream country when Chet Atkins signed him to RCA. He had hits with 'Green River', 'Only Daddy That'll Walk The Line' and 'MacArthur Park', but soon found the existing country scene musically restricting.

By the early Seventies, Jennings had dispensed with house producers and began to make his own, fine, country-rock albums like *Lonesome, 'Ornrey And Mean*. He toured with the Grateful Dead and was recognized as a member of the loose 'Nashville underground' circle which included Willie Nelson, Tompall Glaser and Billy Joe Shaver. Shaver contributed several songs to the 1973 album, *Honky Tonk Heroes*, which featured Jennings' road band rather than the conventional Nashville session men. Jennings is married to Jessi Colter, who had a country crossover hit in America with 'I'm Not Lisa' (Capitol, 1975).

Jethro Tull was formed in 1968 with Ian Anderson (flute, vocals, born in Edinburgh on Aug. 10, 1947), Clive Bunker (drums, born Dec. 12, 1946), Mick Abrahams (guitar, born April 7, 1943) and Glen Cornick (bass guitar, born April 24, 1947). Anderson spent the early Sixties in various bands in and around his native Blackpool, but formed Tull in London. He taught himself flute about six months before, his early playing owing much to Roland Kirk.

They were an immediate success in the clubs and their first single on Island Records, 'Song For Jeffrey', was a hit. Changing to Chrysalis Records they continued to enjoy singles success in Britain, though none made a dent in America, where the albums took off instead. Anderson's penchant for a tatty overcoat and manic stage presence – playing the flute while dancing on one leg becoming an early trademark – gave him instant appeal to both critics and public. By early 1969, however, changes were happening. Mick Abrahams left to form Blodwyn Pig, being replaced by Martin Barre (born Nov. 17, 1946); Clive Bunker left to form the ill-fated Jude, to be replaced by Barriemore Barlow (born Sept. 10, 1949); Glen Cornick left to form Wild Turkey and was replaced by Jeffrey Hammond-Hammond (born July 30, 1946). In 1971 John Evans (born March 28, 1948) joined on keyboards.

Anderson attempted his first concept album in 1971 with *Aqualung*, questioning organized religion and lamenting social injustice. These themes were further developed in *Thick As A Brick* (1972), which introduced stage props, low humour and film. As Tull continued moving further from the concept of a rock band playing music their audiences grew by quantum leaps, though critics were turning the other way. In 1973 *A Passion Play* was greeted with universal critical scorn and sell-out tours; Anderson took the criticism to heart and announced the end of the band, apparently counting on a huge fan response which never materialized. In 1974 the group returned to performing their peculiar brand of rock, theatre and puerile comedy and in 1975 recorded the awful *Minstrel In The Gallery*.

The group is named after the inventor of the seed drill.

Billy Joel, from Hicksville, Long Island, emerged in 1974 with a gold single and album, 'Piano Man'. A songwriter, singer and pianist, he recorded with the Hassles on United Artists in 1968. Forming a duo, he moved to Epic as Attila for another album, before signing to Artie Ripp's Family Productions in 1971. The result was *Cold Spring Harbor* (Family/Philips 1972), a somewhat sombre collection of his own songs.

Legal and managerial problems led to Joel's absence from recording for nearly two years, playing anonymously in piano bars, an experience which provided the basis for 'Piano Man'. In 1973 he signed with Columbia, and by 1975 had released two Michael Stewart-produced albums, *Piano Man* and *Streetlife Serenade*.

Elton John, one of the most successful rock entertainers of the Seventies, was born Reginald Kenneth Dwight on March 25, 1947 in Pinner, Middlesex. He began his career as a weekend pub pianist at the Northwood Hills Hotel for £1 a night in 1964. He spent four years as organist with the soul group, Bluesology, which backed visiting American acts such as Major Lance, Patti Labelle and the Bluebelles, Billy Stewart, and the Ink Spots. He wrote and sang the group's first Fontana single 'Come Back Baby' in 1965. Bluesology became Long John Baldry's backing band in 1967, the year of Baldry's British No. 1 hit with the ballad 'Let The Heartaches Begin' but Dwight, who had changed his name to Elton John – taken from Elton Dean, the group's saxophonist, and John Baldry – grew eager to leave. He failed a Liberty Records audition but was put in touch with Bernie Taupin, a lyricist from Lincolnshire, whom he finally met after six months of putting music to his lyrics. Helped by Caleb Quaye, they got a three-year writing contract with DJM for £10 a week each and John left Bluesology.

Taupin and John tried unsuccessfully to write Top Forty material and John performed on Marble Arch and Music For Pleasure budget albums covering current hits, while he released one single, 'I've Been Loving You', in 1968 and recorded an unreleased album of flower power material. Encouraged by DJM song-plugger Steve Brown, they wrote 'Skyline Pigeon', 'Lady Samantha' and finally the first album *Empty Sky* (DJM) released to warm reviews in the summer of 1969. Producer Gus Dudgeon and arranger Paul Buckmaster transformed the sound of the second album, *Elton John* (1970), which, containing 'Your Song' and 'Border Song', revealed John as a romantic and sensitive performer. However, it gained little British success. A band comprising two former Spencer Davis sidemen, drummer Nigel Olsson (born Feb. 5, 1949) and bassist Dee Murray (born April 3, 1946) caused a stir when premièred at the Rock Proms backing John's exuberant showmanship.

In 1970, the trio opened above David Ackles at Los Angeles Troubadour Club to an ecstatic reception, swiftly echoed in New York and Philadelphia with the effect that *Elton John* on MCA swept into the *Billboard* album charts at No. 17, a feat repeated later in the year by the third album *Tumbleweed Connection* (1970) steeped in Taupin's obsession with the American Old West. In Britain the American reaction was reflected by the chart entry of the second and third albums in spring, 1971.

Meanwhile a film soundtrack *Friends* on Paramount, a live tape of a New York Radio show *17-11-70*, and the grandiose *Madman Across The Water* were released in quick succession in 1971. *Madman* introduced guitarist Davey Johnstone from Magna Carta, and its doomy melodramatic arrangements were almost Buckmaster's last fling. A critical backlash greeted the flood of product in Britain but in

America it made Elton John the first artist since the Beatles to have four albums simultaneously in the Top Twenty.

His music, a synthesis of current styles that betrays his fan-like mentality but fails to project a distinct musical persona, arrived at a time when the distinction between pop and rock was beginning to blur. His easygoing command of a multiplicity of styles, his flair for outrageous showmanship, and his appeal to romantic sensibilities enabled him to become highly successful on stage and record. Lyricist Taupin developed from his earlier poetic pretensions to a more direct, jaunty vein on the next album, *Honky Château*, recorded in France and released in 1972. With *Don't Shoot Me, I'm Only The Piano Player* (1973) it re-established John's critical and popular appeal on both sides of the Atlantic; which grew even greater in 1973, the year he set up Rocket Records and released the double album *Goodbye Yellow Brick Road* arranged by Del Newman, which showed a broadening musical range and Taupin's increased interest in film mythology. Despite the mediocre *Caribou*, 1974 saw his popularity increase until his monthly royalties cheque surpassed the Beatles' earnings at their peak. In 1975, the autobiographical *Captain Fantastic And The Brown Dirt Cowboy*, dealing with his and Taupin's early career, shipped platinum for American sales in excess of one million units, the first album ever to do so, and he augmented and reformed his band. It was followed later in the year by *Rock Of The Westies.*

Behind the intimidating statistics, Elton John remains an elusive artist, lacking a defined musical character. Rather, his success reflects his ability to synthesize the prevailing styles and postures in an amiable – and sometimes moving – manner.

Joy of Cooking, a local Berkeley group, started out in 1967 as an outlet for the talents of Toni Brown and Terri Garthwaite, then both at the University of California. It was an unusual group with two girls at the helm; Toni Brown – vocals, keyboards, guitar (born Nov. 16, 1938); Terri Garthwaite – vocals, guitar (born July 11, 1938); Fritz Kasten –

drums, alto sax; Jeff Neighbor – bass (born March 19, 1942); Ron Wilson – congas, bongos, harp (born Feb. 5, 1933). Toni Brown contributed most of the songs. Their first two albums, *Joy Of Cooking* (Capitol, 1970) and *Closer To The Ground* (1971) established their distinctive rhythmic approach building on closely woven patterns between drums, bass, conga, Terri's rhythm guitar and Toni's lyrical piano work. *Closer To The Ground* saw Toni Brown's country leanings coming out in her singing and in the slight shift in the group's direction. But more importantly, behind their rhythmic playing, lay an adult orientation in lyrics, dealing with post-youthful finding your feet/facing the world subject-matters. A third album, *Castles* (1972), was disappointing but Toni and Terri took time out to cut an album together in Nashville, the impressive *Cross Country* (1973). Toni left the group following the release of the album to record a solo album, *Good For You Too* (MCA, 1974), while Terri remained another year before recording her own solo album for Arista (1975). The group, who have since added another guitarist, Glan Frendel, and piano player Steve Roseman, are currently without a record contract.

Judge Dread, born in Britain as Alex Hughes, came to prominence when his lewd 'Big Six' (Big Shot) hit the British charts (1972). Originally a disc-jockey, Hughes, with manager/lyricist Ted Lemon, based the song on Prince Buster's 'Big Five'. In similar vein, 'Big Seven' was even more successful, making the Top Ten later that year and 'Big Eight' followed shortly after that – achieving a trio of hits without any BBC airplay. Since then, he has reaped steady sales with album *Dreadmania*, and earned a British Top Five with a version of Birkin/Gainsbourg's 'Je T'aime' (1975). A character with huge working-class appeal, Judge Dread seems destined for the cabaret circuit.

Juicy Lucy was a British-based blues band formed on the American model in 1969 by steel-guitarist Glenn Campbell. He had previously been with the Misunderstood, whose 'I Can Take You To The Sun' was a cult single among the

London underground. Other members were Chris Mercer (sax, keyboards) – a John Mayall alumnus – Mick Moody (guitar), James Leverton (bass), Rod Coombes (drums) and Paul Williams (vocals), previously with Zoot Money.

Their first single, the Bo Diddley song 'Who Do You Love' (Vertigo, 1970) was a Top Twenty hit, but later records were less successful. Juicy Lucy made four albums (two for Vertigo, one each for Bronze and Polydor) before splitting up in 1972. Campbell returned to his native America, Mercer played sessions and formed Gonzales, while Williams sang briefly with Jon Hiseman's Tempest.

Speedy Keen, born John Keen on March 29, 1945 in Ealing, London, travelled the Continent with various British rock groups before returning to Britain where his composition 'Armenia, City In The Sky' was recorded by the Who on *The Who Sell Out.* Encouraged by Pete Townshend, he formed Thunderclap Newman with Andy Newman and Henry McCulloch and wrote their transatlantic hit, 'Something In The Air' (Track, 1969). After one album, *Hollywood Dream* (1970), the group folded and Keen didn't record again until 1973 when he released an impressive collection of songs, *Previous Convictions* (Track), united by their punkish philosophy of life, also showcased on *Y'Know Wot I Mean?* (Island, 1975).

Eddie Kendricks was born in Birmingham, Alabama on Dec. 17, 1939. An original member of the Temptations, he left the group to go solo in 1971. He scored only minor hits in 1971–72 but in 1973 had an American No. 1 and British Top Twenty hit with 'Keep On Truckin'' (Tamla) on which his normally tender tenor was a little rougher than usual. *The Hit Man* (1975) showed him to be increasingly interested in making albums as well as singles. Kendricks' 1976 album, *He's A Friend*, was produced by Norman Harris with more than a nod towards the Philadelphia sound.

Jerry Kennedy, previously a Nashville session guitarist and independent producer, took over the plum position of Nashville A and R man and production head for Mercury Records from Shelby Singleton in 1967. He had worked for Singleton at his Bayou Record Shop in Shreveport, Louisiana, during the Fifties, and recorded rockabilly for Decca as well as a solo album on Smash in 1965.

Continuing as a guitarist on sessions that he supervises, Kennedy has a personal approach to his production and has provided a string of hits for his top artists, Jerry Lee Lewis, Faron Young and Tom T. Hall, and also for newcomers such as Johnny Rodrigues.

Doug Kershaw, multi-instrumentalist best known for his fiddle playing, is a genuine 'cajun' from French Louisiana. Born Jan. 24, 1936 in Tiel Ridge, he was taught music by 'Daddy Jack' and 'Mama Rita' who appear in many of the hundreds of songs he has subsequently written. Moving from radio spots with his brother in Lake Charles and Shreveport, Rusty and Doug's Music Makers hit Nashville in 1955 and local recordings on Feature were transferred to Hickory. Several hits ensued, including the much-covered 'Louisiana Man'. More recent albums of his personal documentary of cajun life through song have appeared on Hickory, RCA, Mercury and Warner Bros.

Carole King was born Carole Klein in Brooklyn, New York on Feb. 9, 1942. During a brief college career she tried to write songs with Paul Simon, later leaving to become a full-time composer in Don Kirshner's office at the Brill Building. Teaming up with Gerry Goffin, later to become her husband, she wrote dozens of hits between 1959 and 1967, when the partnership ceased. The grateful recipients of Goffin-King pieces included Bobby Vee ('Take Good Care Of My Baby', 'Walking With My Angel', 'In My Baby's Eyes'), Tony Orlando ('Halfway To Paradise', 'I'll Never Find Another You' – both successfully covered in Britain by Billy Fury), the Drifters ('When My Little Girl Is Smiling', 'Up On The Roof'), Shirelles ('Will You Still Love Me Tomorrow'), Little Eva ('The Locomotion'), Cookies ('Chains', 'Don't Say Nothing Bad About My Baby') and Dusty Springfield and the Byrds ('Goin' Back'). She had an international hit herself with 'It Might As Well Rain Until September' (Dimension, 1962). Previously she had recorded unsuccessfully for ABC-Paramount ('Babysittin''), RCA ('Short Mort') and Alpine ('Oh Neil!', her reply to Sedaka's 'Oh Carol!').

But by 1967, it seemed as though the new wave of predominantly West Coast music had swamped the craftsmanlike writers of the early Sixties. While Neil Sedaka and others disappeared from view, Goffin and King found themselves writing 'Pleasant Valley Sunday' for the Monkees, the creation of their old boss, Don Kirshner.

An attempt to form an independent label, Tomorrow, foundered, but a new direction was signalled by 'A Natural Woman', the Carole King song recorded in 1967 by Aretha Franklin. In contrast to the earlier teenage love songs, it showed a new insight and maturity, already suggested by 'Goin' Back'. The opening lines seemed suffused with a very personal feeling – 'Looking out on the morning rain / Sometimes I feel so uninspired' – an impression confirmed when King herself recorded it on *Tapestry* (1971).

Before that came the City, a group including Danny Kortchmar (guitar), Charlie Larkey (bass – her second husband) and Jim Gordon (drums). An unsuccessful album for Lou Adler's Ode label was followed in 1970 by *Writer*, a Carole King album. It introduced the by now familiar instrumental sound, dominated by King's richly chorded piano, and was the prelude to *Tapestry* (1971), an international hit album which eventually sold over ten million copies. Containing 'You've Got A Friend', 'So Far Away', 'Smackwater Jack' and a low-key version of 'Will You Love Me Tomorrow', it placed Carole King at the forefront of the emerging school of 'singer-songwriters', alongside James Taylor, who took 'You've Got A Friend' to No. 1.

The initial critical welcome for *Tapestry* faded when *Music* (1971) and *Rhymes And Reasons* (1972) seemed little more than reiterations of the new formula. With *Fantasy* (1973), King tried with mixed success to deal with wider social issues as well as the themes of love and friendship which dominated earlier. The 1974 album, *Wrap Around Joy*, contained 'Jazzman' (with a solo by Tom Scott), her first No. 1 for three years. Despite the anti-climax of some of her more recent records, *Tapestry* remains a nodal album, marking the point at which rock lyrics proved themselves capable of handling adult themes as well as teenage ones.

Jonathan King, born Dec. 6, 1944 in London, was a Cambridge University student when his nonsense protest song, 'Everybody's Gone To The Moon' (Decca, 1965), was a surprise British and American Top Twenty hit. Rather than attempt a career as a singer and performer he turned to writing for and producing other groups, such as Hedgehoppers Anonymous, whose 'It's Good News Week' was a transatlantic hit in 1965. He briefly became a pop columnist, deejay and television personality before taking a part-time job as assistant to Sir Edward Lewis, the head of Decca Records, in the late Sixties.

During this period, King released the occasional record, such as the bizarre 'Let It All Hang Out' (1969) and a version of Dylan's 'Million Dollar Bash' (1970). In 1970 he started his own production company with a policy of looking for one-off pop hits, rather than artists, and leasing the masters to other record companies. He was immediately successful, scoring several British Top Twenty hits in 1971, some of which were by him under different names: 'Sugar Sugar' (Sakharin, RCA), 'Johnny Reggae' (the Piglets, Bell), 'The Same Old Song' (the Weathermen, B&C), 'Keep On Dancing' (Bay City Rollers, Bell) and 'Leap Up And Down (And Wave Your Knickers In The Air)' (St Cecilia, Polydor).

In 1972 King set up UK Records and was soon in the charts with Shag's 'Loop Di Loop'. However, such success was short-lived: he failed to break into the American market and his 1972 album, *Bubble Rock Is Here To Stay*, was excessively self-indulgent. For a while the mainstay of UK was 10cc, whose only debt to King was their name – they wrote and produced their own records. Following the departure of 10cc and the failure for King of discoveries like Marty Wilde's son Ricky, who was intended to capture the then vast teenybopper market, he reverted to a more traditional notion of a record company. In 1975 he signed one of the bright hopes of the pub circuit, the Kursaal Flyers, staying with them after the commercial failure of their first album, *Chocs Away* (1975). The year also saw him back in the British Top Twenty with a cover of George Baker's 'Una Paloma Blanca' (UK). In 1976 the self-appointed Prince of Plasticity and scourge of 'progressive rock' released a collection of old and new tracks: *Jonathan King: Greatest Hits, Past, Present And Future.*

King Crimson were the prototype British 'progressive' band of the late Sixties. Based on the lyrics of Pete Sinfield and the music and mellotron of Robert Fripp (born in 1946), Crimson first attracted attention at a Rolling Stones free concert in 1969. With Ian McDonald (flute, keyboards, born in 1946), Greg Lake (bass, vocals, born in 1948) and Mike Giles (drums, born in 1942), Fripp cut *In The Court Of The Crimson King* (Island, 1969). Its baroque extravagances of word and sound set the tone for emerging progressive bands like Yes and, later, ELP, which included Lake.

From then on, a series of major personnel changes made Crimson's progress somewhat erratic. Only Fripp remained constant, with even the wordsmith Sinfield quitting in 1972 after *Islands*, the fourth album. The latter went on to produce the first Roxy Music album, make a solo record (*Still*, 1973) and publish a book of poems. The resulting line-up – Fripp, Mel Collins (saxes), Boz Burrell (bass) and Ian Wallace (drums) was more jazz-oriented and toured America in 1972, recording *Earthbound*, a live album.

The next year, Fripp reconstituted King Crimson with Bill Bruford, the former Yes drummer (born on May 17, 1950), John Wetton (born in 1950), the bass player from Family who would later join Uriah Heep, David Cross (vocals, mellotron, born in 1948) and Jamie Muir, an *avant-garde* percussionist. They made *Larks' Tongues In Aspic* (1973) and the effective *Red* (1974) before Fripp announced the end of King Crimson in October, 1974, declaring that he would now become 'small, intelligent and highly mobile'. He remains an enigmatic presence in British rock, having produced a body of work which includes much that is eccentric and pretentious as well as genuinely experimental, including *Pussyfootin'* (Island, 1974), a collaboration with Brian Eno.

King Tubby, a Jamaican-born producer, Sound System operator and engineer *extraordinaire*, was one of the most influential individuals in reggae of the Seventies. Pioneering the 'dub' sound in his studio, and featuring top deejays U Roy, and (later) I Roy, on his *No. 1* Sound System, he, virtually single-handed, revolutionized the Jamaican music scene. Exploiting treble, in a bass-dominated music, Tubby produced a sound that perfectly complemented the direction in which reggae was moving – solid, heavy and immensely powerful. By 1975, virtually every dub recorded was engineered at Tubby's studios, many being dedicated to him: notably Augustus Pablo's 'King Tubby Meets The Rockers Uptown'.

Kinney Warner Communications. A giant conglomerate, Kinney National Service is known today as Warner Communications. It was started in the late Forties by three businessmen, Caesar Kimmel, Sigmund Dornbusch and Emmanuel Rosenstein. Originally just a parking lot on Kinney Street, Newark, New Jersey, it diversified into funeral parlours and building maintenance. During the early Fifties, Kinney took long-term parking lot leases and made a fortune during the building boom which followed. The company went public in 1962 and bought out Warner Bros in 1969. The deal gave Kinney both the film and record company, which included the WEA group. For convenience, the company changed its name to Warner Communications in 1971 under the presidency of Steve Ross.

Today they control the Warner/Atlantic/Elektra/Asylum/Nonsuch group of record companies; Warner Bros movies and TV; Warner Bros music publishing; Warner books; EC Publications, which distribute the Batman, Superman comics plus *Mad* magazine; Cable TV Communications, the second largest cable system in the States. Warner

Communications also have controlling interest in the Garden State National Bank of Hackensack, N.J., which has $500 million in assets. Recent acquisitions include Jungle Habitat Wildlife Park in New York and the NYC Cosmos, North America's leading soccer team which boasts the legendary Pelé amongst its players.

Gladys Knight (and The Pips). Born in Atlanta, Georgia, on May 28, 1944, Gladys Knight was a child singer with the Morris Brown and Wings Over Jordan gospel choirs before joining her elder brother, Merald (born Sept. 2, 1942) and cousins William (born June 2, 1941) and Elenor Guest to form the Pips in 1952. It is reputed that she sang with the Magnificents on Vee Jay (1956–57) and some of their tracks have been reissued as by Gladys Knight, but she has since denied any part in them. Her 1958 debut release with the Pips – when another cousin, Edward Patten (born Aug. 2, 1939), replaced Elenor – was 'Whistle My Love' on Brunswick. Three years later, their beautiful revival of 'Every Beat Of My Heart' recorded for Atlanta-based Huntom (and leased to Vee Jay), and a re-recording for Bobby Robinson's Fury label, gave them simultaneous hits with different versions of the same song. Further recordings for Robinson (on Fury, Enjoy and Everlast, 1961–63) included the fine 'Letter Full Of Tears', a Top Twenty Record in 1961. They next appeared on Maxx in 1964–65 with several excellent soul ballads (including 'Giving Up' and 'Either Way I Lose') written and arranged by Van McCoy, but remained unrecognized until a contract with Tamla-Motown in 1966 introduced them to a worldwide audience.

After minor success with 'Just Walk In My Shoes' they were placed with producer Norman Whitfield, who gave them nine exciting hits, including the first hit version of 'I Heard It Through The Grapevine' (1967), a wailing 'It Should Have Been Me' (1968), a revival of 'The Nitty Gritty' and the powerhouse 'Friendship Train' (1969). Later, several stunning ballad performances ('If I Were Your Woman' – 1970, 'Make Me The Woman That You Go Home To' – 1971, 'Help Me Make It Through The Night', 'Neither One

Of Us' – 1972) finally brought Gladys recognition as one of the great female soul singers of our time.

In 1973 they transferred to Buddah and continue to win international acclaim with hits like 'Where Peaceful Waters Flow', 'Midnight Train To Georgia' (1973), 'The Best Thing That Ever Happened To Me' (1974), and 'The Way We Were' (1975).

Robert Knight, born on April 24, 1945, in Franklin, Tennessee, first sang lead vocal with the Paramounts – Neal Hopper, Peter Hollins, Richard Simmons and Nashville super session man, Kenny Buttrey – on Dot in 1961. 'Young thrush sings lead on slow rockaballad' was how *Billboard* described their only disc. After solo sides for Dot – including 'Free Me' which Johnny Preston covered – Knight enrolled at Tennessee State University. In 1967, he was signed to Rising Sons by Mac Gayden and Buzz Cason who immediately wrote him a Top Twenty smash hit, 'Everlasting Love', which was covered in Britain by the Love Affair. Knight's other light, frothy and magnificently danceable hits included 'Blessed Are The Lonely' (1968) and 'The Power Of Love', whose flip, 'Love On A Mountain Top', made the British charts in 1974. In the interim, Knight who also recorded for Elf (e.g. 'Isn't It Lonely Together', 1968), continued an academic career in chemical research.

Terry Knight, born in Flint, Michigan, on April 9, 1943, was probably the most influential manager/entrepreneur in rock during the early Seventies, along with Bill Graham and possibly Steve Paul. He began his career as a disc jockey on CKLW, Detroit's biggest station, becoming the city's most popular DJ by the age of twenty. Fired for airing his controversial views, Knight joined a Flint group called the Pack, changing their name to Terry Knight and the Pack and scoring a national hit with 'I (Who Have Nothing)' on Lucky Eleven in late 1966. As a singer he was fair, but as a businessman and self-promoter he was brilliant. After an abortive solo career, he was contacted by the Pack early in 1969. They were failing badly, needed a new direction, and then agreed to give Knight complete control of their career. He renamed them Grand Funk Railroad, and by virtue of his ruthless management and flair for sensationalism, they became America's biggest-selling group in 1970.

Following the success of Grand Funk, Knight took on another group, the Texas band Bloodrock. They also became extremely popular, but by early 1972 both groups had left him, resulting in monstrously complicated lawsuits. By the time they were settled Knight had launched Brown Bag Records and several new groups including Mom's Apple Pie and Wild Cherry. Brown Bag, distributed and backed with large advances by United Artists, was a colossal failure. Knight announced his withdrawal from the music business, to concentrate on his other activities, ranging from ecology action to oil speculation.

Leslie Kong, born in Jamaica, ran a record shop, Beverleys, when Jimmy Cliff, desperate for financial backing, introduced him to Derrick Morgan and the music industry in 1963. With Morgan supervising the sessions, Kong produced Jimmy Cliff's 'Hurricane Hattie', Eric Morris's 'Cinderella', and Derrick's own 'Forward March' and 'Be Still': all hits. By the late Sixties, Kong's Beverleys studio was among the island's biggest. He had been responsible for the earliest records of Desmond Dekker and John Holt, while among his biggest successes were Ken Boothe's 'Freedom Street' and the Melodians' 'Rivers Of Babylon'. He died shortly after.

John Kongos flitted very briefly through the British charts in 1971 when both 'He's Gonna Step On You Again' and 'Tokoloshe Man' reached No. 4, on Fly. Born in Johannesburg, South Africa, in 1946, he settled in 1969 in Britain. The lead guitarist and vocalist with Scrugg, as well as other South African groups in Britain, he eventually branched out on his own as a writer/producer/performer. His music – mostly stamping, multi-tracked incomprehensible chants – was excitingly infectious but the public quickly tired of it.

Kool and the Gang is a seven-piece black band led by bassist Robert 'Kool' Bell, who disciplined their preference for free-form jazz to produce one of the hottest disco funk bands of the Seventies. Formed in Jersey City, New Jersey, in 1964 as The Jazziacs, they also doubled as The Soul Town Revue and The New Dimensions before adopting their present name in 1968 and signing to Gene Redd's De-Lite label the following year. After scoring minor hits with many ragged derivations of Sly Stone themes – 'Kool And The Gang' (1969), 'Let The Music Take Your Mind' (1970) and several loose albums, they tightened up to produce the million-selling 'Funky Stuff' (1973), the first of many equally exciting riffs ('Jungle Boogie', 'Hollywood Swinging', 'Higher Plane' – 1974; 'Spirit Of The Boogie' – 1975) tailor-made for the growing disco boom.

Kris Kristofferson, born in Brownsville, Texas on June 22, 1936, was a country music fan from an early age. He went as a Rhodes Scholar to Oxford University in 1958 where he had a couple of novels rejected by publishers and briefly became 'genuine American' rock'n'roller, Kris Carson. Returning home he joined the army for four and a half years, before eventually, in 1965, reaching Nashville, where his creative drive and love of country music could work for each other.

The next four years were spent hustling songs he was writing, with increasing success. Several were recorded by country stalwarts, he got a publishing contract, provided hits for Ray Stevens and Roger Miller, and finally started to cut his own demos. Around the turn of the decade he made several successful albums, the first and best of which, *The Silver Tongued Devil And I* (Monument, 1971), featured the fine musicianship of Nashville friends, Kris' less notable voice, and songs written with a fine turn of phrase, revolving around traditional country themes of travelling through broken love affairs and drunken despairs. His most famous songs, like 'Me And Bobby McGee' and 'Help Me Make It Through The Night', have swiftly become contemporary standards. Over the last few years he has produced little of note, working (*Kris And Rita*, 1973) and living with Rita

Coolidge whom he married in 1973. He is seemingly set for a career in films with impressive appearances in, among others, *Cisco Pike*, *Pat Garrett and Billy The Kid*, and *Alice Doesn't Live Here Anymore.*

Labelle. From high heels, bouffants and Broadway show tunes to sci-fi fashion, revolutionary image and aggressive 'black rock', Labelle's metamorphosis is one of the most extraordinary phenomena of the Seventies. Patricia Holt (alias Patti Labelle, born Oct. 4, 1944) and Cindy Birdsong grew up together in Philadelphia. They joined the Ordettes, while their friends Sarah Dash (born May 24, 1942) and Nona Hendryx (born Aug. 18, 1945) joined the Del Capris. The four girls amalgamated as the Blue Belles and Newtown Records hit the Top Twenty with their 'I Sold My Heart To The Junkman' in 1962. As Patti Labelle and the Bluebells the group became an established part of the girl group scene of the Sixties, regularly playing the Apollo Theater, visiting Europe and hitting with 'You'll Never Walk Alone' (Parkway, 1964) and 'All Or Nothing' (Atlantic, 1965). But their stream of discs featuring Patti's high, nasal voice became less and less successful. Cindy Birdsong took up an offer to replace Florence Ballard in the Supremes and the team regrouped as a trio.

With new manager Vicki Wickham (late of Britain's *Ready Steady Go* TV programme) and a new, streamlined name – Labelle – the girls moved first to Warner Bros in 1972 and then to RCA where their image sharpened up with the use of strong material, like Gil Scott-Heron's 'The Revolution Will Not Be Televised', instead of cabaret standards. A contract with Columbia/Epic brought forth the *Nightbirds* album produced by New Orleans mastermind Allen Toussaint. With the million-selling 'Lady Marmalade' their rebirth was complete.

Ronnie Lane left the Faces in mid-1973, formed his own backing group, Slim Chance, and had a hit with his first single release, 'How Come' (GM, 1973). He then undertook an overambitious tour, the Passing Show, using a circus big top, which financial pressures forced him to abandon uncompleted, and his band, which included Benny Gallagher and Graham Lyle, broke up after recording *Anymore For Anymore* (GM, 1974). Later that year he re-formed Slim Chance with Ruan O'Lochlainn (keyboards, saxophone, guitar), Charlie Hart (keyboards, violin, accordion), Steve Simpson (guitar, mandolin, violin), Brian Belshaw (bass), and Colin Davey (drums), for *Ronnie Lane's Slim Chance* (Island, 1975), but has been at his best on stage where his eccentric and eclectic range of material is imbued with the jollity of a knees-up in a London East End boozer. In 1976, the same line-up, minus O'Lochlainn, released *One For The Road.*

Denise Lasalle, chunky and funky, during the early Seventies vied with Ann Peebles as the raunchiest writer/songstress out of Memphis. Born Denise Craig in Greenwood, Mississippi, she eventually settled in Chicago where she cut her first, unsuccessful, records for the Chess (1967) and Parka (1970) labels. After forming Crajon Productions with husband Bill Jones, sessions with Willie Mitchell and Gene Miller in Memphis yielded the first of several compulsive hits on Westbound, including 'Trapped By A Thing Called Love' (1971), 'Now Run And Tell That' and 'A Man Size Job' (1972). Recording now in Muscle Shoals, she continues to release the occasional hit but concentrates on songwriting/production for other artists.

Led Zeppelin was formed in October, 1968 by Jimmy Page (guitars, born April 9, 1944), Robert Plant (vocals, Aug. 20, 1948), John Paul Jones (bass, keyboards, Jan. 3, 1946), and John Bonham (drums, May 31, 1948). Page had had the idea for the band throughout the last months of the Yardbirds; he knew John Paul Jones from session work and a friend recommended Birmingham-based Robert Plant, in whose Band Of Joy John Bonham drummed. They recorded their first album in thirty hours and then toured Scandinavia fulfilling old Yardbirds obligations.

On their first American tour in early 1969 they supported

Vanilla Fudge and played club dates. Their second, headlining tour came shortly after and the next shortly after that; by March, 1970, they were performing their fifth tour. *Led Zeppelin* was released in February, 1969 by Atlantic Records; within two months it was No. 8, and remained in the Top Twenty for six months. *Led Zeppelin II*, released in October, 1969, became Atlantic's fastest selling album, moving at 100,000 per week. This record was broken by the group's latest album, *Physical Graffiti*, which at one point was selling 500 an hour. All the group's albums are platinum.

The first group to establish a world reputation by heavily touring America while playing only sporadically elsewhere, a situation created partly by an initial lack of interest in them in Britain, much of their success lies with manager Peter Grant who has guided the group's career with almost mechanical efficiency and timing. His policy of them working only every other year has kept the group in demand, a situation not hindered by the endless quest for perfection that held up release of an album for several months due to cover problems, the year and a half of recording *Physical Graffiti*, or the endless delays of their feature film.

By 1975 they were the most successful group in the world, filling football stadiums across America and five days at London's 20,000-seat Earl's Court with an awesome display of lights, smoke, dry ice and laser beams. The group's focus is Plant and Page. Onstage they are opposites and complements, Plant a golden ringleted Adonis marvellously parodying the sexual superstar while singing in a voice of limitless power, Page a dark, fragile guitarist of immense versatility and command clothed in black velvet and rippling dragons.

Albert Lee, as Chris Farlowe's guitarist in the Thunderbirds, earned a legendary reputation in London in the mid-Sixties among other musicians, though Farlowe's lack of recording success – apart from 'Out Of Time' (Immediate, 1966) without the Thunderbirds – denied him wider acclaim. When Farlowe finally broke up his backing group in 1968, Lee spent eighteen months with Country Fever, during which time he also recorded as Poet and the One Man Band with

Tony Colton and Ray Smith. He later worked briefly with Fotheringay and recorded with Steve Gibbons before rejoining Smith and Colton as Heads, Hands And Feet together with Mike O'Neill and Pete Gavin for three albums, *Heads Hands And Feet* (Island, 1971), *Tracks* (1972) and *Old Soldiers Never Die* (Atlantic, 1973). He subsequently worked with the Crickets and in 1975 rejoined Farlowe for the latter's comeback tour. He remains one of the most accomplished and underrated British guitarists.

Laura Lee, one of the first soul singers to champion liberated women, her early records (Chess, 1967–68) chastised ('Dirty Man'), and advertised ('Wanted: Lover, No Experience Necessary', 'Up Tight Good Man', 'A Man With Some Backbone'). She was equally convincing on romantic songs like Jerry Butler/Curtis Mayfield's 'Need To Belong' and 'He Will Break Your Heart'. After a year with Cotillion she enjoyed greater success on Hot Wax with even more forthright material, including 'Wedlock Is A Padlock' (1970), 'Woman's Love Rights' (1971), 'Rip Off', and 'Crumbs Off The Table' (1972), but later releases on Invictus ('If I'm Good Enough To Love – I'm Good Enough To Marry') seem to indicate a change of heart.

John Lennon has been the most prolific ex-Beatle, and the most controversial. While Paul McCartney and George Harrison adopted conventional rock star personae (one a show business personality, the other a recluse), Lennon, often with Yoko Ono, tried a variety of strategies, often linked with the artistic or political *avant garde*. By 1974, though, his work seemed to be re-joining the rock mainstream as 'Mind Games' and 'Whatever Gets You Through The Night' gave him his biggest hits as a solo artist.

Although the Beatles' split was not officially confirmed until 1970, Lennon had already taken his distance from the others in the previous year when he embarked on a series of 'Bed-Ins' and albums with Yoko which partook of the 'Happenings' philosophy then abroad in the New York artistic community. Three albums were released jointly by John and

Yoko, consisting primarily of electronic and 'found' sounds (press conference tapes, for instance): *Two Virgins* (Apple, 1968) – with the celebrated nude photographs of the couple on the sleeve – *Unfinished Music No. 2: Life With The Lions* (1969) and *Wedding Album* (1969).

However, by 1969, the Plastic Ono Band had emerged as the definitive vehicle for his more conventional musical activity. A shifting group of musicians centred on John and Yoko, its performance at the Toronto Rock Revival show, with Eric Clapton, Klaus Voorman (bass) and Alan White (drums), was released as *Live Peace In Toronto*. Included were rock'n'roll oldies, two of Yoko's wailing compositions and 'Give Peace A Chance', the prototype of the other side of Lennon's new music – a simple, populist song, intended to be sung on the streets.

A further stage in Lennon's self-renewal was reached with *John Lennon/Plastic Ono Band* (1970). Described later as Primal Scream music (after Lennon revealed his treatment by Arthur Janov), the songs dug back into his formative childhood relationships ('Mother', 'My Mummy's Dead') and the Beatle experience ('Working Class Hero' and the riveting 'God', which coined the phrase 'the dream is over'). By comparison, *Imagine* (1971), produced by Phil Spector, was calmer and more contained. The title song was to become the most widely known of Lennon's compositions, while 'How Do You Sleep' was interpreted by many as an attack on Paul McCartney's solo work.

The re-election of Nixon in 1972 and pressures to have Lennon deported from America were perhaps contributory factors to the political commitment which was the driving-force behind *Some Time In New York City* (1972). Lyrics about the oppression of women, the Attica prison riots and Northern Ireland were attacked as simplistic and extremist, but the album's powerful musical impact was enhanced by spirited rock'n'roll backings from the New York group Elephant's Memory. It was packaged with a second record containing material from two live sessions, with the Mothers Of Invention and a 1969 band, at London's Lyceum, including Eric Clapton, Keith Moon and Delaney and Bonnie.

With *Mind Games* (1973) and *Walls And Bridges* (1974), John Lennon returned to more conventional themes of love and personal interaction on meticulously crafted albums using top New York session musicians. 'Mind Games', with a powerful wall of sound behind Lennon's penetrating voice, was a Top Ten hit in America, while the starker 'Whatever Gets You Through The Night' reached No. 1 in America in 1974. In 1975, Lennon made his contribution to rock's re-examination of its own past when, on *Rock'n'Roll*, he re-affirmed his commitment to the archetypal strengths of Fifties music, which have always been prominent in his own work.

Gordon Lightfoot is perhaps the most prolific and consistent Canadian singer/songwriter of the last decade. Unlike some of his compatriots (notably Joni Mitchell and Neil Young), he remains based in Toronto where he has his own studio.

Born in Orillia, Ontario on Nov. 17, 1938, his early albums for United Artists reflected his background in the Yorktown folk scene, Toronto's equivalent to Greenwich Village. 'Canadian Railroad Trilogy' was an epic tribute to the building of the transcontinental lines, while 'Early Morning Rain' became a folk standard, recorded by Peter Paul and Mary, Bob Dylan and many others.

In 1970, Lightfoot moved to Warner Bros, to start a fruitful relationship with producer Lenny Waronker. His first album for the company, *If You Could Read My Mind* included the original recording of Kristofferson's 'Me And Bobby McGee' and Randy Newman and Ry Cooder were among the musicians involved.

His popularity increased throughout the Seventies as he developed a fluid style in which voice, melody and lyrics were merged in a resonant but seldom bland way. The title track of *Sundown* (1974) provided him with his first No. 1 single.

Limmie and the Family Cooking – really a family – are perky purveyors of soul-influenced bubblegum. They are

Limmie Snell and his sisters, Jimmy and Martha, though Limmie and Jimmy swopped names when they started the group, to avoid gender confusion. Born in Dalton, Alabama, the family moved to Canton, Ohio, in 1954. The children sang gospel and Limmie won a recording contract when he was just 11 (recording a series of singles under the bizarre pseudonym of Lemmie B. Good). Eventually he formed a group with his sisters singing by night, working in factories by day. Discovered by Steve Metz, their 'You Can Do Magic' (produced by Metz and Sandy Linzer) proved a small US and a big UK hit for Avco Records in 1972 and 1973 respectively. Subsequent discs have ranged from the catchy, 'A Walking Miracle', to the inane, 'Lollipop'.

Lindisfarne. This all-Newcastle band – Alan Hull (born Feb. 20, 1945), Rod Clements (Nov. 17, 1947), Ray Jackson (Dec. 12, 1948), Simon Cowe (April 1, 1948) and Ray Laidlaw (May 28, 1948) – was signed to Charisma Records in 1968 after a series of successful appearances at various festivals. Their first album, *Nicely Out Of Tune* (1969), full of rich Geordie humour and raucous harmonies, preceded their great moment of popularity but remains their best album.

The band reached their peak in 1971–72. With Nashville producer Bob Johnston, they recorded *Fog On The Tyne* which eventually became the best-selling album in Britain, 1971–72 – though despite two visits to America they were unable to find sympathetic ears for their music – and had Top Five hits with 'Meet Me On The Corner' and a re-release of 'Lady Eleanor' in 1972.

They remained with Bob Johnston but Alan Hull lost the flair for writing and their final album *Dingly Dell* (1972) was salvaged only by resurrecting some of the old, never before recorded material. An arduous Pacific tour eventually took its toll and the band split into two, Alan Hull and Ray Jackson retaining the name Lindisfarne. The new Lindisfarne, despite its greater musical strength, lacked the necessary temperament and dedication, and split up in 1975 after recording two further albums for Warner Bros.

Little Feat was formed in 1970 by Lowell George (guitar, vocals), Bill Payne (keyboards, vocals), Roy Estrada (bass) and Ritchie Hayward (drums). Estrada and George had been with the Mothers Of Invention, Hayward with the Fraternity Of Man, while Payne had played with various Texas groups.

With Ry Cooder, Sneaky Pete Kleinow and producer Russ Titelman, they cut *Little Feat* for Warner Bros in 1970. The majority of the tracks, including the much-covered 'Willin' ', were written or co-written by Lowell George. After a second album, *Sailin' Shoes* (1972), Estrada left to join Captain Beefheart. Little Feat was augmented by three new members: Ken Gradney (bass), Sam Clayton (congas) and Paul Barrere (guitars).

This line-up made *Dixie Chicken* (1973), but the lack of commercial success caused a lull in the band's activity soon afterwards, with George returning to session work. In 1974, they returned to the studio for their most commercially successful album *Feats Don't Fail Me Now*, which was followed by *The Last Record Album* (1975).

Despite their relatively small sales so far, Little Feat is an admired band among other musicians and critics as a Californian equivalent of the Band (for the elaborate but fluid interplay between guitars and rhythm section) and for the surreal imagery of George's best songs.

Dandy Livingstone, born in Jamaica but resident in Britain since the early Sixties, began his career as one half of the popular Sugar'n'Dandy soul/ska act – alongside Sugar Simòne (now Tito Simon) – with regular gigs at the Flamingo club in Soho. During the rock-steady era, having gone solo, he cut some fine albums, notably *Musical Doctor*; but success eluded him until the 1972 release of an album titled *Consciousness* and single 'Suzanne Beware Of The Devil' (Horse), a British Top Twenty hit. Since then his music has been less interesting and he has concentrated on producing and songwriting.

Lobo (real name Kent Lavoie) was born in 1943 in Tallahassee, Florida. He began playing guitar in high school with a band called the Rumors, moved on to the Sugar Beats whose 'What Am I Doing Here With You' was a local hit around St Petersburg, then after a stint in the Army joined Me And The Other Guys, one of the more popular groups in the area. Three years later, he teamed up with Phil Gernhard (who had successfully produced the Royal Guardsmen, another Florida group, as well as Dion and many other Laurie artists) as a solo act, signing with the new Big Tree label.

His first single for the label, 'Me And You And A Dog Named Boo', was a million-seller in early 1971, followed by several large hits over the next two years including 'She Didn't Do Magic', 'I'd Love You To Want Me', 'Don't Expect Me To Be Your Friend' and 'Standing At The End Of The Line'. These records established Lobo as one of AM radio's most consistent stylists, identifiable by his smooth, rhythmic approach, acoustic guitar, warm vocals, and uncomplicated songs. He was in many ways a one-man Bread. Although he maintains a low profile, seldom tours, and shuns the teen magazines, Lobo has remained a steady hitmaker, has made five well-received albums, and has also co-produced hits for another Floridan, Jim Stafford.

Nils Lofgren was born in Chicago in 1952. He went to Washington D.C. where he formed Grin with Bob Berberich (born in Maryland in 1949) on drums from the Reekers, and Bob Gordon (born in Oklahoma in 1951) on bass, and recorded *Grin* (Spindizzy, 1971), which though it was recorded before was released after Neil Young's *After The Goldrush* on which Lofgren was a featured guitarist. After recording with Crazy Horse, Lofgren returned to Grin to record *1+1* (Columbia, 1972) with David Briggs again producing. Divided into a 'dreamy' and 'rockin'' side, the album showcased Lofgren's eloquently eclectic guitar playing and songwriting at their most inventive. For *All Out* (Epic, 1973) the group was enlarged by the addition of Lofgren's elder brother Tom on guitar. A move to A&M produced the disappointing *Gone Crazy* after which Grin folded, and after performing and recording with various members of CSN&Y (notably on

Young's *Tonight's The Night*), Lofgren went solo. His first solo effort, *Nils Lofgren* (A&M, 1975), was a fine example of pop-rock.

Loggins and Messina. When Jim Messina (born Dec. 5, 1947) left Poco to pursue more studio work and less touring, Epic Records introduced him to Kenny Loggins (born Jan. 7, 1948), a young songwriter at the publishing company ABC Wingate. His songs had been recorded by the Nitty Gritty Dirt Band amongst others. Messina produced Loggins' first album using ex-Sunshine Company rhythm men Larry Simms and Merel Bregante, horn men Al Garth and Jon Clarke and keyboard player Mike Omartian. So successful was *Sittin' In* (Columbia, 1971), that the session team, with the exception of Omartian, formed a band to tour.

Since 1971 Loggins and Messina have been one of Columbia's most successful acts, selling more records as the years roll by, though their music lacks the drive and urgency of the first two albums. Four years and five albums later, the personnel has remained unchanged and Kenny Loggins' formula love songs remain compelling MOR items.

Jackie Lomax was born in Wallasey, near Liverpool on May 10, 1944. During the Merseybeat era, he fronted first Dee And The Dynamites, then the Undertakers, who recorded Roscoe Gordon's 'Just A Little Bit' in 1963. He next formed Lomax Alliance, an unsuccessful group, before signing with Apple Records soon after its formation in 1968.

Supervised by George Harrison, Lomax's work for the label – three singles and an album, *Is This What You Want* (1969) – showed him to be a skilful writer and singer. With the demise of Apple, he moved to Warner Bros for the critically acclaimed *Home Is In My Head* (1970) and *Three* (1971), produced by John Simon. With Badger he recorded *White Lady* (Epic, 1974), produced by Allen Toussaint.

Los Angeles' great contribution to rock in the mid-Sixties had been to synthesize pop's rhythmic impact and folk's melodic articulateness, best demonstrated by the early

Byrds. In 1966–67 the vision of social change central to this music moved north to San Francisco, where it became part of a wider community feeling, and so acquired an emphasis on live performance and raw expression. When the vision was made aware of its own limitations on the streets of Chicago and elsewhere in 1968–69, rock's centre of gravity moved out of San Francisco to find several new homes for several new genres under the rock umbrella.

One of these was LA, where former members of the Byrds and the Buffalo Springfield regrouped in a bewilderingly kaleidoscopic series of changes. The most obvious example was CSN&Y, who more than any other group managed to bring together the traditional LA attention to pure craftsmanship and the San Franciscan devotion to live enthusiasm. They were the real superstars, living in the LA canyons, but other ex-Byrds and Buffaloes, together with an influx of country-influenced musicians like Sneaky Pete Kleinow, Bernie Leadon and Al Perkins, were gathering in clubs like the Troubadour.

Country music was *the* new influence. The Byrds, who had electrified Dylan's folk songs, now electrified his retreat into the country, creating the 'country rock' which would form the core of LA's music in the first half of the Seventies. The Flying Burrito Brothers, Manassas, The Eagles, Loggins and Messina, would all follow, relying on a small pool of well-known musicians to create a rhythmic sound that featured country-associated instrumentation, like the pedal steel guitar and the mandolin. In between group sessions these same musicians would make the odd solo album, and join together to back a steady stream of female vocalists which included Linda Ronstadt, Wendy Waldman, Maria Muldaur, and Bonnie Raitt.

Of the pre-folk rock groups only the Beach Boys remained, still touring and making records, still in part under the direction of the genius recluse Brian Wilson. Other solo artists existing outside the main pool from the early days were Randy Newman, Harry Nilsson, and the ever-imaginative Tim Buckley.

The main pool has produced only one solo superstar,

Neil Young. He, and two relative newcomers, Joni Mitchell and Jackson Browne, form a triumvirate of singer/song-writers who continue the LA tradition of 'topical' music, exploring in song the state of America mirrored in their relationships with loved ones and their audiences. All three are principally concerned with the alternatives available in the aftermath of the Sixties' failure to realize its dreams.

However, country rock is also in part topical, in that it mirrors the retreat from the urban problems that the rock culture failed to solve. What is most interesting about LA music is the small number of people with whom it has been associated for over a decade, and their musical responses during that time to what was going on around them, from Randy Newman's black irony to the Beach Boys' ecological harmonies, from Joni Mitchell's self-doubts to the Eagles' smooth-flowing 'Tequila Sunrise'.

Love Unlimited, primarily known as backing group to the heavy-breathing Barry White, consists of sisters Linda and Glodean James (White's wife) and Diane Taylor. From San Pedro, California, the trio sang together in church. When Uni released their first single, 'Walking In The Rain', in 1972 it was an immediate million-seller. Subsequently signing to 20th Century Records they did extraordinarily well with their *Under The Influence Of . . .* and *In Heat* albums. They sing in shrill, sometimes soulful, but more often bland, three-part harmony while their sequin-gowned, bewigged, stylized glamour seems to symbolize perfectly the White concept of slickly packaged sexuality.

Loretta Lynn, born March 14, 1940 in Butcher's Hollow, Van Leer, Kentucky is, simply, the best country girl singer of the past decade in the tradition of Molly O'Day and Kitty Wells.

She began recording on Zero in 1960, transferred to Decca in 1962, and by 1966, with hits like 'Don't Come Home A' Drinkin'', 'With Lovin' On Your Mind', 'First City' and 'You're Not Woman Enough (To Take My Man Away From Me)' and a regular TV guest spot with the Wilburn

Brothers, she had established the image of the simple country girl who could fight back. She recorded with established star Ernest Tubb. During the Seventies she developed as a vocalist and writer to produce classic country albums like *Coal-miner's Daughter* (MCA).

Jeff Lynne, born in Birmingham, England on Dec. 12, 1947, was an active participant in the local group scene from about 1964. He started in school bands, picking up guitar, keyboards and bass, then replaced Roy Wood in Mike Sheridan's Nightriders, one of Birmingham's top groups of the mid-Sixties, along with the Moody Blues, the Uglys, Keith Powell and The Valets, and Carl Wayne and The Vikings. In late 1966, Sheridan went solo, leaving Lynne in charge of the Nightriders. He reorganized them as the Idle Race, who went on to become one of Britain's most impressive late-Sixties progressive-commercial groups. Although they never had a hit, their two United Artists albums, *Birthday Party* (1968) and *Idle Race* (1969), and several additional singles are among the most prized collectors' items of their era, and hold up amazingly well.

After three years of going nowhere with the Idle Race, Lynne joined the Move in 1970. His influence became immediately apparent, as he co-produced the next two albums, with *Looking On* in particular reflecting Lynne's Idle Race sound. He wrote the B-sides to their 1970–71 hits, and the A-side of their biggest American hit, 'Do Ya'. His real interest, though, was the Electric Light Orchestra; an idea proposed by Carl Wayne (who ironically left the Move before Lynne's arrival). Wayne saw the ELO as a conceptual outgrowth of the Move, playing rock with a large classical orchestra, presumably with himself singing arias upfront. Wood and Lynne took the idea further, hoping to develop a fairly small group of rock musicians who could mix classical ideas and motifs into a rock format, using limited instrumentation but creating a sound with the fullness of a symphony orchestra.

A first album laid the groundwork for the ELO, with Lynne writing and singing at least half, including the British hit singles '10538 Overture' and 'Roll Over Beethoven' (1973). Soon after, Wood went off on his own, claiming that Lynne's approach to the ELO lacked the proper amount of rock'n'roll raunch, forming Wizzard to prove his point. In Lynne's hands, the ELO went on to develop the classical/rock synthesis, and became one of the most successful progressive groups of the early Seventies with albums like *Eldorado* (Warner Bros, 1974) – their first big American hit – and singles like 'Evil Woman' (Jet, 1975). Lynne's only outside project in recent years has been to collaborate with Del Shannon (who, along with Bobby Vee and Jerry Lee Lewis, he credits as his greatest influence) on several songs.

Lynyrd Skynyrd was founded by lead singer Ronnie Van Zant, from Jacksonville, Florida, in 1965. With fellow high-school students, guitarists Allen Collins and Gary Rossington, he named the group after an unpopular teacher. In 1972, with Ed King (guitar), Billy Powell (keyboards), Leon Wilkeson (bass) and Robert Burns (drums), they signed to Al Kooper's newly formed Sounds Of The South label.

The band soon won a reputation as a fundamentalist Southern boogie unit, their name being linked with the Allman Brothers Band. Their music, however, made no concessions to sophistication, with Van Zant's songs concentrating on established themes, including the notable 'Sweet Home Alabama' (a Top Ten hit in 1975 on MCA), which effectively responded to Neil Young's anti-redneck 'Southern Man'. Two tours of Britain endeared them to big beat boogie fans there.

Paul McCartney. Following the break-up of the Beatles and the release of two low-key solo albums, *Paul McCartney* (Apple, 1970) and *Ram* – with his wife Linda – (1971), McCartney formed Wings – Paul McCartney, bass, vocals (born June 18, 1942); Linda McCartney, keyboards, vocals (born Sept. 24, 1942); Denny Laine, guitar, vocals (born Oct. 29, 1944); Henry McCullough, guitar and Denny Seiwell, drums – in 1971. With the group he recorded a series of successful, but generally uninteresting, singles – 'Give Ireland

Back To The Irish', 'Mary Had A Little Lamb' (1972), the BBC-banned 'Hi Hi Hi' and its inoffensive flip 'C Moon', 'My Love', 'Live And Let Die' (both American chart toppers), 'Helen Wheels' (1973) – and two albums – *Wild Life* (1971) and *Red Rose Speedway* (1973) – which were streaked with his by then familiar mawkishness and lack of consequence, before the release of the superior and highly successful *Band On The Run* at the end of 1973. By this time McCullough and Seiwell had left, and Wings continued as a three-piece until the arrival of guitarist Jimmy McCullough and Joe English (drums) for the weak but even more commercially successful *Venus And Mars* (1975).

McCartney is generally thought to have precipitated the demise of Apple through his dispute and lawsuit with the other Beatles and their business nominee, Allen Klein. He nevertheless enjoyed the largest and most varied following of any as a solo artist, and by the mid-Seventies was a major figure within, and influence on, mainstream pop.

Charlie McCoy was born in Oak Hill, West Virginia on March 28, 1941. He is recognized as the best harmonica player in country and country-rock music. A one-time member of Stonewall Jackson's back-up band, he became one of the top Nashville session players in the early Sixties, playing on hundreds of country records as well as every Bob Dylan album from *Highway 61 Revisited* to *Nashville Skyline*.

As an instrumentalist, McCoy was heard to good effect on the two albums by Area Code 615, the Nashville session supergroup, during 1969–70. Following a minor 1961 hit ('Cherry Berry Wine', on Cadence), he signed to Monument as a solo artist in 1963, though his own records, such as *The Nashville Hit Man* (1974) tend to be less effective than his work with others.

Van McCoy, born in Washington D.C., recorded unsuccessfully with the Starlighters on End before forming his own record label, Rockin' Records, for which he recorded the smooth ballad 'Hey Mr DJ' (1959) It was picked up for national distribution by Scepter Records, whom he joined as an A&R man, but left after a year to work freelance – he arranged the Drifters' small 1963 hit for Leiber and Stoller, 'Rat Race' – and record for Columbia and Epic ('Keep Lovin' Me', 'I Started A Joke') in a Johnny Mathis vein.

At Maxx he produced a couple of sophisticated soul hits for Gladys Knight and the Pips, including the Top Forty 'Giving Up' (1964), before returning to Columbia as a producer and writer. There he produced an unlikely hit for Chad and Jeremy ('Before And After', 1965) and a series of syrupy tunes for Peaches and Herb (1966–67), and wrote 'Baby I'm Yours' for Barbara Lewis. In 1967 he formed Van McCoy Productions (VMP) and Vanda Records, which had an immediate Top Forty hit with Chris Bartley's smooth recording of 'The Sweetest Thing This Side Of Heaven'. After Vanda folded, he continued working as an independent producer, masterminding such hits as 'I Get The Sweetest Feeling' (Jackie Wilson, 1968), '5-10-15-20 (25-30 Years of Love)' (the Presidents, 1970), and 'Right On The Tip Of My Tongue' (Brenda and the Tabulations, 1971) before settling down to work virtually full-time with the Stylistics as their arranger, following the departure of Thom Bell. Though his work with the group over-sentimentalized their sound, the records were phenomenally successful and Hugo and Luigi, the group's producers, invited him to record an album of symphonic versions of soul hits for Avco. That sold only moderately well, but in the wake of the disco boom he recorded a further instrumental album, *Disco Baby* (Avco, 1975), which included the transatlantic smash 'The Hustle'. Subsequently, Van McCoy combined solo projects with productions for Faith, Hope and Charity amongst others.

Joe McDonald. Born on Jan. 1, 1942, in El Monte, California, Joe McDonald spent much of his youth listening to R&B on the radio, and absorbing the political outlook of his parents, who were organizers for the local Communist Party. After enlisting in the Navy for a few years, McDonald's next major influence was the early work of Bob Dylan, and by 1965 he had formed his own group, Country Joe and the

Fish, in Berkeley, successfully amalgamating electric music with the campus sensibility of dope, political protest, and personal explorations.

After the demise of the Fish, McDonald returned to his roots and recorded *Thinking Of Woody Guthrie* (Vanguard, 1970), a superbly vital collection of the songs of America's seminal political folk singer, backed up by some of Nashville's finest session players, who also worked on his tribute to country music, *Tonight I'm Singing Just For You* (1971). *War War War* (1971), his next album, set Robert Service's First World War poems to music, providing a pertinent comment on both the Vietnam war and McDonald's own experience of the mystique and monotony of military life. It was followed by *Incredible Live*, perhaps his most straightforwardly political record, made when he was working in the FTA anti-war show with Donald Sutherland and Jane Fonda. In 1973 he released *Paris Sessions*, a collection of songs dealing primarily with the oppression of women and the manipulative powers of the media (including the rock-music industry). It was a powerful, and frequently painful, contrast with the zany exuberance of the songs that the Fish recorded, and confirmed McDonald's position as one of the few musicians who not merely survived the Sixties, but actually analysed and placed the failures of the Acid Test culture in a wider American context. *Paradise And Ocean View* (Fantasy, 1975) was a less impressive album.

Roger McGuinn was born on July 14, 1942 in Chicago. After the demise of the Byrds in 1972, he embarked on a solo career. In 1973, his first solo album, *Roger McGuinn* (Columbia), was released, hot on the heels of the unspectacular Byrds reunion album, which featured the five original members of the group. A subsequent solo album, *Peace On You*, was released in 1974. After a British tour the same year, McGuinn formed a band – Steve Love, Richard Bowden, Greg Attaway and David Lovelace – consisting of ex-members of Shiloh and the Stone Canyon Band with whom he recorded *Roger McGuinn And Band* (1975). In 1976, after touring with Dylan's Rolling Thunder revue, McGuinn folded his own group to form a band with bassist Rob Stoner.

McGuinness Flint was formed in 1969 by ex-Manfred Mann guitarist Tom McGuinness (born on Dec. 2, 1941) and former John Mayall drummer Hughie Flint (March 15, 1942). With singer Dennis Coulson and multi-instrumentalists and songwriters Gallagher and Lyle, they had considerable success with their thoughtful blend of good-time, country and folk music. 'When I'm Dead And Gone' (Capitol, 1970) and 'Malt And Barley Blues' (1971) both entered the Top Five in Britain.

Soon after, Gallagher and Lyle left, to be replaced by bass player Dixie Dean. *Lo And Behold* (DJM, 1972) was a selection of obscure Bob Dylan material, continuing the Manfred Mann tradition of recording unknown Dylan songs. By 1974, Coulson had left to try a solo career, and the group added Lou Stonebridge (keyboards, vocals) and Jim Evans (pedal steel, fiddle). Their final album, *C'est La Vie* (Bronze, 1974) was an interesting collection of original songs, produced by veteran session guitarist Big Jim Sullivan.

John McLaughlin was born in 1942 in Yorkshire and began to play the guitar at the age of 11. During the Sixties he played with various London jazz and rock combos, including the Graham Bond Organization (which included Jack Bruce and Ginger Baker) and released his first solo album, *Extrapolation* (Polydor) in 1969. McLaughlin's guitar style utilized elements from blues, jazz, and Eastern musical modes. He combined a dazzlingly fast technique with an ability to use space and unexpected chord configurations in his solos. In 1969 McLaughlin moved to New York; the day after his arrival he played on Miles Davis' *In A Silent Way* sessions. McLaughlin's 'open-ended' guitar sound was well matched to the musical areas Davis was beginning to explore: more metrically free, using a dense variety of sound textures emphasized by electronic manipulation. On Davis' *Bitches' Brew* (1970) albums, McLaughlin developed a more integrated style fusing blues/rock riffs with spiralling solos. On

Carla Bley's jazz opera *Escalator Over The Hill* (1971), McLaughlin's abrasive guitar work (again accompanied by Jack Bruce) was played off against the sparse, Eastern textures of Don Cherry's trumpet work.

In 1972 McLaughlin formed his own group, the Mahavishnu Orchestra, which was extremely successful both critically and commercially, and whose identity was dominated by McLaughlin's devotion to religion. In 1974 he recorded an intermittently powerful album with Carlos Santana, *Love Devotion Surrender* (Columbia), dedicated to their religious teacher Sri Chimnoy, and strongly influenced by the work of the late John Coltrane.

Don McLean, born in New Rochelle, New York on Oct. 2, 1945, suddenly burst onto the scene in 1971 with his epic lament 'American Pie' which topped both the British and American charts; he had been a folk-singer since 1963.

In 1969 he accompanied Pete Seeger, Louis Killen, Gordon Bok and a crew of musicians on the Hudson River sloop, *Clearwater*, in a campaign to clean up the Hudson River. His first album for the United Artists subsidiary Mediarts, *Tapestry*, paved the way for *American Pie* (1972). McLean followed up his overnight success by touring all over the world. He was called awkward, over-emotional, unco-operative, but it was basically a refusal to change his music that characterized McLean. His interest was in folk music, and when the record company wanted a follow-up to his second international hit single, 'Vincent', McLean instead put out an album of standards, *Playin' Favourites. Homeless Brother* (1974) saw McLean returning to a more traditional notion of folk in his songs – the celebration/examination of the hobo – and instrumentation – banjo and acoustic guitar.

Ralph McTell is one of the best songwriters to emerge from the British folk revival of the early Sixties, though the success of his song 'The Streets Of London' has tended to overshadow the rest of his work.

Born in Farnborough, Kent, he was a blues and ragtime guitarist in the London clubs before cutting his first Transatlantic album *Eight Frames A Second* (1968). *Spiral Staircase* (1969) contained 'Streets', a re-recorded version of which was a hit at Christmas 1974.

By the time McTell moved to Paramount/Famous in 1971, he had completed the transition from folk-singer to a singer/songwriter of intelligence and commitment. *You, Well Meaning, Brought Me Here* was, in some ways, his best album. Produced by Gus Dudgeon, it contained songs dealing with militarism and political commitment, as well as the whimsy of 'Old Brown Dog'.

Moving to Warner Bros, McTell made *Not Till Tomorrow* (1972), which included the perceptive 'Zimmerman Blues'. By 1975, after two more albums, a successful national tour and his surprise hit, McTell decided to leave Britain for America, returning later in the year.

Mahavishnu Orchestra. Formed in 1972 by guitarist John McLaughlin (Mahavishnu being the name that McLaughlin was given by his religious adviser Sri Chimnoy), the Orchestra swiftly became the most successful fusion, commercially and critically, of jazz and rock. Their ability to integrate virtuoso solo work within a tightly disciplined instrumental framework made their second album, *Birds Of Fire* (Columbia), one of the few masterpieces of this rather nebulous genre. The Orchestra featured the violin of Jerry Goodman (ex Flock), the pyrotechnically dazzling drumming of Billy Cobham, and Jan Hammer's keyboard and synthesizer work, but was dominated by McLaughlin whose aura of burning spiritual zeal was conveyed by superfast tempos and an *ethereal* heavy metal sound. The original group disbanded in 1974, and was replaced by a larger line-up, including violin maestro Jean-Luc Ponty.

The Main Ingredient, known in the late Fifties as the Poets, consisted of Donald McPherson (born July 9, 1941), Luther Simmons Jr. (born Sept. 9, 1942), and Tony Sylvester (born Oct. 7, 1941). McPherson, the lead singer, sang in a very high 'false' tenor with a velvety texture reminiscent of the Impressions. After a period with Leiber and Stoller's Red

Bird label and a No. 2 R&B record with 'She Blew A Good Thing' in 1966 on Symbol, they changed their name to Main Ingredient and linked up with producer/writer Bert De Coteaux, who specialized in full, lush orchestration in the Thom Bell mould.

Hits followed in 1970–71 with 'I'm So Proud', 'Spinnin' Around' and 'Black Seeds Keep On Growing' the latter written just before McPherson's death from leukaemia on July 4, 1971. A new lead, Cuba Gooding (born April 27, 1944), brought the group far greater commercial success (the million-selling 'Everybody Plays The Fool', RCA, 1972) and hit albums *Afrodisiac* and *Euphrates River*), though their sound moved towards fussily orchestrated, rather bland, middle-of-the-road soul. Tony Sylvester left in 1974 to pursue a successful career as a producer.

Harvey Mandel was born in Detroit on March 11, 1945, but spent his formative years in Chicago, where he learnt blues guitar in similar clubs to the then nascent Paul Butterfield/ Mike Bloomfield school of white blues. Since 1968, he has made solo albums for Philips, Ovation, Dawn and Vanguard, as well as playing at various times during the late Sixties and early Seventies with Canned Heat and the ever-changing John Mayall's Bluesbreakers. As a session guitarist, he has played on records by such diverse talents as the Ventures and Love, as well as more obvious contemporaries like Charlie Musselwhite and Barry Goldberg. *Cristo Redentor* (Philips, 1968) remains his finest solo work.

The Manhattans, formed in Jersey City in 1964, were George 'Smitty' Smith, Winfred 'Blue' Lovett (born in 1940), Sonny Bivins (1941), Kenny Kelly (1948), and Richard Taylor (1939). Spotted at an Apollo Theater talent contest the group were signed to Carnival Records and launched into a successful singles career, interspersing doowop ballads with Motown dance beat discs. R&B hits included 'I Wanna Be (Your Everything)' (1965) and 'Can I' (1966). Moving to King's Deluxe label, more soul hits occurred like the lovely 'If My Heart Could Speak' (1970) before tragedy struck –

Smith, whose poignant lead shaped the group's sound, died of spinal meningitis in 1970. But Gerald Alston (born in 1951) has proved a fine replacement, singing on the beautiful, Philly-recorded 'There's No Me Without You' (1974) and 'Hurt' (1975) – both American hits on Columbia. The Manhattans are unquestionably sweetly superior soul music.

Arif Mardin, born in Istanbul, Turkey on March 15, 1932, is a leading record producer for Atlantic, noted for the clarity of his work. In 1958 he was awarded a jazz scholarship and was later a teacher at the Berklee School of Music. Since joining Atlantic in 1963 in a production capacity, he has reached the position of vice-president and musical director of the company. Over the years he has produced, co-produced and/or arranged for such artists as The Average White Band, Bee Gees, Danny O'Keefe, Cher, King Curtis, Aretha Franklin, Bette Midler, Willie Nelson, Laura Nyro, Lulu, John Prine, the Rascals, Doug Sahm, Herbie Mann, MJQ, Stephen Stills, Dizzy Gillespie and Wilson Pickett. He is responsible for dozens of top-selling Atlantic albums, among them *The Average White Band*, *The Best Of King Curtis*, *Aretha's Gold*, *Greatest Hits*, *Spirit In The Dark*, *Live At The Fillmore*, *Young, Gifted And Black* (Aretha Franklin), *Roberta Flack and Donny Hathaway*, *The Divine Miss M* (Bette Midler), *Groovin'* (The Rascals) and *Stephen Stills*. In addition, he has cut two solo albums, *Glass Onion* and *Journey*.

Bob Marley and the Wailers, a reggae band from Kingston's Trench Town district in Jamaica, won critical acclaim with their first Island album *Catch A Fire* (1973). Two years – and two albums – on, they had achieved international recognition and Marley was being hailed as 'the black Bob Dylan'. The Island contract meant a number of departures for the group, to the increasing dissatisfaction of founding members Peter 'Tosh' Mackintosh and Bunny Livingstone – later replaced by Al Anderson, Tyrone Downey and the I Three female back-up trio – but Marley's music retained much of its earthiness.

The Wailers came together in 1964, with Junior Braithwaite (vocal), to cut 'Simmer Down' for Coxon Dodd; Robert Nesta Marley, born in St Ann, Jamaica in 1945, having previously recorded 'Judge Not' and 'One Cup Of Coffee' for Leslie Kong. The group remained with Dodd until 1967, establishing itself with songs of love and rebellion, rudie style, like 'It Hurts To Be Alone', 'Rule Them Rudie', 'Put It On' and 'Bend Down Low'. Braithwaite having split, Marley became an ethnic hero in Jamaica. Following a series of false starts, they joined Lee Perry in 1970; adding two Upsetters, brothers Carlton and Aston 'Family Man' Barnett, to record 'Small Axe', 'Duppy Conqueror' and 'Trench Town Rock'.

Success hasn't blunted Marley's songwriting skill, as *Natty Dread* (1975) amply illustrates. He continues to preach love, sex, rastafarianism and anti-establishment politics with consummate passion. Cuts like 'No Woman No Cry' and 'So Jah Seh' are confirmed classics. His 'I Shot The Sheriff' was an American chart topper for Eric Clapton in 1975.

John Martyn was signed by Island Records in 1968. At that point, Glasgow-born Martyn was playing acoustic guitar and singing his own songs in the London folk clubs. His first two albums were typical examples of the British folk genre of the time, but *Stormbringer* (1970) and *The Road To Ruin* (1970), featuring his wife Beverley, presented a more individual talent. The first was produced by Joe Boyd in Woodstock and included Garth Hudson among the musicians, while on *Road To Ruin*, Martyn introduced a jazz influence which would play a great part in the development of his style.

On *Bless The Weather* (1971) and particularly *Solid Air* (1972), the amplified guitar with electronic accoutrements accompanied Martyn's unique, scat-style singing. He also began to tour extensively, accompanied by ex-Pentangle bassist Danny Thompson. *Inside Out* (1973) and *Sunday's Child* (1975) found Martyn's approach fully formed, with its roots in various folk and jazz modes. A live album was released by Island in 1975, and distributed by the artist by mail order.

Dave Mason, born May 10, 1945 in Worcester, went through several Worcester/Birmingham bands (the Jaguars, the Hellions, Deep Feeling, Julian Covey and the Machine) and jobs (including being a roadie for Spencer Davis) before he, Winwood, Capaldi and Wood retired to Berkshire to form Traffic. 'Hole In My Shoe', the first song he ever wrote, was the group's biggest single hit, reaching No. 2 in Britain. He left after the release of the first album in December, 1967 to go to Greece but returned to produce the first Family album. He rejoined Traffic in May 1968 to cut the *Traffic* album but left again to pursue a solo career and cut a single, 'Little Woman', only to team up again with Capaldi and Wood in the short-lived Mason, Capaldi, Wood and Frog. He moved to the States and played with Delaney and Bonnie and eventually used many of their associates to record the classic *Alone Together* (Blue Thumb, 1970). Over the next few years he played with Mama Cass (1971) and Derek and the Dominos before rejoining Traffic for the six live dates that resulted in *Welcome To The Canteen.*

He returned to the States and formed a band only to discover that his record label, Blue Thumb, had decided to release some unfinished tapes (*Headkeeper*) totally against his wishes. Contractual problems of that sort plagued him until he signed to Columbia in late 1972. To date he has made three competent albums – *Dave Mason* (1974), *It's Like You Never Left* (1973) and *Split Coconut* (1975) – without ever reaching the heights of *Alone Together.* He remains, none the less, a remarkably fluid and graceful guitarist.

Matthews Southern Comfort was originally the title of the first solo album by former Fairport Convention singer Ian Matthews (Uni, 1970). Written and produced by pop songwriters Howard and Blaikley it was an exciting amalgam of folk and country music, including 'I've Lost You', later a hit for Elvis Presley. Characterized by Matthews' high, clear voice and Gordon Huntley's pedal steel guitar, the critical acclaim for the album led to the formation of a band with the same name.

The line-up of Matthews, Huntley, Mark Griffiths (harmony vocals), Andy Leigh (bass, vocals), Carl Barnwell (guitar, vocals) and Ray Duffy (drums) soon had a No. 1 hit with a version of Joni Mitchell's 'Woodstock', launching their career as Britain's first West Coast-style country-rock band.

But within a year it was all over. After three MCA albums, the temperamental Matthews quit the band to go solo. American Carl Barnwell kept the remainder together as Southern Comfort through three further Harvest albums which lacked the authority of the Matthews-led recordings. They disbanded in 1972.

Ian Matthews. Since leaving Southern Comfort in 1970, the career of Matthews, potentially one of Britain's best singer/songwriters and interpreters in the country/folk idiom, has been erratic. Six albums of his work have appeared on three different labels, involving three sets of accompanists. None has achieved the commercial success of his earlier work with Fairport Convention or Matthews Southern Comfort.

A solo contract with Vertigo produced two low-key albums during 1971, *If You Could See Thro' My Eyes* and *Tigers Will Survive.* Relationships between artist and label were soon strained, however, and the third record made under this agreement, *Journeys From Gospel Oak* did not appear until 1974 when producer Sandy Roberton released it through Mooncrest.

Matthews' next venture was Plainsong, a group involving Andy Roberts (guitar), Dave Richards (bass) and Bob Ronga (guitar). After one Elektra album (*In Search Of Amelia Earhart*, 1972), the restless Matthews left for America. In Los Angeles he linked up with Mike Nesmith who produced his next solo venture (*Valley Hi*, Elektra, 1973). After a further Elektra record, the fine *Some Days You Eat The Bear* (1974), Matthews quit the label to join Columbia.

Curtis Mayfield, after twelve years as mainstay of the Impressions, in 1970 launched a solo career with the highly acclaimed *Curtis* album on Buddah, followed the next year by a live recording and *Roots*, establishing himself as a leading figure in the new wave of soul stars. Combining his old skill for lilting melodies and simple, effective lyrics with a keener view of society's confusion, Mayfield (born in Chicago in 1942) reflected life's ups ('The Makings Of You', 'Move On Up', 'Beautiful Brothers Of Mine') and downs ('If There's A Hell Below', 'Stone Junkie', 'Underground') with a compelling grace that reached its peak in 1972 with his soundtrack for *Superfly* (including the million-seller 'Freddie's Dead'). Although he scored other successful soundtracks, *Claudine*, for Gladys Knight (Buddah, 1974) and *Let's Do It Again* for the Staple Singers (Curtom, 1975), his own releases lost direction and by the end of 1974 he was jumping on every available bandwagon with songs like 'Kung Fu' and 'Sweet Exorcist'. However, *America Today* (1975) was one of his strongest albums, refuting any suggestion that he had finally run out of ideas.

Mel and Tim – Mel Hardin and Tim McPherson – are cousins and lifelong buddies. Brought up in Holly Springs, Mississippi, they moved to St Louis where they mixed with all the big names on the southern soul scene. Working with veteran artist/producer Gene Chandler they had a Top Ten hit with the Stax-influenced 'Backfield In Motion' (1969), written by Tim and released on the small Scepter-distributed Bamboo label owned by Chandler. Another big hit, 'Good Guys Only Win In The Movies', followed in 1970. After contractual fights the duo began recording in the Muscle Shoals studio where they cut the beautiful, lilting ballad, 'Starting All Over Again'. Written by Phillip Mitchell, and leased to Stax Records in Memphis, it was a major soul hit in 1972 but subsequent releases (including two Muscle Shoals recorded albums) have had less success.

Melanie was born Melanie Safka in New York on Feb. 3, 1947. Emerging in 1969, she carried the obligatory acoustic guitar of the singer/songwriter, though her unusual vocal style owed most to jazz and to the French *chanteuse* approach of Edith Piaf.

Her first big hit was a hoarse, dramatic rendition of the Rolling Stones' 'Ruby Tuesday', which reached the Top Ten in Britain in 1970. Other hits on Buddah followed, including 'Look What They've Done To My Song Ma' and 'Brand New Key', an American chart topper in 1971. Her songwriting sometimes tended towards the coy and some found her on-stage warmth embarrassing.

In 1972, Melanie formed Neighbourhood Records with her husband and producer Peter Schekeryk. She moved away from the girlish persona of some of the early work on albums like *Madraguda* (1974), *As I See It Now* (1974) and *Sunset And Other Beginnings* (1975) which contain a mixture of Safka originals and contemporary standards.

Harold Melvin and the Blue Notes, featuring the exhortative soulful wail of Theodore 'Teddy' Pendergrass, are perhaps the group most closely identified with the black Philly Sound. Originally a street corner group, their early work included 'If You Love Me' (Josie, 1956) and 'My Hero' (Value, 1960). Club work on the chittlin' circuit led to a slicker tie'n'tails approach (at Martha Reeves' suggestion) and the white supper club circuit. 'Get Out' was an R&B hit in 1965 on Landa. When offered a chance to work with Gamble and Huff, at the same time as lead John Atkins left to make way for Teddy, the group – Bernard Wilson, Lloyd Parkes, Lawrence Brown, Melvin and Prendergrass – began to produce the brand of sweepingly symphonic yet utterly soulful music that is now their hallmark. Starting with a soul hit, 'I Miss You', they progressed to smoulderingly poignant international hits, 'If You Don't Know Me By Now' (1972), 'The Love I Lost' (1973) and 'Where Are All My Friends' (1974). Their next album *To Be True* was certified gold.

The Meters, a clinically precise rhythm section from New Orleans, comprise veteran keyboard player Art Neville, with Leo Nocentelli (guitar), George Porter (bass), and

Joseph Modeliste (drums). Their distinctive, choppy back-beat has driven countless Allen Toussaint productions (including hits by Lee Dorsey, Betty Harris, and Dr John) and given them several minor hits in their own right, on Josie: 'Sophisticated Sissy' (1968), 'Cissy Strut', 'Look-ka Py Py' (1969), 'Chicken Strut' (1970), 'Good Old Funky Music' (1971), and Reprise: 'Cabbage Alley' (1972), 'Chug Chug Chug-A-Lug' (1973), 'Hey Pocky-A-Way' (1974). However, their rhythms have been too tricky and their sound too thin to compete with the most popular disco bands, though since their signing to Reprise, their albums – *Cabbage Alley* (1972), *Rejuvenation* (1974) and *Fire On The Bayou* (1975) – have attracted interest among the (white) rock audience.

Miami. Despite its many small companies and obscure record labels, the city's musical output stems almost entirely from two sources – Criteria (a modern studio associated with Atlantic but used for outside productions), and Tones/TK (a converted attic in Henry Stone's distribution/production company). Stone arrived in Miami in the early Fifties, started the Rockin' label, and shared interests in Federal and DeLuxe with King Records. By 1960 he'd relinquished these to concentrate on distribution, continuing to run smaller labels (Glades, Marlin, Dade) for local consumption. Throughout the Sixties, he used producers Brad Shapiro and Steve Alaimo but failed to secure any notable hits, although it was Alaimo who discovered Sam and Dave, later to find fame with Stax Records of Memphis.

Meanwhile, two black writer/producers, Willie Clarke and Johnny Pearsall, started the Deep City and Lloyd labels, featuring local acts including Frank Williams, Little Beaver, Paul Kelly, Helene Smith, and later, Betty Wright. Clarke teamed with singer/songwriter Clarence Reid and together they joined Henry Stone in 1968. After scoring national success with Betty Wright ('Girls Can't Do What The Guys Do', 1968), Reid, Clarke, and Alaimo gradually fostered more hits, until by the early Seventies various Stone labels (Alston, Glades, TK, Cat, Dig) represented two aspects of a popular 'Miami sound': deep soul and the new wave of disco music. Featured artists included J. P. Robinson, Jimmy 'Bo' Horne, Timmy Thomas, Benny Latimore, Little Beaver, K. C. and The Sunshine Band, and, most successfully, George and Gwen McCrae.

Simultaneously, Criteria emerged as one of the most popular studios in the south (along with Muscle Shoals, Alabama). Shapiro left Stone in the late Sixties to work there with arranger Dave Crawford, producing many sessions for Atlantic, while other top names (from Aretha Franklin to Steve Stills, James Brown to Dr John) regularly placed the studios in the credits of best-selling albums.

Middle of the Road. Originally called Los Caracas and playing Latin-American music, Eric Lewis, Ken Andrew, Ian Lewis and Sally Carr, from Scotland, became Middle Of The Road in 1971 after they heard Lally Stott's 'Chirpy Chirpy Cheep Cheep' while touring Italy, and decided to record it. Despite competing versions by Stott and Mac and Katie Kissoon, their record took off in Spain and Belgium and ended up selling over five million, worldwide.

The group's appeal, besides Carr's pure, fresh voice and appearance, lay in their lightweight, melodic, cheery approach to pop. Subsequent hits on RCA including 'Tweedle Dee Tweedle Dum' and 'Soley Soley' (1971) established them among the most successful purveyors of simple, inoffensive pop in the early Seventies.

Frankie Miller. After the demise of Jude, the group Robin Trower formed with him after leaving Procol Harum, Miller, born in Glasgow, began playing the London pub circuit, eventually touring and recording *Once In A Blue Moon* (Chrysalis, 1972) with Brinsley Schwarz as his backing group. That album showed his blues-influenced singing style, but it wasn't until *High Life* (1973), produced by Allen Toussaint in New Orleans, that he fully revealed his feisty, gravel voice and his songwriting abilities. A critical success, the album produced hit singles for Three Dog Night and Betty Wright, but sold poorly. In 1975, Miller, an erratic and infrequent performer, formed the Frankie Miller Band with

Henry McCullogh and Mick Weaver from the Grease Band on guitars, Chris Stewart from Spooky Tooth on bass, and Stu Perry on drums, and released *The Rock*, again to critical success and poor sales.

Joni Mitchell. Born Roberta Joan Anderson on Nov. 7, 1943 at Fort McLeod, Alberta, she was an art student turned folksinger in the heyday of Toronto's Yorktown. From there she became a regular on the East Coast folk circuit in 1967, with her folksinger husband Chuck Mitchell. Some early songs were recorded by Judy Collins and Tom Rush, and minus her husband, she moved west to Los Angeles, to make her first album, *Joni Mitchell* (Reprise, 1968) under the guiding hand of ex-Byrd David Crosby.

Her main assets at this stage were a quirky self-taught acoustic guitar style, a voice with an exceptionally wide range, and her poetic talent. In the meantime, her first album and the two that followed – *Clouds* (1969) and *Ladies Of The Canyon* (1970) – were most notable for the delicate mirror they held to the Californian peace and love ethos, a theme that culminated in her apocalyptic song of the festival, 'Woodstock'. Most of the time, though, the rather fey approach to reality was more than compensated for by her melodic originality, a gift for words, and her singing.

In 1970, Joni took a year off, went to Europe, went sailing with Nash and Crosby on the latter's boat. She returned to make *Blue* (1971), an album which marked a change in emphasis, shared by *For The Roses* (1972) and *Court And Spark* (1974).

A major impetus for all her work has been the struggle to make sense of a personal failure to find lasting satisfaction in any of her well-publicized relationships. The central dilemma she has experienced in these relationships – caught between security and freedom, between her consciousness and her emotional needs – was first expressed on her first album. Staring warily at each other over the accumulated paraphernalia of the hippie dream are the two Jonis – in 'I Had A King' the one who finds romance restrictive, in 'Cactus Tree' the jet-setting lady who finds freedom insufficient.

These two personae fight each other with increasing sophistication, awareness, and musical skill through all her albums.

Progress in her lyrics has been matched by the music. *Ladies Of The Canyon* saw piano share predominance with acoustic guitar for the first time, and since then her musical range has steadily expanded. *Blue* had more of a rock rhythm; *For The Roses* (Asylum, 1972) and *Court And Spark* (1974), overlaid this with Tom Scott's immaculate woodwind and brass playing. Through this progress Joni's melodies have grown ever more imaginative and her singing reached new heights of expressiveness on the luxuriant *Hissing Of Summer Lawns* (1975). The power of her live performances accompanied by Scott's LA Express is captured on *Miles Of Aisles* (1974).

Her subsidiary theme reflects her subsidiary relationship – that with her audience. Like Neil Young she has produced a string of songs exploring the paradox of selling her personal life-history. 'For Free' and 'For The Roses' explore, as the titles suggest, the two sides of the coin: playing for oneself, to one's own standards, and being part of the corporate machine churning out product. 'Carey' and 'Free Man In Paris' both lament the conflict between a lost freedom and the rewards it brings.

Her privileged position in one way adds to the power of her music. Being a woman free of the usual costs of living in a male-dominated society, like financial dependence and lack of opportunity for self-expression, her songs of relationships have probed a deeper conflict, that between romantic love and the liberation of women. *Court And Spark* explores this area, of a woman 'raised on robbery', but looking for love, and showing how the singer herself connives against her own aspirations, caught in a double bind of a heart seeking romance and security that offends her mind, and a mind seeking freedom to find only the painful transience of love affairs.

The prairie girl in LA, love and freedom in search of each other, the need to communicate and the costs of success – all these come together in an overall vision of a generation caught between past and future for whom 'old bonds have broken down', and for whom 'love is gone', yet who still search for love and the new relationships which the Sixties optimistically looked forward to. Joni Mitchell has explored this situation with insight, and with musical expertise that has deepened with every album.

Willie Mitchell, a writer/producer/arranger turned company executive, led Al Green and Hi Records along the same trail from Memphis to international success that Otis Redding and Stax had blazed a few years earlier. Born in Ashland, Mississippi, in 1928, Mitchell was raised in Memphis where he learned trumpet at high school before playing professionally with the Tuff Green and Al Jackson dance bands. In 1954, he formed his own R&B combo whose popularity throughout the South led to a recording with vocalist Billy Taylor (Skipper, 1960) and a contract as house band with Home Of The Blues records.

His work behind R&B stars like Roy Brown and the Five Royales and his own instrumental releases (including 'One Mint Julep', 1961) brought him to the attention of Hi's owner Joe Coughi. Within a year of his signing in 1963, Mitchell's hits were competing with the company's only other regular sellers, Bill Black's combo and Ace Cannon. For a while he aped the winning formulas of Stax's bands ('20–75', 'Percolatin'' in 1964, 'Buster Browne' in 1965) or Tamla's Junior Walker ('Everything Is Gonna Be Alright', 'That Driving Beat', both 1966), but by 1968 hits like 'Soul Serenade' and 'Prayer Meeting', and his outside productions for O. V. Wright (Back Beat), Syl Johnson (Twinight), and Otis Clay (Cotillion), were beginning to display the steady, rolling rhythms and simple brass figures that typified all his later triumphs.

After becoming Hi's vice-president in 1969, Mitchell and arranger Gene 'Bowlegs' Miller groomed two new signings, Ann Peebles and Al Green, to project their Memphis Sound. The following year, 'Part Time Love' (Peebles) and 'I Can't Get Next To You' (Green) were the first successes of the new formula. Since then, Green has scored a dozen smash hits to become one of the top five black stars in America while Ann Peebles followed in his wake. Hi has continued to expand its roster of talent, while many outside artists (including Denise Lasalle and the Detroit Emeralds) have successfully used Mitchell's band and studio. But, while the hits keep rolling, it is already being argued that his productions are degenerating into repetition.

The Moments are purveyors of a peculiarly lilting brand of sweet soul which some have dubbed the New Jersey or All Platinum Sound. The original group, featuring the falsetto lead of Mark Greene, hit with 'Not On The Outside' but were quickly replaced by a completely new trio featuring Billy Brown (born June 30, 1946), Al Goodman (March 31, 1947) and Johnny Morgan. A string of stentorian falsetto-led hits began with 'Sunday' (1969) and 'Love On A Two-Way Street' (1970), the latter selling a million and really establishing the New Jersey-based Stang/All Platinum company. Another million-seller, 'Sexy Mama', followed in 1973. The group today mainly feature the lead of Harry Ray (born Dec. 15, 1946) and write and produce their own material with Goodman producing soul hits by other acts including Shirley and Co and Retta Young.

The Moody Blues were formed in Birmingham in 1964 by Mike Pinder (keyboards, vocals, born in Birmingham on Dec. 19, 1942), Graeme Edge (drums, born in Rochester, Staffordshire on March 30, 1942), Ray Thomas (vocals, harmonica, flute, born in Stourport-on-Severn on Dec. 29, 1942), Denny Laine (guitar, born in Jersey on Oct. 29, 1944) and Clint Warwick (bass, born in Birmingham on June 25, 1949).

Originally an R&B group, they had a British No. 1 hit the next year with the Bessie Banks song, 'Go Now', on Decca. Subsequent singles were unsuccessful and in 1967 Laine and Warwick left to be replaced by guitarist Justin Hayward (born in Swindon in 1946) and bass-guitarist John Lodge. The group changed direction with *Days Of Future Passed*, a concept album making full use of electronic and orchestral effects, which was hailed as a successful fusion of rock and classical music. Hayward's 'Nights In White Satin' was issued as a single, reaching the British Top Twenty in 1968. On re-release in 1975, it was an even bigger hit.

There followed a series of six gold albums, developing the *Days Of Future Passed* formula which included Peter Knight's lush strings, quasi-philosophical lyrics of greatly varying quality and the high, vulnerable vocal tones, mainly of Hayward and Thomas. The whole was held together by the immaculate production techniques of Tony Clarke, 'the sixth Moody'. The occasional single was released, with 'Question' (1970), 'Isn't Life Strange?' (1972) and 'Singer In A Rock And Roll Band' (1974), the most successful.

The Moody Blues' following is vast and intensely loyal, although after *Seventh Sojourn* in 1972 and its attendant world tour, the group members concentrated on separate projects, with Hayward and Lodge working together as the Blue Jays and the others as solo artists. The resulting albums appeared in 1975 on the group's Threshold label. 'Blue Guitar', by the Blue Jays, was a major hit single.

Doug Morris, a producer, songwriter and record executive, has been one of the more significant behind-the-scenes record men of the Sixties and early Seventies. Born in 1938 in New York, Morris entered the business around 1962, writing songs for some of the artists on Laurie and soon becoming involved in production, working with Elliott Greenberg, one of the label's owners. One of his first productions was 'Send Her To Me' by Gary 'US' Bonds, followed by records with many of the other Laurie/Rust/Legrand artists. His biggest hits were in 1966, with the Chiffons' 'Sweet Talkin' Guy' and the Barbarians' 'Are You A Boy Or Are You A Girl?' both of which he wrote and produced.

In 1970, Morris started his own label, Big Tree, whose first hit was Lobo's 'Me And You And A Dog Named Boo' in April, 1971. Distributed by Ampex, the label had other hits with Dave and Ansel Collins' 'Double Barrel' (one of the first reggae hits in America) and 'White Lies, Blue Eyes' by Bullet, but their biggest hitmaker was Lobo. In 1972, Big Tree switched distribution to Bell, and in two years issued over fifty singles which included, besides Lobo's hits, records by April Wine, Duane Eddy, Thundermug, the Happenings, and their biggest hit, 'Smokin' In The Boys' Room' by Brownsville Station. Distributed since 1974 by Atlantic, Big Tree has continued releasing many singles, having hits with Fancy's 'Wild Thing' and Hot Chocolate's 'Emma', while Lobo and Brownsville Station remain consistent sellers. In an era dominated by albums and record business bureaucracy, Big Tree is one of the last important independent singles labels.

Van Morrison, born in Belfast, on August 31, 1945, developed an early interest in blues and jazz, and left school at 15 to play music. He formed Them in 1963, but after two hit singles and an American tour, Morrison became disillusioned with the music business, and returned to Ireland. Later, producer Bert Berns invited him back to America to record for his new Bang label. Morrison agreed, and his first single, 'Brown Eyed Girl', reached the American Top Ten in 1967. Two solo albums were released on Bang, including the classic *Blowin' Your Mind* (1968).

Until then, Morrison's music had been heavily rooted in R&B. Them used it to express a distinctively punk *angst*, and although the Bang recordings showed Morrison maturing both as a singer and a songwriter, his talent still appeared derivative rather than original. *Astral Weeks* (1968), his first album for Warner Bros, changed all this. It remains unique amongst his work: fresh, subtle and infinitely delicate. The lyrics are stream-of-consciousness romanticism, magically evoking a wealth of moods, feelings, locations, all superbly enhanced by the music. Swelling and tumbling gently, guitar, flute, sax, drums (Connie Kay) and flowing acoustic bass (Richard Davis) create a finely textured backdrop for Morrison's vocals, which in turn make brilliant use of scat and repetition.

Moondance (1970) saw him bring together the emotional vigour of his earlier, R&B-influenced work and the lighter, jazzy sound of *Astral Weeks.* All his subsequent albums, including *His Band And Street Choir* (1971), *Tupelo Honey*

(1971), *St Dominic's Preview* (1972) and *Veedon Fleece* (1974) have built on the musical synthesis of *Moondance*, central to which is the work of guitarist John Platania. Morrison's music continues to show a love of blues, country, jazz and soul; while his lyrics further explore the many moods of a singular romanticism. In 1973, he embarked on his first full-scale tour of Europe and North America, backed by a ten-piece band, the Caledonia Soul Orchestra, which included a string quartet.

At his best, Morrison is a compelling performer. Nervous, intense, he stands motionless midstage, eyes closed, while his voice seems first to take him over, then enrapture the entire theatre. Luckily, some of these performances are available on the double album, *It's Too Late To Stop Now* (1974).

Above everything, Van Morrison is a great singer. He can take a few phrases and repeat them over and over, weaving his voice around the music, gradually working his way deeper into the listener's consciousness. When this comes off, on tracks like 'Madame George', 'Stoned Me' or 'Listen To The Lion', his music is truly spellbinding.

Mother Earth started out in that melting-pot of music, Texas, in 1967. They were: Tracy Nelson (born on Dec. 27, 1944 in Madison, Wisconsin), piano, vocals, once a folk singer with a debut album on Prestige behind her; R. Powell St John, singer, once part of a bluegrass band (with Janis Joplin) which was resident at the legendary Threadgill's Bar in Austin; Mark Naftalin, keyboard player, then fresh out of the Butterfield Blues Band; Bob Arthur, bass; John 'Toad' Andrews, guitar; George Rains, drums – once three-quarters of a Texas University R&B band, the Wigs, completed by Boz Scaggs. Rains, like the final member of the group, Martin Fiero, an accomplished sax player, had been with the Sir Douglas Quintet.

Their first recorded work was on *Revolution*, a soundtrack album from the film about San Francisco, their adopted home by 1968. Along with Doug Sahm, Mother Earth were the most successful in drawing from the wide Texas musical experience – blues, cajun, soul, rock and country –

and in creating a strong group identity highlighted by Tracy Nelson's full-throated singing and R. Powell's distinctive guttural tones, and by playing which was rough without being ragged, warm and mellow without being too laid back.

Their first album, *Living With The Animals* (Mercury, 1968) is deeply rooted in both soul and blues in a highly personalized manner. If anything, their second album *Make A Joyful Noise* (1969) was even more impressive with a city side and a country side, the latter a fascinating blend of dobros, fiddle and bottlenecking offsetting Tracy Nelson's singing and an early exposition of country rock. John Andrews' funkier guitar-playing fitted surprisingly neatly into the country mould. Augmented by Nashville players they cut *Tracy Nelson Country* the same year, 1969, the group having moved to Nashville from 'Frisco. They went through numerous personnel changes, with only Tracy Nelson and Andrews remaining constant, and produced a series of weaker albums, the best being *Bring Me Home* (Reprise, 1972) featuring Boz Scaggs, then arousing interest with the same rich-textured sounds Mother Earth music always conveyed. Tracy Nelson's solo albums have been relatively undistinguished.

Mott the Hoople. Mick Ralphs (guitar, born May 31, 1944), Dale 'Buffin' Griffin (drums, born Oct. 24, 1948) and Pete 'Overend' Watts (bass, born May 13, 1947) first started playing together in the Hereford area in the mid-Sixties. By 1969 they had added Verden 'Phally' Allen (organ, born May 26, 1944) and were calling themselves Silence. Ralphs shopped demo tapes around London, striking gold with Island Records A&R man Guy Stevens. He changed their name to Mott the Hoople after a book by Willard Manus, and since vocalist Stan Tippens was retiring suggested they replace him with a singer/pianist. Ian Hunter (born June 3, 1946), an avid Dylan fan who knew only two songs on the piano, was finally chosen. From the first album his constant wearing of sunglasses (due to weak eyes), long curly hair and his blatant Dylan stylings provided the group with a focal point. In 1972 – after four albums, notably *Brain Capers* (1971) –

they broke up due to bad luck and debts, but were encouraged by David Bowie to re-form and they signed with Columbia Records. Bowie penned 'All The Young Dudes', their first hit in 1972. Hit singles continued in Britain – notably 'All The Way From Memphis' (1973), 'Roll Away The Stone' (1974) – while albums took off in America – *Mott* (1973) and *Mott The Hoople* (1974).

In early 1973 Verden Allen left; later that year Mick Ralphs left to join Bad Company. He was replaced by Ariel Bender (Luther Grosvenor). Later, Blue Weaver (organ) and Morgan Fisher (piano) were added. In mid-1974 Weaver and Bender left; Fisher took over the keyboards while Bender was replaced by Mick Ronson. In December the pressures became too much for Hunter and without warning he and Ronson left to pursue a career together. After several months of auditions they were replaced by Ray Majors (guitar) and Nigel Benjamin (vocals), the name being shortened to Mott.

Mountain comprised Leslie West (guitar, born in New York on Oct. 26, 1945), Felix Pappalardi (bass, born in New York in 1940), Steve Knight (keyboards), and Corky Laing (drums, born in Montreal, Canada on Jan. 26, 1948). A heavy guitar-led outfit, they were based on the Cream model, Pappalardi having produced several of the British band's albums.

Formed in 1969, they had a Top Thirty hit the next year with 'Mississippi Queen' (Windfall), and in their three-year existence produced five albums, all acceptable to Cream fans starved of their heroes. In 1972, Pappalardi left to be replaced by Jack Bruce. As West, Bruce and Laing, the new trio cut two further albums during 1972–73. To complete the circle, the original Mountain re-formed in 1974 to cut *Avalanche* (Windfall).

Mud, a run-of-the-mill group adopted by songwriters Nicky Chinn and Mike Chapman to complement their interest in Sweet, Mud – Les Gray (vocals), Rob Davis (guitar), Roy Stiles (bass), Dave Mount (drums) – were altogether more homely than their flash stablemates. The collaboration with

Chinn and Chapman produced a series of hit singles between 1973 and 1975, starting with 'Crazy' (RAK, 1973) and culminating in the clever Presley parodies, 'Lonely This Christmas' (1974) and 'The Secrets That You Keep' (1975). Dissatisfied with the slim financial return from enormous record sales, the group split with Chinnichap and RAK early in 1975. Their departure was followed by the release of two hit singles from their old partnership, 'Oh Boy' and 'Moonshine Sally'. None the less, their first self-produced singles on Private Stock, 'L-L-Lucy' and 'Show Me You're A Woman', easily made the Top Twenty.

Maria Muldaur, born in New York's Greenwich Village, has blended jazz, blues, gospel, bluegrass and country music into a successful hit formula. Influenced by the records of Bessie Smith and the early bluegrass musicians, she started singing in local folk clubs, and at sixteen formed a girl group, the Cashmeres. They signed with Gone records and did some back-up work for other artists. Maria later became interested in Appalachian music as performed by Doc Watson and others. She learned to play fiddle from the great Gaither Carlton, Watson's father-in-law. At 21 she joined the Even Dozen Jug Band in New York which included John Sebastian, Stefan Grossman and Josh Rifkin. They cut an album, played two shows at Carnegie Hall, did some TV work, and then disbanded. She recorded as Maria D'Amato.

Maria moved to Cambridge and married Geoff Muldaur, a member of Jim Kweskin's Jug Band. She soon became a full-time group member, staying with them for six years and recording several albums. When the band broke up, Maria and Geoff moved to Woodstock and cut two albums for Reprise – *Pottery Pie* and *Sweet Potatoes*. When her marriage faltered, Maria struck out on her own. Her first album, *Maria Muldaur*, released in June, 1974, was well-received and included the hit single 'Midnight At The Oasis', a Top Twenty success on both sides of the Atlantic. Produced by Lenny Waronker and Joe Boyd, the album features an assortment of musicians including Dr John, Ry Cooder, Clarence White and Amos Garrett, who played the exceptional guitar solo break on 'Midnight'. Her second album, *Waitress In A Donut Shop*, released in December, 1974, included three songs arranged and conducted by the eminent jazz saxophonist Benny Carter, who was joined by some of the best jazz musicians in the world. Maria has since become well-known in jazz as well as rock circles, her wispy, fragile voice and Bohemian looks winning her a top-of-the-bill spot at the 1975 Newport and Montreux Jazz Festivals.

Mungo Jerry had a constantly changing line-up of skiffle revivalists dominated by the personality of lead singer Ray Dorset (born in 1946 in Ashford, Kent). Originally known as Good Earth (Dorset, Colin Earl, Paul King, Mike Cole) they were the hit of the Hollywood (Newcastle) Festival in 1970 and simultaneously released their million-seller 'In The Summertime' (Dawn). The majority of their subsequent singles have been successful, notably 'Baby Jump' (1972) and 'Allright, Allright' (1973). When critics attacked the group's music for being very monotonous, Dorset brought out a solo album (*Cold Blue Excursion*, 1972) in which he experimented unsuccessfully with a variety of styles.

Anne Murray, born in Spring Hill, Nova Scotia, Canada on June 20, 1946, started singing professionally when she was signed by Brian Ahern – now her producer – for a season on Canadian TV's folksy *Sing-Along Jamboree.* She joined Arc Records and then Canadian Capitol with whom she had her first hit, 'Snowbird', in 1970. In America it was also a big country hit and inaugurated a series of country hits: e.g. 'Talk It Over In The Morning', 'Cotton Jenny' (1972) and 'He Thinks I Still Care' (1974).

However, while her country hits and singles like 'Danny's Song' (a Top Ten hit in 1973) and 'Love Song' (1974) show the pleasant and gentle side of her singing, album tracks like her soulful version of Barbara George's 'I Know' and singles like the Top Ten 'You Won't See Me' – originally the flip of 'He Thinks I Still Care' – show her also to be a strong interpretative and expressive singer. Unlike many of the new breed of MOR/country singers, Murray (and producer

Ahern) have not allowed her early successes to set the pattern of her career. Thus she continues to live in Canada and to support Canadian writers like Bruce Cockburn.

Richard Nader was born in 1940 in Masontown, Pennsylvania, and was already playing the oldies of 1956 on a local radio station in 1958. By the time he entered college he was hosting weekly record hops on WMBS, which were the biggest events in that part of the country until 1964, when Nader was drafted. He continued with an oldies show in Korea, and on his return he tried to interest Frank Barsalona of Premier Talent in the idea for a series of 'rock'n'roll revival' concerts. Barsalona didn't buy it, but he hired Nader as an assistant promoter. With that experience behind him he formed his own company and on October 18, 1969 Nader presented the first of his own revival shows at New York's Felt Forum, starring Bill Haley, Chuck Berry, the Shirelles, and the Platters.

The show was a sellout, the first of nearly a hundred, all over the country. Nader's name became synonymous with the rock'n'roll revival that was one of the biggest trends of 1969–72, culminating in the film *Let The Good Times Roll.* Of all the promoters, he showed the commitment of a true fan, going to great lengths to locate and reunite such legendary groups as the Five Satins and the original Platters, who like many Fifties groups had scattered widely after breaking up. Although these shows helped get many Fifties acts back into the business, revival concerts as a trend had run out of steam by 1973, when Nader failed badly with a tour of English Invasion artists, although he was probably somewhat ahead of his time as well. Little has been heard from Nader since 1973, but when the Sixties Revival picks up, he's sure to be there.

Graham Nash, born in Blackpool on Feb. 2, 1942, was a leading member of the Manchester group, the Hollies. He sang high harmony on, and co-wrote, most of that group's single successes in the mid-Sixties. Becoming disenchanted with their commercialism and his own lack of recognition, he joined Stills and Crosby in 1968 as CSN, where more lasting music and stardom were to come. His songs for CSN/CSN&Y and on his solo albums – *Songs For Beginners* and *Wild Tales* – straddle the line between a powerful emotional simplicity and a naïve sentimentality. 'Lady Of The Island' and 'Our House' are good examples of the two poles. Nash's main problem has always been that his superb harmony voice is not really suited to extensive lead singing; for this reason he has always been at his best in a group.

Johnny Nash, born in Houston, Texas on Aug. 19, 1940; John Lester Nash Jr. has been into more bags than a wrongly addressed envelope. As the (black) teenage star of KPRC's *Matinee,* he broke the Houston TV colour bar and attracted the attention of ABC-Paramount, for whom he scored with 'A Teenager Sings The Blues', 'A Very Special Love' (Top Fifty in 1957), 'The Teen Commandments' (Top Thirty in 1958) on which he shared the vocal chores with Paul Anka and George Hamilton IV, and 'As Time Goes By' (Top Fifty in 1959).

While Nash went on to star in films like *Take A Giant Step, Key Witness* and the Swedish *Love Is Not A Game,* his recordings – which hovered unsuccessfully between soul and night-club easy listening – appeared on a variety of labels including Warner Bros (1962–63), Groove, Argo (1964) and MGM (1970). His own labels, Joda and Jad, which operated intermittently between 1965 and 1970, brought him back to the charts with 'Let's Move And Groove Together' (1965) and the even more successful Byron Lee Jamaican studio recordings, 'Hold Me Tight' (a No. 5 in 1968), 'You Got Soul' and 'Cupid' (1969). Nash subsequently built his own studio on the island and established himself as the leading exponent of commercial reggae with internationally successful discs for Epic, including 'Stir It Up' (1971), 'I Can See Clearly Now' (an American No. 1), the eloquent 'There Are More Questions Than Answers' (1972), 'Tears On My Pillow' and 'Let's Be Friends' (1975). His composition for Joey Dee, 'What Kind Of Love Is This', hit the Top Twenty in 1962 and he also produced Sam and Bill's Hot Hundred entry, 'For Your Love', in 1965.

Nashville is still identified as the 'country sound' recording centre, but in reality it is much more than that and has catered to the needs of popular singers increasingly throughout the Sixties. Then, in 1968, came a watershed. The Byrds came to town to record with country session men and the classic *Sweetheart Of The Rodeo* album resulted. Then came Bob Dylan to record *Nashville Skyline*, including a duet with an established Nashville figure, Johnny Cash.

The story of Nashville since 1969 has been that of the further development of these two trends: the country-pop confluence and the country-rock tributary. The popular music of the Seventies has made increasing use of the steel guitar behind ballad singers and country artists like Tammy Wynette, Faron Young and Charlie Rich have topped charts internationally – while Olivia Newton-John managed to do the same thing by copying the Nashville approach in London.

Apart from the forays of west-coast groups, including the important recordings of the Nitty Gritty Dirt Band in Nashville, the city has also produced its own brand of 'modern' singer/songwriters like Kris Kristofferson, Mickey Newbury, Tom T. Hall, Waylon Jennings and Billy Swan. Instrumentally, a group of 'Nashville Sound' musicians formed Area Code 615 in the country-rock style, and bluegrass veteran Earl Scruggs has been recording with folk and rock artists like Joan Baez and the Byrds.

However, the music business itself largely remains in the hands of the same major labels and publishers, though several new independent labels have emerged in the mainstream country field, like Mega, Stop, Chart and the temporarily successful Cinnamon.

Nazareth. When they moved to London from Fife, Scotland, Nazareth were able to prove one of the fundamental formulas of rock – that heavy rock projected with the aid of the right business expertise was a guaranteed success. The band was launched at a fashionable Soho strip club but it was frequent touring throughout Britain and Europe that produced success.

They had to wait eighteen months for their first Top Ten hit, 'Broken Down Angel'. Then it all came at once for them – a headline British tour, follow-up hits 'Bad Bad Boy' and 'This Flight Tonight', and hit album, *Razamanaz* (Mooncrest, 1973). They had the right stage image, projecting sex and mean rock through their singer Dan McCafferty and guitarists Pete Agnew and Manny Charlton.

They gradually moved into the heavy metal bracket and suffered from overkill in 1974 but 1975 saw them back in the charts with a version of 'My White Bicycle', while McCafferty released a solo album, *Dan McCafferty* (Mountain), and Nazareth's 'Love Hurts' hit the American Top Twenty.

Willie Nelson is currently the reluctant head of a Texas country-rock 'movement' that grew around him and centred itself on Austin. He and his songs are in the country mainstream, but his importance was in rebelling against the Nashville business centre.

Born on March 30, 1933 in Fort Worth, Texas, Nelson worked as a band member with Ray Price and wrote hits like 'Nightlife', 'Family Bible' and 'Funny How Time Slips Away'. Having previously recorded for Betty, D, and Bellaire, he joined Liberty in 1962 and hit with 'Touch Me', and again on RCA in 1965 with 'The Party's Over' and 'Once More With Feeling'. Later, wishing room to experiment and develop his more than usually complex phrasing and melody lines within traditional country themes, he moved to Austin, and to Monument and Atlantic Records. His albums, *Phases And Stages* and *Shotgun Willie* (Atlantic, 1973), are the classic statement of his style, paving the way for his greatest commercial success, for Columbia in 1975, with 'Blue Eyes Crying In The Rain' and 'Red Headed Stranger'.

Michael Nesmith is the only former Monkee to establish himself as a solo artist. An orchestral album for Dot (*When The Wichita Train Whistle Sings*, 1968) and the Top Twenty success of Linda Ronstadt with his 'Different Drum' led the formation of the First National Band in 1970. With

Orville 'Red' Rhodes (pedal-steel guitar, born in East Alston, Illinois on Dec. 30, 1930), John London (bass, born in Bryan, Texas on Feb. 6, 1942) and John Ware (drums, born in Tulsa, Oklahoma on May 2, 1944), Nesmith made a 'trilogy' of albums of country music, California-style: *Magnetic South* (RCA, 1970), *Loose Salute* (1970) and *Nevada Fighter* (1971).

Subsequently Nesmith formed a Second National Band, retaining Rhodes but bringing in drummer Jack Rinelli and bass-player Johnny Meeks, formerly with Gene Vincent's Blue Caps and Merle Haggard's Strangers. The idea was again to cut three albums, but only *Tantamount To Treason Vol. 1* (1972) appeared. The next Nesmith/Rhodes album, *And The Hits Just Keep On Comin'* (1972) is generally considered their best work to date. The title was a wry joke, since of the plethora of Nesmith recordings, only two singles – 'Joanne' and 'Silver Moon' – had reached the Top Fifty.

In 1972, Elektra offered Nesmith his own label, Countryside. Putting together a house band led by Red Rhodes, Nesmith produced four albums by Garland Frady, Ian Matthews, Rhodes himself and Nesmith's own final RCA album, *Pretty Much Your Standard Ranch Stash* (1973). When David Geffen replaced Jac Holzman at Elektra, Countryside was axed, leaving the talented but wayward Nesmith to plan his third attempt at a concept recording, released in 1975 as *The Prison*.

Mickey Newbury opened the Seventies with a Top Thirty hit, 'American Trilogy' (Elektra, 1971), a reworking of traditional songs, concerned, as the title suggests, with America. It is, however, untypical of his recordings which in the main deal with personal relations in the singer/songwriter country-rock genre. Born in Houston, Texas, on May 19, 1940 Newbury left behind the small club bands to move to Nashville and starve there as a songwriter during the mid-Sixties. Eventually, he wrote hits for Ray Price ('Sweet Memories') and Jerry Lee Lewis ('She Even Woke Me Up To Say Goodbye'). Encouraged, he recorded himself for RCA, Mercury and Elektra. Though he has written fine songs like 'San Francisco Mabel Joy' and 'How I Love Them Old Songs', sustained success has so far eluded him, despite a big push by his record company, Elektra, in 1975.

Randy Newman. Once described as the Mark Twain of rock, Newman (born Nov. 28, 1943) is a humorist who has chosen the pop song as his medium. An adept song craftsman, he learnt his trade working in Los Angeles for Metric Music alongside Glen Campbell, Leon Russell, Jackie de Shannon, David Gates and others, and became a session arranger for Warner Bros in 1967. A year later he recorded his first solo album, *Randy Newman* (Reprise) with the help of Van Dyke Parks and although it sold so badly that the company was forced into giving it away as an advertising gimmick, it set the tone of his later work. One of the chief reasons for public indifference, then as now, was his voice, cracked and discordant, which perfectly matched the spirit and tone of his songs, which were alternately cynical, ironic and serio-comic in effect.

Unlike most of his songwriting contemporaries, Newman is one writer whose style is personalized rather than strictly personal: he rarely writes about his own situation. This may set him somewhat apart from the world of rock and it is true to say that he is equally at home writing in a jazz, country or ragtime vein as in rock, and in albums like *12 Songs*, *Sail Away* (1973) and *Good Old Boys* (1974) he has helped immeasurably to broaden the scope of the pop song in terms of subject matter by exploring the other side of sex in his songs – inadequacy, impotence, even perversion. Although never likely to be commercially successful as a performer he maintains a healthy cult following and is, remarkably, the biggest selling foreign artist in Holland. His songs have been covered successfully in America by Three Dog Night ('Mama Told Me Not To Come') and in Britain by Alan Price ('Simon Smith And His Amazing Dancing Bear').

New Riders of the Purple Sage. Formed out of the New Delhi River Band – the name was supposedly developed by numerological transposition – in 1969, they initially attracted attention through the presence of part of the Grateful Dead – Jerry Garcia, Mickey Hart, Phil Lesh and even Robert Hunter have at some time played for the band though only Garcia is featured on (their first) record, *New Riders Of The Purple Sage* (Columbia, 1971). The nucleus of the band has always been David Nelson and John Dawson; Buddy Cage replaced Garcia on pedal steel in 1971, Spencer Dryden (from Jefferson Airplane) joined as drummer and Skip Battin (from the Byrds) became bassist. Their albums range from country and rockabilly (*Powerglide*, 1972; *Gypsy Cowboy*, 1973) to good-time rock'n'roll (*Home Home On The Road*, 1974).

The New Seekers were formed in 1969 to cash in on the demise of the Seekers, a soft-harmony 'folk' group that had four million-sellers in the mid-Sixties, including 'I'd Never Find Another You' (1965) and 'Georgy Girl' (1965), by Keith Potger, the guitarist with the original group. Comprising Eve Graham (born in Perth, Scotland on April 13, 1943), Lyn Paul (born in Melbourne, Australia on Feb. 16, 1949), Peter Doyle (born in Melbourne, on July 28, 1949), Marty Kristian (born in Leipzig, Germany on May 27, 1947) and Paul Layton (born in Beaconsfield, England on Aug. 4, 1947), the New Seekers' first hits were 'Look What They've Done To My Song Ma' (Elektra, 1970) in America and 'Never-Ending Song Of Love' (Phillips, 1971). Then they recorded Cook and Greenaway's Coca-Cola jingle, 'I'd Like To Teach The World To Sing' (Polydor) in 1972 and immediately secured themselves a worldwide cabaret and TV audience. Other MOR hits followed, including 'Beg Steal Or Borrow' and 'Circles' in 1972 which was followed by a carefully prettied-up version of 'Pinball Wizard/See Me Feel Me' in 1973. They disbanded in 1974.

Olivia Newton-John was born in Cambridge into an academic family. In Australia, where she went at the age of four, she formed a singing group, the Sol Four, in her teens before going solo and winning a trip back to Britain in a talent contest sponsored by Johnny O'Keefe, Australia's

Elvis Presley. In Britain, she temporarily teamed up with another Australian, Pat Carroll, to work as a duo in TV and cabaret, before her MOR cover of Dylan's 'If Not For You' (Pye International, 1971) won her a place in the British Top Ten and the American Top Thirty on UNI. She followed this with British Top Twenty versions of 'Banks Of The Ohio' (1971), 'What Is Life' (1972) and 'Take Me Home Country Roads' (1973) and at the same time consolidated her TV and cabaret career, often appearing with Cliff Richard.

Then in late 1973 John Farrar's production of her 'Let Me Be There' (MCA) astounded the world by becoming first a country hit and then a pop hit in America while missing in Britain. Having happily hit the precise meeting point of country and MOR music in time and style, Newton-John, with her pleasant light voice and Farrar's clean and sympathetic production behind her, continued plugging away. The result was hit after hit – 'If You Love Me Let Me Know', 'I Honestly Love You' (a No. 1 in 1974) and 'Have You Never Been Mellow' (another No. 1 in 1975) – in America where in 1974 she won three Grammies, two of which were for the Best Female *Country* vocalist – much to the chagrin of more traditional elements in Nashville – and Best Female *Pop* Performance.

New York. Strange though it seems, major cities such as New York and Los Angeles have seldom developed the kind of strong local rock scene or identifiable regional sound that lesser American cities (Memphis, New Orleans, Cleveland, San Francisco, Minneapolis, Atlanta, Austin, etc.) have always boasted. New York's street-corner vocal group scene in the Fifties was a notable exception, but following its demise there was little the city could call uniquely its own.

The Greenwich Village club scene of 1965 produced many local groups, among them the Blues Magoos, Vagrants, Magicians, Fugitives, Fugs, Blues Project, and of course the Lovin' Spoonful. But although some of these rose to national fame, none defined a true local scene. This changed with the arrival of the Young Rascals, who seemed to reflect the attitudes and tastes of New York youth (especially the suburban Long Island contingent) as no group had before, and the Velvet Underground, who explored the extremities of the New York experience, from the self-destructive, burnt-out weariness of the street-corner junkie to the jaded brat from Scarsdale. In a real sense, these two bands *were* New York.

But the bands that followed in the late Sixties fell short of this standard, and what might have been a real New York scene, like the scene in San Francisco around that period, never materialized. Other New York bands, Vanilla Fudge, Mountain, the Insect Trust, the Group Image, the Illusion, the New York Rock And Roll Ensemble, NRBQ and Lothar and the Hand People, either ascended instantly into the ranks of international popdom or disappeared without ever making it beyond the clubs they started in.

It was only with the beginning of the Seventies that a new, vital scene began to emerge from the streets of New York. Concurrent with the rise of the glitter movement in England, New York's trendsetters were evolving a style and scene of their own, a nouveau-freakish bisexual camp, grotesque makeup and torn panty-hose, boys and girls alike posing as dropout sodomists in the Oscar Wilde room of the Mercer Arts Center, where trashy bands thrown together by kids off the street played for the hard-core faithful.

These bands, of whom the New York Dolls quickly became pre-eminent, played hard, basic rock'n'roll, with solid roots in the mid-Sixties British and punk styles. They dressed and acted like their audience, in varying degrees of drag, and they mixed choice oldies with original songs dedicated to the lifestyle of their small following.

By 1973/74 the Dolls had spawned a large number of imitators, among them Wayne County, the Brats, Teenage Lust, the Miamis, the Harlots Of 42nd Street, New York Central, and Milk and Cookies. There were also other New York acts with a bold, mid-Sixties or glitter pop approach, such as Elliott Murphy, Kiss, and of course Blue Oyster Cult.

This scene flourished for two years or so, with many small

clubs opening to accommodate these bands, and much national media attention focused on it all. But with the failure of the Dolls and Murphy to break through to a wider audience, and the inability of any of their imitators to establish an identity of their own, the scene as a whole began to taper off.

A third generation of Seventies bands began to appear in New York in early 1975, including such names as the Marbles, Television, the Ramones, the Dictators (whose debut album became another critics' favourite) and the Heartbreakers. Many observers have predicted that without the omnipresent influence of the Dolls, these bands could make more of an individual mark. Meanwhile, with the success of BOC, Kiss, and the signing of street poet Patti Smith to Arista, New York still has a future as one of the leading rock cities of the Seventies.

The New York Dolls. With a repertoire derived from the MC5, Velvet Underground, Shangri-Las and early Rolling Stones, and a blasting double-lead guitar wall of sound, and singer David JoHansen's Jaggeresque voice, they had an impressive (if limited) style. But the group's flashy stage show and gutter transvestite costumes, and their songs of life and cheap love among the trashy New York glitter people, endeared them enormously to their audience.

The original group (late 1971) consisted of guitarists Johnny Thunders and Rick Rivets, bassist Arthur Kane and drummer Billy Murcia. JoHansen joined in early 1972, Murcia died on an early tour of England and was replaced by Jerry Nolan. Rivets was also replaced, by Sylvain Sylvain, before the first album.

Despite a Mercury Records contract (two albums, *New York Dolls* and *Too Much, Too Soon*), two singles ('Trash' and 'Stranded In The Jungle') and numerous tours, the Dolls never caught on nationally. In mid-1975 they broke up.

Nico, born in Germany in 1944, reached New York via a career as a film actress in Italy (Fellini's *La Dolce Vita*) and a model in Paris. After appearing in Warhol's *Chelsea Girls,* she became the 'chanteuse' of the Velvet Underground. Her haunting, deadpan singing of 'I'll Be Your Mirror' and 'All Tomorrow's Parties' on *The Velvet Underground And Nico* (Verve, 1967) secured her a small but slavish following. Her subsequent albums – *The Marble Index* (Elektra, 1969), *Desertshore* (Reprise, 1971) and *The End* (Island, 1974) – have been produced and arranged by former colleague John Cale. They extend her combination of Gothic, stylized singing, haunting harmonium accompaniments, and songs that suggest a glacial mental landscape of terminal psychosis.

Harry Nilsson, born in Brooklyn, New York on June 15, 1941, became something of a cult figure during the late Sixties through his association with the Beatles and his gentle parody of their vocal and songwriting style. His early songs for west-coast pop and R&B artists (such as Bo Pete's 'Baa Baa Black Sheep Parts 1 and 2', Crusader) are deservedly obscure and commercial success did not come his way until 1971 when his recording of 'Without You' (RCA), ironically not one of his own songs but written by Ham and Evans of Badfinger, reached the top of the charts in both Britain and America. Since then his albums have sold consistently well, although his recent recordings have lacked the sheer finesse and offbeat originality of his first single and album releases. His trademark is the soft, melancholic ballad sung in a wistful, hurt voice and while he is arguably a far better singer than he is a songwriter many of his songs have been recorded by other artists, including 'Ten Little Indians' by the Yardbirds and '1941' by Tom Northcott. An above-average pop talent, his main problem appears to be a lack of musical discipline: too often he records simply for the sake of recording. His best albums are probably *Pandemonium Shadow Show* (RCA, 1968) and *Ariel Ballet* (RCA, 1968).

The Nitty Gritty Dirt Band are John McEuen (banjo, mandolin, guitar, born on Dec. 19, 1945); Jeff Hanna (guitar, drums, born on August 11, 1947); Jimmy Fadden (guitar, bass, March 9, 1948); Les Thompson (bass) and Jim Ibbotson (guitar, keyboards, Jan. 21, 1947). The group was formed in 1965 out of various high school bands, basing themselves around Aspen and Denver in Colorado.

Signing to Liberty Records, their records contained an eclectic mixture of blues, jug-band music, bluegrass and original songs by writers including Jackson Browne and Kenny Loggins. *Uncle Charlie And His Dog Teddy* (1970) and *All The Good Times* (1972) showed off the Dirt Band's brand of country-rock to good effect.

They had a surprise Top Ten hit in 1970 with Jerry Jeff Walker's 'Mr Bojangles' but the pinnacle of their success was the widely acclaimed triple album, *Will The Circle Be Unbroken* (1973), recorded in Nashville and including guest appearances by many traditional country veterans.

Jack Nitzsche, born in Michigan in 1937, emerged as perhaps the most innovative pop arranger-composer-producer of the Sixties. At 21 he received a diploma in music and moved to Hollywood where he worked as an independent arranger and music copyist for Sonny Bono. In 1962, he was hired by Phil Spector to arrange 'He's A Rebel' by the Crystals and stayed on as his regular arranger, helping Spector create his famous 'wall of sound'. He arranged and orchestrated most of Spector's biggest hits, including the Crystals' 'Da Doo Ron Ron', the Ronettes' 'Be My Baby' and Ike and Tina Turner's 'River Deep – Mountain High'. Although working primarily with Spector, Nitzsche signed a solo contract with Reprise in 1963, scoring several instrumental successes like 'The Lonely Surfer' (1963), which featured as sidemen such aspiring superstars as Leon Russell and David Gates.

Nitzsche later became friends with the Rolling Stones, playing piano and offering advice on many of their early records, including *Out Of Our Heads* and *Aftermath*. 1968 found him writing the score for the Mick Jagger movie *Performance*. That same year he arranged, produced and played piano on Buffalo Springfield's 'Expecting To Fly', which led to a working relationship with Neil Young. Nitzsche wrote and arranged for Young's debut solo album; arranged and produced 'A Man Needs A Maid' and 'There's

A World' on *Harvest*, and played piano on *Time Fades Away*. He also recorded and toured with Crazy Horse, Young's regular back-up group. 1972 saw a new departure for Nitzsche, who came to London to cut *St Giles Cripplegate* with the London Symphony Orchestra, an album containing a series of classically styled instrumental passages composed and arranged by Nitzsche with production by Elliot Mazer.

However, a year later he returned to a more familiar rock format and presented Reprise with a vocal/instrumental album which was subsequently rejected by the company. Nitzsche's growing dissatisfaction with the direction of rock music clearly showed through on the album, and resulted in his virtual retirement from the rock world. He now works exclusively on movie scores, and his arrangements include the crystal glass orchestration for *The Exorcist*.

Don Nix, born in Memphis on Sept. 27, 1941, is of Cherokee Indian descent on his mother's side. At high school he was part of a band which became the Mar-Keys, the 'house' band for Stax Records during the mid-Sixties, backing Otis Redding, Wilson Pickett and Sam and Dave. In 1965, Nix moved to California, where he lived with Leon Russell and became involved with Delaney and Bonnie whose Stax album, *Home*, he produced. Subsequent production work with Jeff Beck, Albert King, Freddy King and John Mayall, together with three solo albums including the ragged *Living By The Days* (Elektra, 1971) and the masterminding of a tour, titled The Alabama State Troupers, which included Lonnie Mack and Jeanie Greene as well as himself, have made Don Nix a well-known if not hugely successful figure.

Nucleus is the band led by trumpeter Ian Carr who, in his book *Music Outside* (Latimer, 1973), has given a detailed and very entertaining account of its genesis and subsequent life. Having got off to a good start by winning first prize at the Montreux International Festival in 1970, Nucleus established an international reputation for improvised but highly integrated music which stands almost exactly midway between jazz and rock. Among its members have been Karl Jenkins (baritone sax) and John Marshall (drums), who later joined Soft Machine, and guitarist Chris Spedding.

His composition *Solar Plexus*, written for an expanded Nucleus, is the first, and perhaps the only, record in the rock idiom to be produced as the result of subsidy by the Arts Council.

In chronological order, Nucleus' albums become looser, more assured and fluid, with *Elastic Rock* (Vertigo, 1970), *Solar Plexus* (Vertigo, 1970), *Belladonna* (Vertigo, 1972), and *Snakehips Etcetera* (Vertigo, 1975) as high spots.

The Ohio Players, an eight-piece black band almost as well known for their striking album covers as for their music, first hit the big time with a funky riff called 'Pain' on Westbound in 1971. Twelve years earlier the original members (from Dayton, Ohio) had got together as The Ohio Untouchables – the group that supplied the memorable backing to The Falcons' searing R&B hit 'I Found A Love' (Lupine, 1962). After innumerable personnel changes and a name switch they recorded several erratic sides for TRC (1967), Compass (1968) and Capitol (1969) before absorbing the ideas of James Brown and Sly Stone to reach modern audiences. 'Pain' introduced a succession of throbbing variations ('Pleasure', 'Funky Worm', 'Ecstasy') climaxing in a new contract with Mercury and their biggest hit, 'Skin Tight', in 1974. Subsequent releases ('Fire', 'Smoke') enhanced their reputation as one of the tightest bands in the business.

The O'Jays. Eddie Levert, Walter Williams, William Powell, Bobby Massey and Bill Isles formed a doowop group while still at Canton McKinley High School, Eddie and Walter having previously sung as a gospel duo. Renamed The Mascots in 1958, they recorded unsuccessfully before Cleveland disc jockey Eddie O'Jay gave them his name. After a record with producer Don Davis, H. B. Barnum took the group to LA where they cut a small hit with 'Lonely Drifter' (leased to Imperial in 1963).

After a large number of Imperial recordings ('Lipstick

Traces', 1965, 'Stand In For Love', 1966) the group moved on, to Minit and then Bell with producer George Kerr.

The group (by then a quartet) experienced a little success (including 'I'll Be Sweeter Tomorrow', 1967) before signing for Gamble/Huff's Neptune label. There, 'One Night Affair' (1969) and 'Looky Looky' (1970) hit but Neptune was dissolved in mid-1971. Bobby Massey left the group to work in production and the O'Jays (as a trio) tried a little self-produced recording until Gamble/Huff (now with a Columbia linkup) came bouncing back with Philadelphia International Records. The O'Jays signed in 1972 and had a string of big hits with 'Back Stabbers', 'Love Train', 'For The Love Of Money', 'Sunshine' (cut live in London) and 'Give The People What They Want'. Eddie Levert's expressively soulful lead over the vibrant MFSB backings makes O'Jays discs amongst the very finest examples of the famed Philly Sound.

Danny O'Keefe, born in 1943 in Wenatchee, Washington, moved to St Pauls, Minnesota with his family where he started singing folk-blues around the campus coffee houses. He followed the folk club circuit to New York and then Seattle. There he had a motorcycle accident and turned to songwriting while recuperating. He recorded on Jerry Denham's Jerden label ('That Old Sweet Song') and wrote for the Daily Flash before joining Calliope in Los Angeles, with whom he recorded one album for Buddah. Signed to Cotillion by Ahmet Ertegun, he recorded a solo album, *Danny O'Keefe* (1971), before a re-recording of the wryly ironic 'Goodtime Charlie's Got The Blues' (Signpost, 1972) hit the American Top Twenty. That song was included on the Arif Mardin-produced *O'Keefe*, a collection of his own compositions performed in a laconic, blues-influenced fashion that was critically well received. Subsequent albums, including *Breezy Stories* (Atlantic, 1973), have been uneven, showing his songwriting to be occasionally pretentious, while the worth of a song like 'Mad Ruth/The Babe' is obscured by its over-precious backing.

Mike Oldfield was acclaimed as the most significant composer of the decade after the success of *Tubular Bells* (1973). Born in 1954, he first recorded acoustic songs with his sister on *Sallyangie* (Transatlantic, 1968). He later joined Kevin Ayers and the Whole World on guitar and bass. There he met the classically trained *avant-garde* composer David Bedford, who was to orchestrate the later works for occasional live performances.

Signing to Virgin as a solo artist, he recorded *Tubular Bells*, a collage of melodic lines and varied instrumentation (guitar, bass, mandolin, organ, grand piano, voices), held together by the insistent bell motif. That theme was released as 'Mike Oldfield's Single', used in *The Exorcist*, and reached the American Top Ten. Its unexpected and overwhelming international success was followed by *Hergest Ridge* (1974), a more unified but less evocative work.

Both *Tubular Bells* and *Hergest Ridge* received live performances and Oldfield released a humorous single, 'Don Alfonso', with David Bedford, before his next major work, *Ommadawn* (1975). A more ambitious composition, it utilized African drummers, Celtic pipes and a choir of local children. Like Oldfield's previous works, it was a best-seller. Unlike earlier attempts at classical/rock fusions, Oldfield's themes and harmonic progressions are firmly rooted in rock and folk modes. His achievement has been to become the first to extend such themes into coherent symphony-length works.

Yoko Ono, born in Japan on Feb. 18, 1933, moved to America with her parents when 14. She later entered the New York *avant-garde* scene as a poet, film-maker and conceptual artist before meeting John Lennon in London in 1968. They married the following year.

The media blamed Yoko for the Beatles' split; but her relationship with John was only one of several contributory factors, and there can be little doubt that she was vilified chiefly because she was a woman, an Oriental and an intellectual. John introduced Yoko to rock and she brought him her experience with electronic music and jazz. Their first albums together – *Two Virgins* (1968), *Wedding Album* (1969), *Life With The Lions* (1969) – were indulgently esoteric; but their development of the Plastic Ono Band created a new music that was spare, hard, often beautiful, always honest. Yoko's best work is on her *Approximately Infinite Universe* (1973) – cool, anguished, feminist rock that is among the most tough-minded and aware of Seventies music.

Osibisa pioneered African rock music in Britain. Founded in 1970, the group comprised Teddy Osei (tenor sax, flute) from Kumasi, Ghana, Loughty Amao (saxes) from Nigeria, Robert Bailey (keyboards) from Trinidad, Spartacus R (bass) from Grenada, Wendell Richardson (guitar, vocals) from Antigua, Mac Tontoh (trumpet) and Sol Amarfio (drums).

For MCA, Osibisa recorded *Osibisa* (1970) and *Woyaya* (1971), after which the group underwent major personnel changes, with only Osei and Amarfio remaining from the original line-up. A third MCA record (*Heads*, 1972) led to the band being featured on the soundtrack of *Superfly TNT*. In 1973 they moved to Warner Bros, releasing *Happy Children* (1973) and *Osibirock* (1974). In 1976 they had their first British chart success with 'Sunshine Day' (Bronze) by which time lead singer Richardson had re-joined the group.

The Osmonds are the musical progeny of George and Olive Osmond: Alan (born June 22, 1949), Wayne (Aug. 28, 1951), Merrill (April 30, 1953), Jay (Sept. 12, 1955), Donny (Sept. 12, 1957), Marie (Oct. 13, 1959), and Jimmy (April 16, 1963). The first five brothers showed musical inclinations at an early age and were encouraged to sing and play at family evenings. Their local church – they are Mormon and live in Utah – soon heard of the singing family and asked them to perform at various functions. Jay Williams, father of Andy, heard them and recommended his son to audition them for his TV show. They became regulars for the show's four-year history, switching to *The Jerry Lewis Show*, branching into other TV and variety shows, and touring with

Williams, Pat Boone and Phyllis Diller, meanwhile recording for MCA.

Record success began in 1971 with the release of 'One Bad Apple', an American chart topper on the MGM label then headed by Mike Curb, and continued with 'Down By The Lazy River' and 'Hold Her Tight' (1972). In 1972, at the height of their popularity in America, they turned their attention to Britain where astute promotion in the teeny-bopper market secured them an immediate hysterical following of riot-laden proportions. Donny Osmond was the first to score with a chart-topping solo record, 'Puppy Love' (1972) – the first of a stream of Fifties revivals, 'Too Young', 'Why', both Top Ten in 1972, 'Twelfth Of Never' and 'Young Love', both No. 1s, and 'When I Fall In Love' (1973) – before he turned to duets with Marie Osmond with the chart-topping 'I'm Leaving It Up To You' (1974) and 'Morning Side Of The Mountain' (1975).

Donny wasn't the only Osmond to tread the solo path: 'Little' Jimmy had a No. 1 hit in 1972 with his revival of a Beatles cash-in song of the early Sixties, 'Long Haired Lover From Liverpool' and a Top Ten hit with a revival of 'Tweedle Dee' in 1973, while in 1972 Marie Osmond had a huge hit with 'Paper Roses' before opting for 'more adult' duets with Donny.

The successes of these solo projects stemmed not so much from the chart successes of the Osmonds *en masse*, though that was considerable – 'Crazy Horses' (1972), 'Going Home' and 'Let Me In' (1973) were all Top Five records – but from their in-person appearances, in which Donny and 'Little' Jimmy (and later Marie) provided easily identifiable foci for the group's audience. From November, 1972, the date of their first visit to Britain, to the end of 1974 they visited Britain frequently, culminating in an exclusive filmed performance, excerpts from which were shown daily on BBC TV for a week.

By 1975, the group's teenybopper popularity was on the wane in Britain too – significantly they had always sold more photographs of themselves than records. But the Osmonds, still presenting a meticulous, highly polished showbiz-oriented show, broadened their audience in 1974 with a convincing version of Johnny Bristol's 'Love Me For A Reason'.

Gilbert O'Sullivan, a lightweight singer-songwriter from Ireland where he was born in Waterford on Dec. 1, 1946, stands as a perfect example of how a minor but genuine talent can be spoiled by the star system. When he first appeared in England in 1970, singing 'Nothing Rhymed', he was dressed in short trousers and cloth cap, a parody of the working-class environment he was supposedly singing about in his songs, and even his earliest recordings on MAM, the label owned by Gordon Mills, manager of Tom Jones, were marred by excessive easy-listening style orchestrations. The turning point came in 1972 with 'Alone Again (Naturally)', a remarkably unsentimental song about rejection, which broke him in America.

The Ozark Mountain Daredevils are John Dillon (guitars, fiddle, etc.), Randle Chowning (lead guitars, harmonica), Steve Cash (harmonica), Buddy Brayfield (keyboards), Larry Lee (drums) and Michael Granda (bass). All sing, and are from the vicinity of Springfield, Missouri, where they had played in various local bands before forming up in 1973.

Signed to A&M, their first album was produced by David Anderle and Glyn Johns. It was a pleasant amalgam of country and rock, with graceful harmonies and strong compositions. 'Jacky Blue', written by Lee, from their second record, was a major American hit in 1974. A third album, *Car Over The Lake*, recorded in Nashville, was released in 1975.

Gene Page, one of the most recent of soul's 'backroom boys' to go solo, came from a musical family: his brother Billy is a successful songwriter while his composer/pianist father started Gene on classical piano when he was five, in Los Angeles. He won a scholarship to the Brooklyn Conservatory, New York, and began arranging for producers like Phil

Spector ('You've Lost That Lovin' Feeeling'). In LA, Gene arranged Dobie Gray's 'The In Crowd' before being appointed staff arranger for Reprise and then Motown, working with all their big names in the Sixties. He still arranges for Marvin Gaye (the concert which became the *Live* album) and Diana Ross (*Touch Me In The Morning*, 1973), and has worked on movie scores like *Blacula*. But it is his arrangements for Barry White that have brought him most success.

Gram Parsons, born Nov. 5, 1946, in Winter Haven, Florida, formed the International Submarine Band, with whom he recorded *Safe At Home* (LHI, 1967), a precursor of country rock, before joining the Byrds at Chris Hillman's invitation for their first predominantly country-influenced album, *Sweetheart Of The Rodeo*. He left the group in 1968, refusing to tour South Africa, and formed the Flying Burrito Brothers, which recorded the definitive Southern country rock album, *Gilded Palace Of Sin* (A&M, 1969), a unique mixture of black and white Southern music performed from a rock perspective. After one more album with the group, *Burrito Deluxe* (1970), he left to pursue a solo career. Without Parsons the Burrito Brothers veered more and more towards an LA version of country rock.

Signed to Reprise, after a lengthy series of delays he released *GP* (1973), which featured the harmonizing of Emmylou Harris and united him with top session musicians including Byron Berline and James Burton under the direction of ex-Cricket Glen D. Hardin. They formed the nucleus of his Hot Band. *GP* and the following album, *Grievous Angel* (released posthumously in 1974), featured an impressive array of mournful country standards and Parsons originals that translated the traditional concerns of country music into a contemporary context. Though both were critically well received they sold poorly. Following his sudden death on Sept. 19, 1973, Emmylou Harris recorded two plaintive albums, *Pieces Of The Sky* and *Elite Hotel* (Reprise, 1975), and toured with the Hot Band, achieving greater commercial success than Parsons.

Dolly Parton, born Jan. 19, 1946 in Sevierville, Tennessee, is one of the best female singer/songwriters of the Seventies. She operated until very recently solely in the mainstream country circuit (touring with Porter Wagoner) and appeared on Wagoner's syndicated TV show as 'Miss Dolly', projecting both the phenomenal figure and cascading blonde locks of the Southern bombshell, and the down-home innocence integral to straight country. This has disguised the fact that she writes perceptive songs about her background and lifestyle and sings them brilliantly. Recording first for Goldband, Mercury and Monument, she hit with 'Dumb Blonde' in 1967 and joined RCA in 1968. Since 1970, several songs like 'Joshua', 'Jolene', 'Coat Of Many Colors' and 'In My Tennessee Mountain Home' – all country hits – have carried her quivering Appalachian soprano to a wider, international audience.

Patto was an innovative but commercially unsuccessful London band of the early Seventies. Formed from the remnants of Timebox, the group comprised Mike Patto (lead vocals, born Mike McCarthy on Sept. 22, 1942 in Glasgow), Ollie Halsall (guitars, keyboards, born in Southport, Lancashire on March 14, 1949), Clive Griffiths (bass, born May 16, 1945) and John Halsey (drums, born Feb. 3, 1945).

With Muff Winwood producing, Patto cut two albums for Vertigo (*Patto*, 1970, *Hold Your Fire*, 1971) and one for Island (*Roll 'Em, Smoke 'Em, Put Out A Line*, 1972). All featured Halsall's aggressive guitar work and Patto's vocals on hard-edged jazz-influenced songs.

The group split at the end of 1972, with Mike Patto joining Spooky Tooth and Halsall playing with Jon Hiseman's Tempest and later Kevin Ayers as well as establishing himself as a leading session musician. In late 1975, he was reunited with Mike Patto in Boxer, with Tony Newman (drums) and Keith Ellis (bass); their first album was *Below The Belt* (Virgin, 1976).

Billy Paul was born on Dec. 1, 1934 in Philadelphia. He had an early grounding in jazz, through his mother's record collection. He attended Temple University, West Philadelphia Music School and Granoff Music School, amassing an impressive set of qualifications before beginning his recording career as a slick jazz singer on Jubilee.

Paul met writer/producer Kenny Gamble at Philadelphia's Cadillac Club, where they recorded an album. Following Gamble to his Neptune and Philadelphia International labels, he retained his jazz styling but aimed for the pop/soul market. Late 1972 brought him a chart-topping million-seller, 'Me And Mrs Jones', a smoochy but vibrant ballad with 'love-triangle' implications which also reached the British Top Twenty. He continues to record for Philadelphia International in his smooth, jazzy style.

Freda Payne spent many years performing big band jazz standards and slinky bossa novas on the night club circuit, recording in this vein for ABC and MGM. Then, in 1969, she joined ex-Tamla writing team Holland-Dozier-Holland on the Invictus label and reached younger audiences with several bright dancing hits, including 'Band Of Gold', 'Deeper And Deeper' (1970), and 'Bring The Boys Home' (1971). Later releases were less popular, and she re-signed with ABC in 1974.

Ann Peebles, best known for her 1973 hit 'I Can't Stand The Rain', has been one of the finest exponents of Willie Mitchell's Memphis soul sound since joining Hi in 1969. Born in St Louis on April 27, 1947, she debuted on Hi the same month as Al Green with 'Walk Away', the first of many raunchy R&B hits, including oldies – 'Part Time Love', 'I Pity The Fool' (1970–71) – and new songs – 'Somebody's On Your Case', 'Gonna Tear Your Playhouse Down' (1972–73). Releases since 'Rain' have been equally impressive (particularly 'You Keep Me Hanging On') but their formula-bound similarity has inhibited sales. She is married to singer Don Bryant.

Pentangle was a successful British amplified folk group founded in 1967 by Bert Jansch and John Renbourn. Both were already established as virtuoso solo guitarists and the previous year had made an album together for Transatlantic (*Bert and John*). With folk singer Jacqui McShee and jazzmen Denny Thompson (bass) and Terry Cox (drums) they worked up a repertoire of traditional songs, jazz instrumentals, blues and occasional contemporary songs.

Signing with Transatlantic, Pentangle cut five albums between 1968 and 1971. For the most part, Jansch and Renbourn played acoustic guitars into microphones, though a muted electric guitar was introduced on *Cruel Sister* (1970). McShee's soprano voice dominated the singing, sometimes in combination with Jansch's less polished voice.

Frequent tours, at home and abroad, were organized by their manager, Jo Lustig, who signed them to Reprise for *Solomon's Seal* (1972). That proved to be their last record, with Jansch, Renbourn and McShee going into semi-retirement for two years. Thompson formed a successful touring partnership with *avant-garde* guitarist John Martyn. Pentangle's recorded work was uniformly immaculate but often without the fire of Jansch and Renbourn's solo albums, which they continued to record throughout the life of the group.

Lee Perry – also known as Scratch and Upsetter – was born in 1940 in Jamaica, and won international recognition in the late Sixties with a series of rhythmic reggae instrumentals: 'Clint Eastwood', 'Return Of Django' – British Top Five, 1969 – and 'Live Injection', all produced in conjunction with studio musicians, the Upsetters.

An apprenticeship in the Fifties with Coxon Dodd's legendary Downbeat Sound System led Scratch to Studio One where he produced artists Delroy Wilson ('Joe Liges'), Shenley Dufus ('Rukumbine') and himself ('Trials And Crosses'). He left Dodd in 1968, following the inevitable disagreements. He worked alongside producers Joel Gibson and Clancy Eccles, briefly, until the Seventies when he was responsible for the classic Wailers' sides ('Small Axe', 'Duppy Conqueror'), Junior Byles ('Beat Down Babylon', 'Curley Locks'), I Roy, U Roy and many others, as well as recording under his own name ('Station Underground News', etc.). Scratch still lives in Jamaica where he is a revered legend.

The Persuasions – Joseph Russell (born Sept. 25, 1939 in Henderson, North Carolina), Jerry Lawson (born Jan. 23, 1944 in Fort Lauderdale, Florida), Jayotis Washington (born May 12, 1941 in Detroit), Herbert Rhoad (born Oct. 1, 1944 in Bamberg, South Carolina) and Jimmy Hayes (born Nov. 12, 1943 in Hopewell, Virginia) – were formed in New York in 1968. After an inauspicious recording debut on Minit, in 1969, the group adopted an *acappella* singing style (harmony voices without instrumental backing), and Frank Zappa issued their debut album on his Straight label. Further *acappella* albums followed when they signed with Capitol, to be greeted with interest and curiosity but little commercial acceptance. They joined MCA in 1973 for one album, moving to A&M in 1974 with Willie C. Daniels replacing Washington, but their new label put a band behind them in an attempt to gain commercial success.

Mike Pinera was one of America's most popular guitarists in the early Seventies. His forte was the 'overkill' style developed from psychedelic music through boogie and heavy metal, in much the same fashion as Ted Nugent of the Amboy Dukes. He first appeared with Blues Image, a Florida group whose 'Ride, Captain Ride' (Atco) was a Top Ten hit in 1970. From there he joined Iron Butterfly, playing on their later albums, then moved on to Cactus, who remain one of the perennial midwest touring boogie bands. In 1974, Pinera competed against Nugent in the 'Guitar Battle of the Century'. Nobody seems to recall who won.

Poco were formed after the demise of Buffalo Springfield in 1969 when Richie Furay (guitar, vocals, born May 9, 1944) and Jim Messina (guitar, vocals, born Dec. 5, 1947) joined up with Rusty Young (pedal steel, vocals, Feb. 23, 1946), George Grantham (drums, Jan. 20, 1947) and Randy Meisner (bass). Messina left and was replaced by Paul Cotton (May 9, 1944) from the Illinois Speed Press by which time the band had found a regular bass player in Timmy Schmit (Oct. 30, 1947) who replaced Randy Meisner when he left to join Rick Nelson's Stone Canyon Band.

This line-up reached a highpoint with Poco's fifth album *A Good Feelin' To Know* (Epic, 1973) but after *Crazy Eyes* (1973) the group's leader Richie Furay quit to join forces with Chris Hillman and J. D. Souther.

They signed with ABC in 1975, and *Head Over Heels* was their biggest album success for some time.

The Pointer Sisters are Ruth, Anita, Bonnie and June Pointer born in Oakland, California's black ghetto in 1946, 1948, 1950 and 1954 respectively. They became a camp *succès d'estime* after years of failure (including back-up work and two Atlantic singles in 1972) when they replaced a cancelled act at LA's Troubadour Club in May, 1973, causing an overnight sensation.

Guided by manager David Rubinson, their exuberant nostalgic mix of jazz, gospel and R&B harmonies, owing much to Lambert, Hendricks and Ross and performed in exotic Forties costumes, catapulted them from rags to riches with TV work, tours, a hit single, two gold albums (produced by Rubinson on Blue Thumb) and finally in 1974 a Grammy Award for Best Country Single with their self-penned 'Fairy Tale'. With a broadening appeal they have moved into the lucrative Las Vegas cabaret circuit.

Polydor Records. In 1961 Deutsche Grammophon Gesellschaft, the company formed by Joseph and Emil Berliner, who invented the flat disc in 1897, formed Polydor Records to complement its Deutsche Grammophon label. In 1965 Polydor opened a manufacturing plant in Britain – all previous records, such as Tony Sheridan's (and the Beatles') 'My Bonnie', a minor hit in 1963, being imported from Germany. Soon after, the company signed production and distribution deals with Robert Stigwood (which resulted in the short-lived Creation and Reaction labels, a string of British hits from the Bee Gees and Cream, and finally RSO Records), Kit Lambert and Chris Stamp (Track Records and hits for the Who, Jimi Hendrix and Thunderclap Newman) and Giorgio Gomelsky (the short-lived Marmalade label) and licensed Atlantic and Stax in Britain.

Although Polydor soon established itself in Britain, it wasn't until much later that it formed its own A&R department and began signing groups such as Slade (1971) and the New Seekers (1971). An American label was formed in 1967 which also pursued a policy of licensing other labels and buying other record companies (MGM-Verve in 1972).

One of the few major record companies to have little or no image, despite its involvement in British and American rock – it licenses or distributes Capricorn, Jonathan King's UK Records, Phil Spector International and Kudu/CTI amongst others – its biggest success in the Seventies is James Last whose succession of MOR albums have sold in even vaster quantities than records by Slade and the Osmonds.

Billy Preston, a child protégé turned superstar's sideman, was already an experienced veteran by the time mass audiences bought 'That's The Way God Planned It' (Apple, 1969). Born in Houston, Texas, Sept. 9, 1946, he was raised in Los Angeles where he first played organ behind gospel queen, Mahalia Jackson, before making a cameo appearance in the film *St Louis Blues* at the age of ten. Through the early Sixties, he toured with Little Richard and Sam Cooke while recording organ instrumentals for Contract Derby and Vee Jay. Later recordings, on Capitol, regular appearances on the American TV show *Shindig*, and tours with Ray Charles brought him to the attention of the Beatles whom he accompanied on 'Get Back' and 'Let It Be' while recording in his own right for their Apple label. Singles like 'I Wrote A Simple Song', the Top Ten 'Outta Space', 'Will It Go Round In Circles' (1972) and several versatile albums (including *Music Is My Life* and *Everybody Likes Some Kind Of Music* on A&M) continued to display his diverse talent, but it was still as an accompanist that he received most attention, notably on recordings by Sly Stone and as special guest on the 1975 Rolling Stones tour of America.

Alan Price was born on April 19, 1942 in Jarrow, England. He founded and led Newcastle's Alan Price Combo, which became the Animals en route for London and success early in 1964. Price employed a driving organ technique to good effect as a foil to Eric Burdon's vocals. He left the group in May 1965 and did not re-emerge until almost a year later with his own Alan Price Set, whose line-up included John Walters (trumpet, flugelhorn), Clive Burrows (baritone), Steve Gregory (tenor), Boots Slade (bass), and Roy Hills (drums). His first single, 'I Put A Spell On You' (Decca, 1966), led to a string of hits, which introduced the British public to the songs of Randy Newman, notably 'Simon Smith And His Amazing Dancing Bear'.

Following a number of popular 'guest' appearances on television with Georgie Fame, the pair had their own series in 1970, later extending their partnership into cabaret and recording, though without ever taxing their abilities. In 1973 he wrote several songs for the soundtrack of Lindsay Anderson's *O Lucky Man* and his bit part as a musician in the same film earned him a starring role in *Alfie Darling* (1975).

His 1974 album *Between Today And Yesterday* (Warner Bros) and the Top Ten single taken from it – 'Jarrow Song' – found him in fruitful contact with his Tyneside roots. The following album – *Metropolitan Man* (Polydor, 1975) – was disappointing by comparison.

Charley Pride has become, in the last decade, a country music institution. The ex-construction and refinery worker, Army veteran and pro-baseball player from Sledge, Mississippi, where he was born in 1938, signed with RCA in 1966 and recorded as a ballad singer some forty successful albums in the wake of singles like 'All I Have To Offer You Is Me' and 'Kiss An Angel Good Mornin'' which also entered the pop charts. Pride's voice is average and not very expressive. He is also the first and (so far) only black country music superstar.

John Prine, born in Maywood, Illinois, was misleadingly hailed as a 'new Dylan' when his first Atlantic album appeared in 1971. With his close friend Steve Goodman, he was a graduate of the Chicago folk scene, and the enthusiasm of Paul Anka was instrumental in his recording debut. Cut in Memphis, the first album (produced by Arif Mardin) caused a stir through songs like 'Sam Stone' – a post-Vietnam piece – and 'Illegal Smile'.

Prine's drawling delivery and tight-lipped lyrics led to the inevitable Dylan comparisons, but his later albums – *Diamonds In The Rough* (1972) and *Sweet Revenge* (1973), which revealed a significant debt to country music – had little commercial success. Other performers, however, had begun to record his songs, notably 'Paradise' (Everly Brothers) and 'Hello In There' (Bette Midler and Joan Baez).

Pub Rock, the convenient term used to describe a phenomenon of the early Seventies in Britain, is a dangerous one. It implies that all the bands tagged with it have something more in common than that they have all played in pubs, and it ignores the fact that music has always been an integral part of pub life. Before 1972, pub music was usually a solo pianist, a desultory trio, or a jazz band (jazz of all kinds and standards). Then, the American country-rock band, Eggs Over Easy, managed to get a booking at the Tally-Ho, in Kentish Town, one of the foremost jazz pubs. This paved the way for Bees Make Honey (whose leader, Barry Richardson, was known to the pub for his trad-jazz past), and the seal of approval came when Brinsley Schwarz played there. The Brinsleys, while never gaining the recognition they deserved, were fostering a move away from introspective 'head' music back to simpler roots, influenced by rock'n'roll, country and R&B. If 'pub rock' had a typical sound, it was this; music best designed for jigging about, pint of beer in hand.

With the decrease in the number of small clubs (ironically, often in pub back rooms) it was becoming impossible for up-and-coming bands to gain exposure. Gradually, as more bars moved from jazz to rock (notably The Kensington) and breweries, or their managers, realized that a rock band would boost sales, a loose circuit of small venues arose. After the pioneers, four generations of bands passed through the pub circuit. The first (1972–73) included Ducks Deluxe, Clancy, Ace, Kilburn And The High Roads, Phoenix and Chilli Willi And The Red Hot Peppers; the second (1973–74) Kokomo and Dr Feelgood; the third (1974–75) FBI and the Kursaal Flyers; the fourth (1975–76) Moon and Roogalator. On some nights, a dozen A&R men, record executives and agents would be sniffing out new talent in the same tiny bar. While pub rock has undoubtedly helped to reinject 'good-time' values back into a rock mainstream in danger of becoming overloaded with 'significance' it's sadly ironic to note that many of the bands mentioned above have broken up, though a few (notably Dr Feelgood, Kokomo and Kursaal Flyers) gained a wider audience. It seems likely that the pubs will continue as a training-ground for new talent.

Suzi Quatro was born on June 3, 1950 in Detroit of a musical family and made her debut, at eight, playing bongos with her father's jazz band, the Art Quatro Band and, at fourteen, she was TV go-go dancer Suzi Soul. At fifteen, she formed an all-girl group, Suzi Soul and the Pleasure Seekers, with her sisters Patti and Nancy; they played in mini skirts from Las Vegas to Vietnam. In late 1970 Mickie Most, in Detroit recording Jeff Beck at Motown, heard her and brought her to Britain, where she toured, third on the bill, and released singles that got nowhere. In early 1973, she was teamed with songwriters/producers Chinn and Chapman who wrote and produced 'Can The Can', a British chart topper on RAK. With a new image encasing her five-foot figure in a leather jump suit, the idea of her playing bass guitar in a band of large bruisers – Len Tuckey (guitar), Alistair Mackenzie (keyboards), Dave Neal (drums) – made her an instant success. '48 Crash' and 'Daytona Demon' (1973) and 'Devil Gate Drive' (1974) consolidated that success which went unchallenged until late 1974, when she had two flops in a row. She spent the first six months of 1975 in America, gaining wide recognition via an Alice Cooper tour.

Queen were perhaps the most significant new British band of the mid-Seventies, capturing (as Roxy Music had done before them) a wide-ranging audience including both Top Twenty fans and progressive rock enthusiasts. It was formed in 1972 by two former members of Smile – Brian May (guitar) and Roger Taylor (drums), with Freddie Mercury (vocals) and John Deacon (bass).

The band signed to EMI and released *Queen* (1973). Despite critical approval and heavy publicity, the band did not achieve success until 'Seven Seas Of Rhye', their second single, reached the Top Twenty. Mercury's ingeniously allusive lyrics and Roy Baker's immaculate production ensured the success of the subsequent album, *Queen II*. By the time of *Sheer Heart Attack* (1974), earlier doubts that Queen were simply an androgynous glam-rock spin-off were dispelled, and 'Bohemian Rhapsody' from the fourth album – *A Night At The Opera* (1975) – proved to be one of the most adventurous singles of the year. It also achieved the rare distinction of a million sales in Britain.

Bonnie Raitt, a white blues and soul singer/guitarist who was born in Burbank, California in 1950, began playing as a duo with ever-present bassist, Freebo, on leaving Radcliffe College in 1969, when she recorded her first album *Bonnie Raitt* for Warner Bros. Rougher than her later work, it mixed blues, soul, dixieland and contemporary ballads, including her own compositions. The looser *Give It Up* was recorded in 1972 with Woodstock musicians including Eric Kaz, whose 'Love Has No Pride' is the highlight of the album, and typical of her heartrending approach. Established as a local Boston star with feminist leanings, she appeared at the Ann Arbor Jazz Festival in 1972 with blues singer Sippie Wallace, and played club and college dates alongside bluesmen Otis Rush, Sun House, and Fred McDowell. With Lowell George she produced a classic album, *Taking My Time*, in Hollywood in 1973, featuring songs by Randy Newman, Eric Kaz, Mose Allison and Fred McDowell. Adding keyboards, drums, and another guitar she toured in 1974 and recorded the disappointing *Streetlights* with producer Jerry Ragavoy, but returned to form with *Home Plate* (1975).

Rare Earth, a vocal and instrumental unit from Detroit previously known as the Sunliners, comprised Gil Bridges (sax, flute and vocals), Pete Rivera (drums, vocals), John Parrish (bass, trombone, vocals), Rod Richards (guitar, vocals) and Kenny James (keyboards). Signed to launch the Motown Corporation's Rare Earth label in 1969 they marked the company's entry into the 'heavy rock' field. Though their musical style was a departure from the Motown norm, their initial material wasn't; and it was a revival of the Temptations' 'Get Ready' and '(I Know) I'm Losing You' that brought them Top Ten hits in 1970. More original material was used subsequently, such as 'I Just Want To Celebrate', as the group developed an identity under Norman Whitfield's close supervision. In 1970 Ray Monette replaced Richards, and in 1971 Rivera, Parrish and James were replaced by Pete Hoorelbeke, Mike Urso and Ed Cuzman.

The Raspberries were the focal point of the Ohio music scene in the early Seventies and the inspiration for dozens of other groups in a very active regional scene. As a band incorporating a mid-Sixties style and approach into a distillation of Seventies pop consciousness, they were the embodiment of the basic process of musical rejuvenation that was the most significant formative trend of their era.

Formed in 1971, the Raspberries were Eric Carmen (vocals, piano, bass, born Aug. 11, 1949), Wally Bryson (guitar, born July 18, 1949), Jim Bonfanti (drums, Dec. 17, 1948) and Dave Smalley (guitar, July 10, 1949). They came from a series of groups including Cyrus Erie, the Choir, the Quick, and the Mods that collectively represented the cream of Cleveland's pop scene, which has always stood out from the rest of America as being strongly influenced by the best in British rock. From 1965 on, the various Raspberries had been local idols, adapting little-known records of the Who, Small Faces, Kinks, Move and their other heroes, among them the Beatles, Lesley Gore and the Beach Boys. 'It's Cold Outside' by the Choir was a regional hit in 1967, and remains the best American treatment of the British mid-Sixties sound.

In the Raspberries, these influences all came together in a fresh, dynamic new synthesis. Produced by Jimmy Ienner, their first album came out on Capitol and their second single, 'Go All The Way', entered the Top Ten in September, 1972, becoming one of the year's biggest sellers. On top of influences ranging from the Beatles to Free, Carmen contributed a style of his own, a lush pop romanticism, singing in pure, rich harmony of idealized adolescent love, a theme he reworked through many subsequent songs. The hard rock backing offset the material's latent schmaltz, and created an appealing, truly ingenuous sound.

The Raspberries' peak was during 1973–75, during which they released three brilliant albums (*Fresh*, *Side 3* and *Starting Over*) and had several more hits ('I Wanna Be With You', 'Let's Pretend', 'Tonight', 'I'm A Rocker' and 'Overnight Sensation'). With each new release they became more adept at blending their influences (crashing Who chords, soaring Beach Boy harmonies, violent Keith Moon drumming, powerful Paul Rodgers/Paul McCartney screams) into an overall sound as original and enduring as those they strove to emulate.

As they got better, however, it seemed they became less popular. It wasn't until their final album, *Starting Over* (1975) that critics began raving. But within months the group broke up. Carmen's first solo album for Arista maintained the Raspberries' sound and included a 1976 Top Twenty hit, 'All By Myself'.

Redbone are Lolly Vegas (lead guitar, vocals), Tony Bellamy (rhythm guitar, vocals), Pat Vegas (bass guitar), Peter DePoe (drums). An American Indian band from a Cheyenne reservation in Washington State, formed in 1968, Redbone is an anglicized form of 'rehbone', a cajun epithet for half-breed – they spent their early years travelling between migrant camps, picking crops, backing people like Odetta and John Lee Hooker. Initial success came when the Vegas brothers penned 'Niki Hokey', a hit for P. J. Proby and then Bobbie Gentry. Recording success came to the group in 1970 with the worldwide hit 'Witch Queen From

New Orleans' (Epic). Since then their hybrid 'swamp rock' has mutated into a smooth Las Vegas-oriented sound. Their biggest hit to date has been the 1975 million-seller, 'Come And Get Your Love'.

Helen Reddy, born in Melbourne, Australia on Oct. 25, 1942, topped the American charts in 1972 with her own composition 'I Am Woman' which quickly became associated with the American women's liberation movement. She arrived in America in 1966 as a little-known Australian performer, but her career didn't pick up until her manager (and husband) signed her to Capitol Records in the early Seventies. 'I Don't Know How To Love Him' from *Jesus Christ Superstar* gave her a Top Twenty record in 1971 and then came 'I Am Woman' which inaugurated a series of Top Ten hits: 'Delta Dawn' (1973), 'Keep On Singing', 'You And Me Against The World' and another No. 1, 'Angie Baby' (1974), also a British hit in 1975, 'Emotion' and 'Ain't No Way To Treat A Lady' (1975). Even more impressive than the number of her hits though, are their careful production, the range of material – which goes from the chilling 'Angie Baby' to the cheerful 'Keep On Singing' – and her powerful evocative voice.

Lou Reed, born on Long Island, New York on March 2, 1943, into an affluent middle-class family, led his first punk-rock bands (Pasha and the Prophets, LA and the Eldorados) while at high school. He attended Syracuse University but dropped out and dabbled in courses in journalism and acting. Reed finally integrated these talents into the Velvet Underground.

After writing all the group's material, Reed quit in the summer of 1970. His first solo album, *Lou Reed* (RCA, 1972), contained some strong songs but was weakened by the inept production work of Reed and Richard Robinson. His next album, *Transformer* (1973), lived up to its title: produced by David Bowie and Mick Ronson, just when Bowie was most in the media spotlight, the association gave Reed the publicity he needed, while Ronson's string arrangement made 'Walk On The Wild Side' (an account of Warhol's Factory clan of freaks) into a classic single and a surprise hit: after eight years in the music business, it became Lou Reed's first Top Ten single in 1973.

Berlin (1973), though not as commercially successful as *Transformer*, contained Reed's most compelling and disturbing work since the Velvet Underground: a cycle of songs about a sado-masochistic relationship which culminates in the woman committing suicide and the man wondering where his feelings went. Supported by an all-star cast of musicians, and Bob Ezrin's subtle production, Reed contributed some of the best vocals of his career and songs which were both understated and paralysingly bleak. His live album, *Rock'N'Roll Animal* (1974), combined Velvet Underground with ornate Allman-Brothers-style guitar work, an unexpected but pleasant achievement. By contrast, his double album of electronic music, *Metal Machine Music* (1975), was widely regarded as the worst album ever made by a major recording artist, and understandable only as an act of artistic suicide.

Reggae grew out of rock-steady; which grew out of ska; which, in turn, had roots in secular African/Caribbean musical traditions (*calypso*, *mento*), sacred revivalism and American – particularly New Orleans – R&B. At the same time the emergence of black pride was intrinsic to the music's subsequent development. Ska had been easily absorbed, even touted as a tourist attraction by the Jamaican establishment; rock-steady withheld, the property of the aristocratic rudie; reggae declared its autonomy and became the music of struggle. One reason for this was the hitherto dormant rastafarianism – a general term describing divergent, back-to-Africa cults, peculiar to Jamaica, of a millenarian nature.

The rastafarians saw Ethiopia as Zion and Haile Selassie (Ras Tafari) as the 'Living God'. But even whilst espousing rasta (rastafarianism) in songs like the Ethiopians' 'The Selah', the Charmers' 'Rasta Never Fails' and Prince Jazzbo's 'Step Forward Youth', reggae retained its own particular dynamism.

By the Seventies, the 'blues' had diversified; encompassing rebel music from Junior Byles ('Beat Down Babylon'), Max Romeo, the Wailers; fervid, melodic piety from the Melodians ('Rivers Of Babylon') and Maytals; pop-reggae from the Pioneers and Greyhound; sentimental vocalists John Holt, Pat Kelly, the late Slim Smith; *sufferers* Errol Dunkley, Delroy Wilson, Dennis Brown, etc.

Producers were essential to the Jamaican music industry. Men like Duke Reid and Coxon Dodd pioneered ska and the producers who monopolized Seventies reggae – Niney, Lee Perry, Bunnie Lee, Lloyd Clarke, Rupie Edwards (who had a British hit 'Ire Feelings' in 1975) and Clement Bushay, were as relevant as the artists they engineered. Dramatic vocals and instrumentation embellished clean, hard rhythms, emphasizing reggae's inherent *dread* quality.

In this spirit, the talk-over, originated by Sound Systems DJs, was effected. Talk-over was eulogy – brotherhood, love, or merely self-advertisement – to a *skank* rhythm. Popularized by U Roy around 1970 with a string of hits (including 'Rule The Nation', 'Scandal'), the trend peaked during 1972–73 with, among others, Dennis Alcapone, I Roy and Scotty consistently scoring. Big Youth (Augustus Buchanan) usurped U Roy with successful singles ('Ace 90', 'Foreman v Frazier') and albums (*Chi Chi Run*, *Dread Locks Dread*). Prince Jazzbo, Jah Woosh, Topper Zukie, Jah Lloyd and Jah Ali were later exponents of the genre.

The talk-over engendered 'dub': backing tracks reduced to bass and drums, punctuated with the occasional, arbitrary vocal or guitar riff to make things interesting. Feedback extravaganzas, dubs were ideal DJ fodder and in vogue in 1975 with albums from Keith Hudson and Aston Barrett (*Pick A Dub*) and Rupie Edwards' *Dub Basket* amongst others. Augustus Pablo, who laid wistful melodic passages over throbbing dub ('Tales Of Pablo') was particularly popular. 1974–75 also brought a new breed of rasta 'prophet': Johnnie Clarke ('Move Out A Babylon'), Cornell Campbell ('Gorgon'), Sang Hugh ('No Potion A Gal') and, most auspiciously, Burning Spear (Winston Rodney) who led a trio of the same name and sang, with acute conviction, songs endemic to the Jamaican experience: 'Zion Higher', 'Marcus Garvey' and the extremely moving 'Slavery Days'.

In Britain, the Sound Systems of Duke Reid, Sir Coxsone, Count Shelley in London, and Duke Neville in Birmingham, provided the West Indians with their only escape, the church apart, from a hostile white society. Its popularity in the black clubs often ensured the music's subsequent British release. The metamorphosis of rock-steady into reggae had alienated the music's small white audience – the skinheads. As reggae preoccupations moved from the speedy and aggressive to the stoned and peaceful, they drifted away. The skinheads' brief patronage had been responsible for reggae's early appearances in the British charts, including Dave and Ansell Collins' 'Double Barrel' – No. 1 in 1970 – and 'Monkey Spanner'; Horace Faith's 'Black Pearl'; Harry J's 'Liquidator' and the Pioneers' 'Let Your Yeah Be Yeah'.

Following the demise of ska labels like Bluebeat, Rio and R&B, and with Island wooing the rock market, Trojan Records led the market in the late Sixties. The label's commercial middle-of-the-road music appealed to pop tastes and the company established itself as the largest reggae outlet in Britain. Rivals included Pama, who hit with Max Romeo's 'Wet Dream' in 1969 (despite a BBC ban) and Creole. By 1975, dozens had surfaced, each situated in concentrated immigrant areas. Count Shelley, Lord Koos – both owned by British resident Sound System operators – Atra, Magnet, Ethnic and Dip were among those that established themselves. Attempts by the major companies to corner this market, EMI's subsidiary Rhino, for instance, made little impact on the reggae scene despite their occasional hit records.

Duke Reid was one of the pioneers of the Jamaican music ska. A Sound System operator, he began producing home-grown product when the supplies of R&B music from America began to run dry. His earliest productions were for Derrick Harriott's Jiving Juniors ('My Heart's Desire'), Laurel Aitken ('Judgement Day') and Stranger Cole ('Cow In A Pasture'). He continued to dominate the scene throughout the Sixties, and even with the advent of reggae was still to the forefront with productions like U Roy's 'Rule The Nation'. However, by the mid-Seventies he had been somewhat outstripped by younger men like Bunnie Lee and Niney, and consequently faded.

Terry Reid was born in Huntingdonshire, England on Nov. 13, 1949. At 15, he joined Peter Jay and the Jaywalkers as their soulful lead singer, then leaving to form his own trio. His first album, *Bang Bang, You're Terry Reid* (Epic, 1968), was produced by Mickie Most and featured his hard-edged vocals and aggressive guitar work. *Terry Reid* (1969) included outstanding versions of 'Highway 61 Revisited' and Jerry Ragavoy's 'Stay With Me Baby'.

Settling in America, Reid's live appearances were intermittent and his third album did not appear until 1973. *River* (Atlantic) was disappointing, inconclusive and meandering after the incisiveness of the Most productions.

Charlie Rich is *the* country-pop superstar of the early Seventies. Yet he became so with a style not markedly different from that he had evolved over the previous decades.

Born Dec. 14, 1932 in Colt, Arkansas, Rich grew up with an equal access to classical, blues and country music influences. By the time he was drafted into the Air Force he was playing jazz saxophone and piano and had married a jazz singer. By 1957 he was a staff composer, demo singer and arranger for the rock'n'roll and country stars of the Sun label in Memphis; and his early songs like 'Breakup' and 'It Hurt Me So' were recorded by Jerry Lee Lewis, and 'The Ways Of A Woman In Love' and 'Thanks A Lot' by Johnny Cash.

In 1960, Elvis Presley recorded Rich's 'I'm Comin' Home' and Rich reached the Top Thirty with 'Lonely Weekends'. By now a singer/pianist, he began to alternate between soul-blues and country music. Leaving Sun and Phillips International, he moved to Groove/RCA to work with producers Bill Justis and Chet Atkins and to move towards country. In the mid-Sixties he moved to Smash and recorded R&B for Shelby Singleton, coming up with a Top Twenty hit

'Mohair Sam' in 1965. After a year with Hi Records in 1967, Rich settled for Billy Sherrill's Epic label country sound and he expanded his country – and cult – following with a huge hit in 1973 with 'Behind Closed Doors'. Other hits – 'The Most Beautiful Girl In The World', 'There Won't Be Anymore' and 'A Very Special Love Song' – followed throughout the world.

The Sherrill sound was saccharin enough to move Rich into the international middle-of-the-road market, and perhaps to widen the appeal of music based heavily in country and blues, elements which Rich retains strongly in his own voice and piano style, for example the marvellous 'Feel Like Goin' Home'.

Joshua Rifkin is a pianist and arranger who played a central role in the recent revival of 'classical' ragtime music. An earlier association with Jac Holzman of the Elektra label produced *The Baroque Beatles Book*, a novelty selection of Lennon–McCartney tunes played on the harpsichord in baroque style. Rifkin made a more significant contribution to rock through his string arrangements for Judy Collins' *In My Life* album, which brought strings to 'folk/rock' music for the first time.

Minnie Riperton has, reputedly, the largest vocal range in rock – her voice spans five octaves. Born in Chicago, her first records were with the Gems, a Chess Records session vocal group. In 1966 she cut some unsuccessful solo records as Andrea Davis before joining Rotary Connection, a racially mixed progressive group created by Chess.

From 1968, Riperton sang on six Rotary Connection albums. When the group dissolved, she cut a solo record (*Come Into My Garden*) produced by her husband Richard Rudolph. Next she moved to Epic where 'El Toro Negro' (alias Stevie Wonder) produced a well-received album, *Perfect Angel* (1974), which included the transatlantic hit 'Lovin' You'. *Adventures In Paradise* (1975) was less interesting, with Minnie Riperton's voice more decorative than soulful.

Johnny Rivers was born John Ramistella on Nov. 7, 1942 in New York. At the age of three he moved to Baton Rouge, Louisiana. In the late Fifties Alan Freed changed his name to Rivers and secured him his first record contract with Gone. His big break came when he discovered a successful format of live performance at the Whisky A Go Go in Los Angeles, which could be easily transferred to record. Since 1963 Rivers sold over twenty million records, and had more than twenty chart entries, notably 'Memphis', 'Mountain Of Love' (1964), 'Seventh Son' (1965), 'Secret Agent Man' and the No. 1 'Poor Side Of Town' (1966), 'Baby I Need Your Lovin'' and 'Tracks Of My Tears' (1967), all of which were Top Ten Records on Imperial.

At the end of the Sixties, Rivers formed his own label, Soul City, and the first signings to the label were the Fifth Dimension, who immediately won several gold records. The combination of the production of Johnny Rivers and Bones Howe, the harmonies of the Fifth Dimension, and the songs of the then little-known Jim Webb, became an almost unassailable force during the first few years of Soul City's existence, but when the group left the label, things became quiet enough for Rivers to return to serious record-making on his own account on UA. The hand-clapping disco format was abandoned, replaced by studio bands comprised of the best Hollywood session men, and several successful albums and singles, plus a still remembered European tour, resulted.

His most recent success has been in persuading Brian Wilson to return to the studios, even if only to add distinctive back-up vocals to Rivers' own version of the Beach Boys' classic, 'Help Me Rhonda'.

Andy Roberts is an underrated guitarist and songwriter whose own work has been overshadowed by his association with the various manifestations of poetry, comedy and rock in Britain. From Harrow, London, he joined the Liverpool Scene on its formation in 1967, accompanying the poetry of Adrian Henri and 'playing Spider John Koerner numbers'.

His solo career began with *Home Grown* (B&C, 1970), which included the fine 'Moths And Lizards In Detroit'. In

1972 he formed Plainsong with Ian Matthews. The band made one country-inflected album for Elektra before Matthews' departure caused it to fold. Roberts continued to record for Elektra (*The Great Stampede*, 1973) while playing in the Grimms live show, another mixture of music and humour for which he wrote the theme song, 'Clowns On The Road'.

Rock Movies. Perhaps it was the songs Simon and Garfunkel composed for *The Graduate* (1967) and the atmospheric use of music in *Easy Rider* (1969) that first alerted film producers to the fact that a rock score could enliven a film and maybe help to sell it too. At any rate, by the turn of the Seventies, no movie seemed complete without a trendy chart name in the composing credits. Nilsson did *Skidoo* (1969), Ray Davies did *Percy* (1971), Elton John did *Friends* (1971), and the fashion continues to this day. Curiously enough very few composers, with the notable exception of the Pink Floyd, ever get invited back to work on a second film.

However, a more enduring and more profitable marriage between rock music and the cinema came about with the advent of the concert documentary. *Festival* (1967), a film about Newport, was the progenitor of this but *Monterey Pop* (1970) was the first to succeed, and for the next three years it seemed that no self-respecting garden fête was without its squad of cameramen. The most famous of the cycle and the most accomplished technically was *Woodstock* (1970), decked out with every conceivable gimmick to make one act look different from the next. None the less *Monterey Pop* and *Gimme Shelter* (1971) were of much greater significance and indeed, in their respective ways, offered truer accounts of Rock festivals. By 1973 the market for concert films had been saturated and it was just as well that *Let the Good Times Roll*, an account of a revival concert that featured Haley and Chubby Checker, was the last entry in the field. Many other films of the period were disappointments. *Let It Be* (1970), a documentary about the Beatles at work and play, had to be thrown together for contractual purposes, and looked it. Frank Zappa's uncontrollable flight of fancy, *200 Motels* (1972), was an utter mess. And the film version of *Jesus Christ Superstar* (1973) consisted of a crowd of hippies jumping up and down in the desert *ad nauseam.* During the first half of the Seventies rock stars also seemed particularly reluctant to try their hands at dramatic art. After one or two films apiece Jagger and Dylan showed no interest in continuing; most didn't bother to start. Only one recruit made good, the lugubrious Kris Kristofferson, still in demand for mangy lover rôles (*Alice Doesn't Live Here Anymore*). During 1974–75 there was every indication of a revival of interest in the rock musical. Certainly, for better or worse, *That'll Be The Day* (1973), *Stardust* (1974) and *Flame* (1974) were among the most commercially successful films on the pop music business that Britain has produced. These were films that were as much about rock as they were films that used rock. However, in the mid-Seventies it was the latter category that produced the most interesting films, for example the first Jamaican feature film, *The Harder They Come*, the bizarre *Tommy* (1975), a commercial if not an aesthetic success, *American Graffiti* (1974) which was both, the assured *The Lords Of Flatbush* (1974) and *Nashville* (1975).

Johnny Rodriguez was born in Sabinal, Texas on Dec. 10, 1952. He grew up on honky-tonk Texas country music and rock'n'roll, becoming lead guitarist with Tom T. Hall before gaining his own Mercury contract. 'Pass Me By' (1972) and 'Ridin' My Thumb To Mexico' (1973) were instant country hits, revealing Rodriguez as a sweet but strong ballad singer in the Merle Haggard mould, sometimes emphasizing his Chicano identity by singing parts of songs in Spanish. *My Third Album* (1974) found him widening his musical horizon with versions of George Harrison's 'Something' and Richard Betts' 'Rambling Man'.

Mick Ronson. From Hull, Ronson's musical training began with violin at school (where he also learned to read music) and private piano lessons. Bored with the slowness of the other pupils he began playing his violin like a guitar, soon graduating to the real thing. In the mid-Sixties he formed a local band, the Rats, who recorded singles but didn't gain popular attention.

He left to record with Michael Chapman, meeting David Bowie soon after. He provided the major musical impetus for Bowie's albums *Man Who Sold The World* (1970) and *Hunky Dory* (1971) and was instrumental in forming the Spiders From Mars. Ronson's stinging guitar and spare arrangements attracted much acclaim and were viewed by many as the backbone to Bowie's success. After the demise of the Spiders and the recording of *Pin Ups* in 1973, he turned to a brief solo career. But without other forces and personalities to bounce off, his two solo albums were patchy and disappointing; his solo tours likewise. In mid-1974 he joined Mott the Hoople, leaving in December with Ian Hunter to perform and record as Hunter–Ronson, before touring with Bob Dylan's Rolling Thunder revue.

Linda Ronstadt was an acclaimed but unsuccessful country-rock singer until her potential was realized in 1974 with the Peter Asher-produced album, *Heart Like A Wheel* (Capitol – Asylum in Britain). Born in Tucson, Arizona on July 15, 1946, she started out as a folk singer in the Joan Baez vein, before joining the Stone Poneys in 1965.

A surprise Top Twenty hit came in 1967 with Mike Nesmith's 'Different Drum' (Capitol), but Ronstadt went solo soon after. A series of albums containing reworked versions of country and rock songs followed, foreshadowing the similar approach of other women singers by several years. They included *Hand Sown, Home Grown* (1969) and *Silk Purse* (1970).

Her career was hampered by problems in maintaining a stable line-up in her backing group and by unimaginative record production. In 1974 she signed to Asylum and the new confidence on *Don't Cry Now* produced by John Boylan heralded her later success with the chart-topping singles 'You're No Good' and 'When Will I Be Loved' from the *Wheel* album, her last for Capitol under the existing contract.

Her success continued with a Top Ten album (*Prisoner In Disguise*) and single 'Heat Wave' on the Asylum label.

Diana Ross, born March 26, 1944, grew up in Detroit's ghetto-area Brewster Housing Project and began singing at an early age with neighbourhood friends, Florence Ballord and Barbara Martin. They later formed the Supremes with Mary Wilson. In 1968, the group became Diana Ross and the Supremes, but, despite the phenomenal success of the group, in December, 1969 Diana, by now married to Motown boss Berry Gordy Jr., left to pursue a solo singing and acting career, and the following spring her solo debut 'Reach Out And Touch' was a Top Twenty hit. Autumn, 1970, saw Diana receive another gold disc when 'Ain't No Mountain High Enough' topped the American charts and reached the British Top Ten, while 1973 saw an early peak in her acting career when she was an Oscar nominee for her portrayal of the late Billie Holiday in *Lady Sings The Blues*, the Motown Corporation's first step into the film world. In 1975 she starred in the even glossier *Mahogany*, directed by Gordy, and the following year its theme song, 'Do You Know Where I'm Going To', took her to the top of the American pop – but significantly not R&B – charts.

Roxy Music is a Seventies concept that is the creation of Bryan Ferry (born Sept. 26, 1945). While an art student in Newcastle, Ferry had worked as a deejay and singer with soul band Gas Works before becoming a teacher and occasional artist. He realized the quickest, widest method to gain attention was a rock band, and after teaching himself piano in ten days began putting together Roxy Music. The name was picked from a list of old cinema names and the concept was to be one of elegance and glamour, with a hint of nostalgia rubbing against futuristic rock. The initial line-up was David O'List, from the Nice (guitar), Paul Thompson (drums, born May 13, 1951), Graham Simpson (bass guitar) and Andy Mackay (saxophone, oboe, July 23, 1946). Through Mackay, Eno (May 15, 1948) was employed as sound man, soon graduating to the stage, where he treated instruments, played synthesizer and co-ordinated effects tapes. Signed by Island Records, their first album *Roxy Music* was released in mid-1972 in a blaze of attention. Simpson had been replaced by Rik Kenton (born Oct. 31, 1945) who himself left a few months later to be replaced by a series of guest bassists that included ex-Big Three member John Gustafson. In September 'Virginia Plain' became a top British hit, followed by 'Pyjamarama'.

Meanwhile, the androgynous-looking Eno was attracting attention in his own right, an event not foreseen in the Ferry plan. On *For Your Pleasure* (1973), Phil Manzanera (Jan. 31, 1951) and his 'stun' guitar replaced O'List and subsequently Eddie Jobson (violin, keyboards) replaced Eno, who pursued a studiedly eclectic solo career, while Roxy Music became more streamlined, if predictable. Over the next two years Roxy Music and Bryan Ferry as a solo artist gained considerable attention throughout Britain and Europe, Ferry concentrating more on his solo career, appearing in an endless array of sophisticated, 'smoothie' stage costumes. In America, though, Roxy Music was more slowly accepted. Belated chart successes came in 1976 with their biggest British chart success, 'Love Is The Drug', from *Siren* (1975).

Rufus were originally a West Coast splinter group from Chicago-based popsters, American Breed. They started out as Ask Rufus before personnel changes resulted in a bi-racial soul band featuring the versatile lead vocal of Chaka Khan. Signed by ABC in 1973 they recorded a moderately successful debut album, *Rufus*, from which three singles were drawn, but the breakthrough came with their compelling treatment of a Stevie Wonder song 'Tell Me Something Good' from their second album, *Rags To Rufus*, the following year.

Further personnel changes left Chaka fronting Tony Maiden (guitar), Bobby Watson (bass), Kevin Murphy and Nate Morgan (keyboards), and André Fischer (drums) – the line-up which has gone on to the major league, bridging pop and soul markets with *Rufusized* (1974) and single hits 'Once You Get Started' and 'Please Pardon Me' (1975). Now billed as Rufus featuring Chaka Khan, further hits followed in 1976 starting with 'Sweet Thing'.

Todd Rundgren, master engineer-producer and prototype Seventies recording artist, was born in Pennsylvania on June 22, 1948. He was lead guitarist with various local groups, including Money and Woody's Truck Stop, before making his first albums with the Nazz. Three appeared on SGC between 1968 and 1970, showcasing a band clearly influenced by the British groups of the Sixties. The group had a small hit with 'Hello It's Me' in 1969, which Rundgren re-recorded in 1973 with even greater success.

In 1970, Rundgren changed direction to work as house engineer and producer for the Bearsville label. He was associated with albums by Paul Butterfield, Ian and Sylvia, Jesse Winchester, Badfinger and The Band. He also put together his own recording trio, Runt, with Tony Sales (bass) and Hunt Sales (drums). The result was *Runt* (Ampex, 1970) and *The Ballad Of Todd Rundgren* (1971). The former included a Top Twenty single 'We Gotta Get You A Woman'.

Dropping the Runt tag and working as a solo artist, Rundgren went on to make *Something/Anything,* a double album released in 1972 on the Bearsville label. The title was accurate: the record included neat pop songs like the hit single, 'I Saw The Light', but also self-indulgent pieces of electronic trickery and artless jams. Then came *A Wizard, A True Star* (1973), which he modestly described as 'the first stream-of-consciousness album'. As well as a medley of old soul songs, it included critical lyrics about politicians, rock revolutionaries and Top Forty androgyny.

Todd (1974) was a suitably egocentric title for what many consider to be Rundgren's best album. It again contained socially conscious songs ('Sons Of 1984', 'Number One Lowest Common Denominator') as well as a dazzling tour of various current rock styles. He continued to produce such artists as Grand Funk Railroad, Hall and Oates and Felix Cavaliere, as well as recording two further albums: *Utopia* (Warner Bros, 1974) with his regular road band, and *Initiation* (1975).

Doug Sahm, born in Texas on Nov. 6, 1941, started out playing country music. At the age of five he was a regular on a local radio show. He recorded for the Sarg label and, billed as Little Doug, toured with the big names in early-Fifties country music. He also recorded for Warrior (with The Pharaohs), Harlem (with the Markays), Personality (Doug Sahm and the Spirits) and Renner (as Doug Sahm). The variety of styles he has subsequently mastered is explained by the area in which he was brought up, San Antonio. He heard as much Texas blues as country music (his first band, The Knights, which he formed when he was 14, played blues music) and a Mexican influence is also found in the so-called 'Tex-Mex' music of the Sir Douglas Quintet. The Quintet lasted on and off until the early Seventies, and since then Sahm has occasionally returned to the studios as a solo artist. His *Doug Sahm and Band* (Atlantic, 1973) album features such guests as Bob Dylan, Dr John and David Newman; it is a relaxed and inspired studio jam covering Western Swing, country, blues, R&B and rock. In 1974 he formed his Tex-Mex Trip band with Doug Clifford and Stu Cook (both late of Creedence Clearwater Revival), Link Davis Jr. and Frank Rodarte. The music still ranges wide, but with more emphasis on Sahm's own brand of country-rock, and is well represented on *Groovers' Paradise* (Warner Bros, 1974).

Peter Sarstedt emerged from the shadow of his brother, Eden Kane, one of the minor figures of pre-Beatles British pop, in 1969 with his own composition, 'Where Do You Go My Lovely' which zoomed to No. 1 on UA. It and its follow-up, 'Frozen Orange Juice' (1969), were perfect distillations of middle-class *angst* that temporarily fitted the mood of the times. None of Sarstedt's other projects – which included the forming of a group with his brothers – came to anything, nor have his recent albums for Warner Bros (e.g. *Trees*, 1975) met with any success.

Leo Sayer, with David Essex, led a new breed of rock showmen in the mid-Seventies, combining flamboyant showbiz stage acts with critically accepted songs, and avoiding the camp connotations of Gary Glitter *et al.* Born in Shoreham, Sussex on May 24, 1948, Sayer briefly led a band named Patches, before teaming up as a songwriter with Dave Courtney.

Their work first appeared on Roger Daltrey's debut solo album, from which 'Giving It All Away' was a hit. Managed by Adam Faith, Sayer was signed to Chrysalis, reaching the Top Ten with his first single, 'The Show Must Go On'. He developed a striking stage act using mime and a harlequin outfit. Both *Silverbird* (1973) and *Just A Boy* (1974) entered the British album charts, while the latter also provided him with a transatlantic Top Ten single, 'Long Tall Glasses'. In 1975 Dave Courtney released a solo album, *First Day*, and Sayer, now writing with Frank Farrell, released the more assured *Another Year*, which included the Top Three single 'Moonlighting'.

Boz Scaggs was born on June 8, 1944. His style was developed in Dallas, Texas, and Madison, Wisconsin, where he was one of the singer/guitarists with the Ardells, whose members included Steve Miller and Ben Sidran. After a trip to Europe which produced a hastily made and obscure album, *Boz* (Polydor, 1966), Scaggs joined the Steve Miller Band in its San Francisco heyday, and many regard his time with Miller as having produced the band's most memorable work, *Children Of The Future* (1968) and *Sailor* (1968). After leaving Miller in 1968, Boz made an album at Muscle Shoals, Alabama, *Boz Scaggs* (Atlantic, 1968), produced by Jann Wenner, the editor of *Rolling Stone*, which contained some impressive guitar playing by the then little-known Duane Allman. From that date on, Scaggs has produced a new album every fifteen months, for a small but loyal following.

Gil Scott-Heron, one of the first performers to have integrated the political impetus behind the black struggles of the late Sixties and early Seventies into the mainstream of black music, was born in Chicago in 1950 and grew up in Jackson, Tennessee. He moved to New York and studied at Lincoln

University where he met his later collaborator, Brian Jackson (born in 1954). He published two novels, *The Vulture* (1969) and *The Nigger Factory*, and a collection of 'rap' verses, *Small Talk At 125th And Lennox*, before turning to music with Jackson. He recorded three albums for Bob Thiele's Flying Dutchman label, amongst which were *Pieces Of Man* – which included 'The Revolution Will Not Be Televised', recorded by Labelle – and *Free Will* (1973), before moving to the co-operative Strata/East label. There, with Jackson, he cut *Winter In America* (1974), which included the incisive 'H-20 Gate Blues' and 'The Bottle', a disco discourse on the problems of alcoholism in the black ghetto. They signed with Arista in 1975 and recorded *The First Minute Of A New Day* and *From South Africa To South Carolina* (which included the disco hit, 'Johannesburg'). Both albums sold well. Scott-Heron's music is characterized by the juxtaposition of his declamatory singing and Jackson's jazz-inspired arrangements.

Earl Scruggs was born in Flint Hill, North Carolina, in 1924 into a musical environment where an unusual, three-finger five-string banjo style was prevalent. Scruggs perfected this style and brought it to Bill Monroe's band in 1945, contributing much to the formative recorded statements of 'bluegrass' music. Later, with Lester Flatt, he contributed songs like 'Foggy Mountain Breakdown' to the legacy of bluegrass, and soundtracks to the *Beverly Hillbillies* and the movie *Bonnie And Clyde*. In the Seventies, he formed a widely different band, the Earl Scruggs Revue, electric and eclectic, playing folk, college and rock venues with artists like Arlo Guthrie, Bob Dylan, the Byrds, Linda Ronstadt and Joan Baez. His most recent records were for Columbia, including *Anniversary Special* (1975).

Troy Seals was born in Big Hill, Kentucky on Nov. 16, 1938. A guitarist, singer, writer and producer, he is one of the first in a long line of Southern artists who have been equally involved in both country and black music. Seals is married to Jo Ann Campbell. He toured with her as part of the Dick

Clark Revue in the late Fifties and early Sixties and recorded the powerful 'I Found A Love, Oh What A Love' (as Jo Ann and Troy, Atlantic, 1964), a Top Forty entry in the R&B charts in 1965. He next joined the Dapps, an eight-piece band whose members included Lisz Asch, David Parkinson, Ronald Geismar, Timothy Hedding, William Bowman, Eddie Setser and Tim Drummond (now with Neil Young). The band occasionally backed James Brown (in 1967–68) and recorded for King. His songs have been recorded by Lonnie Mack (with whom he's also recorded and produced), Percy Sledge (the magnificent 'Stop The World Tonight'), Dobie Gray and Mentor Williams (both of whom he's also produced), Sammi Smith ('Girl In New Orleans') and Kenny Price ('You Almost Slipped My Mind') among many others. His most recorded song is 'We Had It All', which he wrote with Donnie Fritts. Only intermittently a performer and recording artist in his own right, he recorded an uneven solo album for Atlantic, *Now Presenting Troy Seals* (1973), and is currently with Columbia.

Seals and Crofts, both born in Texas in 1940, were former members of the Champs, an instrumental group from the late Fifties (they had a major hit with 'Tequila' in 1958) who re-emerged in the Seventies as a successful singer-songwriter duo.

Dash Seals and Jimmy Crofts signed first to TA and then to Warner Bros and began recording a series of albums whose sound owed much to the recently disbanded Simon and Garfunkel, with lyrics often expressing the duo's newly found Bah'ai faith. Critics found them unenterprising and sanctimonious, but Seals and Crofts had clearly found a college audience as Top Ten hits like 'Summer Breeze' (1972) and 'Diamond Girl' (1973) demonstrated.

John Sebastian, born on March 17, 1944 in Greenwich Village, wrote some of the finest hit records of the day – 'Daydream', 'You Didn't Have To Be So Nice', 'Younger Girl', 'Do You Believe In Magic' – for the Lovin' Spoonful before the group broke up in 1968. During the era of the festivals he often stole the show with impromptu performances notably at Woodstock, and by the time he appeared at the Isle of Wight in 1970 he had coined the phrases 'Cheapo Cheapo' and 'Mr Tie-Dye'.

His first solo album, *John B. Sebastian* (Reprise, 1970), suffered a long gestation period because of contractual problems but it remains his best post-Spoonful album. John abandoned his life on the road as told on *The Four Of Us* (1971) to settle down in a Los Angeles suburb and work with a small backing combo. The people's champion appears to be sitting back awaiting middle age without much resistance.

Bob Seger is a high-energy white rocker, singer, composer and guitarist who was born in 1947. He has failed to achieve more than local success since his first band, Last Heard, formed in his native Detroit in 1964. Critical acclaim and local sales of around 50,000 greeted each of his singles, in particular the seminal 'Heavy Music' (Cameo-Parkway, 1966), the anti-war '2+2=?' (Capitol, 1967) and 'Ramblin' Gamblin' Man' (Capitol, 1968) but they barely dented the national charts. He retreated to college in 1969, returning for a year with local duo Teagarden and Van Winkle in 1970 before re-forming his own band for two Reprise albums, *Back In '72* and *Seven*, which saw the flowering of his songwriting – autobiography, ballad, and social commentary – as hard driving rock. In 1975, he returned to Capitol for the reflective *Beautiful Loser*, toured with Bachman Turner Overdrive and seemed on the verge of reaching the wider audience that had eluded him for so long.

Sha Na Na (Scott Powell, Johnny Contardo, Frederick Dennis Greene, Don York, Rich Jeffe, Elliot Cahn, Chris Donald, Bruce Clarke, Screamin' Scott Simon, John Banman, Lonnie Baker, Jacko Marcellino and Vinnie Taylor) had been performing in New York coffee bars for two years before a brief appearance in *Woodstock* (1970) brought them international recognition. Since then their act has changed little: astute, hilarious parodies not only of the music of the Fifties but also of the teenage aggression associated with the era. Publicizing themselves as hoodlums, the band (once nicknamed 'the Dirty Dozen' but now reduced to a fluctuating membership of between eight to ten players) is a troupe of talented actors and musicians. However, they've not yet succeeded in capturing on their albums and singles for Kama Sutra the fun of their stage act. Guitarist Vinnie Taylor died in 1974 and Elliott Randall joined as replacement.

Bobby Sherman, the most successful teen idol of the late Sixties, filled the fan magazines during the gap between the Monkees and Donny Osmond. His biggest hits included 'Little Woman', 'La La La (If I Had You)', 'Easy Come, Easy Go', and 'Julie, Do Ya Love Me' (all 1969–70 on Metromedia). His bland personality and appearance (he looked a bit like Bobby Goldsboro) made him a star with the pre-teen girls and their mothers, helped along by endless promotions in the teen magazines. Born in 1944 in Santa Monica, California, Sherman was 'discovered' at a party by Sal Mineo and in 1965 became a regular on *Shindig*, interpreting popular hits and making a few singles of his own on the side. His real popularity began after *Shindig* went off the air in 1966, when he got a leading part in another TV series, *Here Come The Brides*.

Billy Sherrill, as head of recording policy for Epic/Columbia in Nashville, is one of the most powerful figures in the recording industry of that city. He joined Epic in 1964 as a producer and was responsible for many country hits until, in the Seventies, he manufactured hits for three superstar country artists – Tammy Wynette, Charlie Rich and Tanya Tucker.

Born in Winston, Alabama, Sherrill came into music as a saxophonist and pianist with a local white R&B band in the mid-Fifties. Moving to Nashville in 1958, he played some sessions and recorded rockabilly for Mercury ('Like Makin' Love', covered in Britain by Marty Wilde) and other smaller labels, before joining Sam Phillips' Sun label as producer in charge of the new Nashville studio. This lasted from 1960 to 1964, when Phillips sold the studio, but Sherrill had the chance to work with top names like Jerry Lee Lewis and Charlie Rich. On joining Epic, Sherrill moved more into mainstream country and by 1968 had worked out a classic, sparse yet dramatic country sound to suit the tear-jerking songs of Tammy Wynette. With his Spectorish production of songs like 'Stand By Your Man' (Wynette) and 'Delta Dawn' (Tanya Tucker) he became country music's biggest hit maker.

In 1968 too, Sherrill acquired Charlie Rich for Epic. They had worked briefly at Sun, but now Sherrill directed Rich at the middle-of-the-road country pop market and scored massive hits with 'Nice'n'Easy', 'Behind Closed Doors' and 'The Most Beautiful Girl' etc. However, if Sherrill's production enhanced Tammy Wynette's singing only too often it did the reverse for Charlie Rich, drowning him in a sea of melodrama and saccharin.

Carly Simon was born on June 25, 1945 in New York. She first performed and recorded with her sister Lucy as the Simon Sisters in the mid-Sixties, having a small hit with 'Winkin' Blinkin' And Nod' (Kapp, 1964). They did folk-oriented material, playing only in the New York area where Carly was still at college. When Lucy married they stopped performing and it was several years before Carly was 're-discovered' at a party and given an Elektra contract in 1970.

In the intervening years she had started to write music, and met Jacob Brackman, lyricist and screenplay writer, with whom she started a lengthy collaboration. Their most famous song, from her first album *Carly Simon* (1971) was the successful 'That's The Way I've Always Heard It Should Be'. Its theme – the conflict between aspirations inherited in childhood and the adult reality – has been consistently pursued by Carly throughout the four albums that have followed, notably on the second, *Anticipation* (1971). Her greatest asset has always been her strong and confident singing voice, and if the level of insight on her album has declined over the years, the standard of musicianship, and in particular Richard Perry's productions, has increased. Since her huge international hit with 'You're So Vain' in late 1972 her albums (*No Secrets*, 1972, *Hot Cakes*, 1974, *Playing Possum*, 1975) have sold consistently well. She is married to James Taylor, and duetted on her 1974 hit, 'Mockingbird', the old Inez and Charlie Foxx song.

John Simon was born in Norwalk, Connecticut on August 11, 1941. After studying music in college, he took a job with Columbia Records. His first record was *Point Of Order*, a documentary account of the McCarthy hearings. Simon gradually moved into the pop world, producing 'Red Rubber Ball', a sizeable 1966 hit for the Cyrkle. He went on to produce sessions with Simon and Garfunkel and Leonard Cohen before finally leaving Columbia to work on the soundtrack of *You Are What You Eat*; for it he wrote 'My Name Is Jack', which later became a Top Ten hit for Manfred Mann in Britain in 1968.

Moving to Woodstock he met The Band and produced their first album, *Music From Big Pink* (1968). Later that year Simon cut his first solo album for Warner Bros, *John Simon*, an appalling blend of lyrical fantasy and reality, with Simon's piano and vocals set against a loose-jazz rhythm. An even bigger flop was *The Journey*, his second Warners album cut in 1972. However, it is as a producer that Simon has distinguished himself, with albums by Gordon Lightfoot, Blood, Sweat And Tears, Seals and Crofts, Electric Flag, Jackie Lomax, John Hartford, Cass Elliott and Bobby Charles amongst others.

Paul Simon survived the dissolution of his enormously successful partnership with Art Garfunkel in 1970 with his reputation as a songwriter, if anything, enhanced. His output as a solo artist has been small – one live and three studio albums by 1975 – but marked by meticulous attention to detail unequalled in rock.

The first record (*Paul Simon*, Columbia, 1971) was hailed as a significant personal statement, shedding the whimsy of much of the Simon and Garfunkel music. More significantly, it showed Simon exploring a wide range of musical forms, including reggae ('Mother And Child Reunion') and even the middle-of-the-road ballad ('Everything Put Together Falls Apart' – a song whose lyrics contradicted the chosen musical style).

This process continued on *There Goes Rhymin' Simon* (1973), with the inclusion of the Dixie Hummingbirds gospel group among the accompanists for 'Loves Me Like A Rock', while the Peruvian group Urubamba appeared in live performances recorded on the *Live Rhymin'* album (1974). At the insistence of Columbia, singles were release from the first album, with both 'Me And Julio Down By The Schoolyard' and 'Mother And Child Reunion' reaching the Top Thirty. A bigger hit came with 'American Tune' from the second album, chosen by *Rolling Stone* as the song of the year, for its ability to capture the mood of Watergate-era America.

During the Seventies, Simon has had to withstand pressures for a resumption of the Simon and Garfunkel operation, conceding to the extent of recording one track with his ex-partner ('My Little Town') which appeared on both singers' 1975 albums. Simon's *Still Crazy After All These Years* also produced more hits with 'Gone At Last', a duet with Phoebe Snow, and the American No. 1, '50 Ways To Leave Your Lover'. A craftsman in his attitude to songwriting, record production and public performance, Simon has, however, never sacrificed the cutting edge of the best of Sixties rock for the blandness of mainstream pop. On the contrary, he has continued to mirror and interpret the feelings of his first generation of listeners.

Peter Skellern was born in Bury, Lancashire in 1947. His musical apprenticeship embraced church choir, pop group and the Guildhall Academy of Music in London, where he studied piano. His first Decca single, the unusual 'You're A Lady' (1972) reached No. 3 in Britain and entered the American Top Fifty.

Skellern's vocals were a unique mix of balladeer (Hoagy Carmichael) and regional inflexion (George Formby), though, unlike Gilbert O'Sullivan, his was not a novelty voice. His three Decca albums suggested an equally wide range of genres. After *You're A Lady* (1972), *Not Without A*

Friend (1973, produced by Derek Taylor) included ragtime tunes and intimate ballads, while *Holding My Own* (1974) paid homage to music-hall comedy.

In 1974, Skellern had another major hit with 'Hold On To Love', while simultaneously developing a parallel career as a writer for the stage, composing the score for a revue and a musical. His first Island album, *Hard Times*, was released in 1975.

Slade. Converted by Chas Chandler from an undistinguished club band into one of the biggest pop phenomena of the early Seventies via an unbroken string of hits that included six No. 1 singles and two No. 1 albums, Slade – Noddy Holder (vocals, guitar, born June 15, 1946), Dave Hill (guitar, born April 4, 1952), Jim Lea (bass, born June 14, 1950), Don Powell (drums, born Sept. 10, 1950) – started out in the Midlands in the Sixties as the In-Betweens before changing their name to Ambrose Slade and thence, at Chandler's suggestion, to Slade.

As Slade they initially received attention because of their skinhead image, but as success rapidly followed their first hit single, a revamping of Bobby Marchan's 'Get Down And Get With It' (Polydor, 1971), this was modified into a kind of aggressive glitter. The development of Holder and Lea as composers of all the group's subsequent hits encouraged comparisons with early Lennon–McCartney, which were reinforced by the closeness of Holder's voice to John Lennon's. But more importantly, the dynamism of early hits like 'Mama Weer All Crazee Now' (1972) and 'Cum On Feel The Noize' (1973) paralleled Pete Townshend's anthems for a previous teenage generation. In an effort to enlarge their public beyond teenyboppers and boot boys, they spent the second half of 1974 working on a film, *Flame*. From it came the haunting semi-ballad 'Far Far Away', a British chart topper, which suggested a change in direction for the group. After a less successful year in 1975, in 1976 they returned to their stomping sound with 'Let's Call It Quits'. Never a success in America, Slade nevertheless remain the most articulate of the new wave of British pop groups of the Seventies.

Patti Smith was born in Chicago in December, 1946 and grew up in South New Jersey. In 1967 she moved to New York to study painting at the Pratt Institute and began writing poetry that was heavily influenced by the world and images of rock'n'roll. By 1970 this developed into poetry read against rock'n'roll backing, and following after-hours performances/recitals, notably at the Mercer Arts Center with rock critic Lenny Kaye, and the publication of her poems in *Creem* magazine in 1971, she formed an occasional group with Kaye (guitar) and Richard Sohl (piano) to record her first single 'Piss Factory/Hey Joe' (MER, 1974). In 1975, Ivan Kral (guitar) and Jay Dougherty (drums) were added to the group and she was signed to Arista. *Horses*, produced by John Cale, appeared later that year.

Sammi Smith, born on August 5, 1943 in Orange, California, had a string of minor country hits on Columbia from 1968 onwards. 'Foxy Dan' and 'Brownsville Lumberyard' showed off her interesting, wide-ranging voice, used to even better effect in 1970 on Kristofferson's 'Help Me Make It Through The Night' (Mega). This interpretation went to No. 1 in the country chart and reached the national Top Ten. A singer with Waylon Jennings' band in the early Sixties, Sammi Smith is now, with Jennings and Willie Nelson, regarded as part of 'new wave' country music.

Joe South was born in Atlanta, Georgia on Feb. 28, 1940. Work locally as a session guitarist and singer led to a minor hit in 1958 with 'The Purple People Eater Meets The Witch Doctor' (NRC), a none-too-subtle attempt to cash in on the recent novelty song craze. Another small success came three years later with his version of the country classic 'You're The Reason' (Fairlane).

Throughout the Sixties, South worked on many sessions in Atlanta and elsewhere, including Dylan's *Blonde On Blonde* and records by Simon and Garfunkel, Aretha Franklin and Tommy Roe. As a songwriter, he had hits with 'Untie Me' (The Tams, 1962), 'Down In The Boondocks' (Billy Joe Royal's Top Ten hit of 1965), 'Hush' (by Royal in 1967 and

Deep Purple in 1968) and 'These Are Not My People' (Johnny Rivers, 1969).

Joe South made his mark as a performer with *Introspect* (Capitol, 1968). A classic set of blue-eyed soul songs often aimed at the intolerance and hypocrisy of Southern society (straight and hip), it included two Top Ten hits: 'Games People Play' for South himself and Lynn Anderson's 'Rose Garden'.

The next album, *Don't It Make You Want To Go Home*, was in the same righteous vein, producing more hits with 'These Are Not My People' and South's 'Walk A Mile In My Shoes'. Later Capitol releases were less successful and in 1975 he signed to Island.

Sparks were the vehicle for the bizarre songs of Ron Mael (born in Culver City, Los Angeles, in 1948) as shrieked by his brother Russell (born in Santa Monica, Los Angeles, in 1953) which stirred Britain during 1974. The Maels, ex-child models, formed their first group, Halfnelson, while studying at UCLA but were dissatisfied with the American rock scene after two Bearsville albums in 1971–72, and accepted an offer to come to Britain, where they put together the definitive Sparks. The new line-up's first single, 'This Town Ain't Big Enough For Both Of Us' (Island, 1974), had a startlingly unnatural quality, and the Maels performed it (and three more hits) with a fine sense of theatre. Following a series of uneven albums (including *Propaganda*, 1975) and diminishing chart success, the Maels disbanded the group and returned to California.

Chris Spedding, ace British session guitarist, was born on June 17, 1944 in Sheffield. He joined Pete Brown's Battered Ornaments in 1967 after an apprenticeship in dance and jazz bands. On its break-up in 1970, he recorded two solo albums and began to play sessions. In 1971, he joined the Jack Bruce Band, playing on both solo Bruce albums, and introduced the rock guitar to the jazz-rock fusions of Mike Gibbs, Mike Westbrook and Ian Carr's Nucleus with whom he spent eighteen months.

His prolific and catholic session career was interrupted when in late 1972 he formed Sharks with Free bassist Andy Fraser. A rock band also comprising Canadian drummer Marty Simon, and Snips, a hoarse-voiced singer from Hull, Sharks were continually plagued by internal dissent. Fraser left after the first album to be replaced by Buster Cherry Jones, bass, and Nick Judd, keyboards. Always promising more than it delivered, Sharks broke up in late 1974 after a third album produced by the Who's John Entwistle was rejected by Island. In 1975 Spedding toured with John Cale and Roy Harper and began to release singles through Mickie Most's RAK label, scoring a minor hit with 'Motorbiking'.

Spirit, formed in the summer of 1967, comprised Ed Cassidy (drums, born in Bakersfield, California in 1930), John Locke (piano, born in Los Angeles on Sept. 25, 1943), Randy California (guitar), Mark Andes (bass, born in Philadelphia in 1947) and Jay Ferguson (vocals, born in Burbank, California on May 10, 1947). All the members had been musically active for some time: Cassidy first as a jazz sideman and then with the Rising Sons, Andes first as a session man – he was on Bobby Pickett's 'Monster Mash' – and then with Ferguson and California in the Red Roosters, and Locke with the New World Jazz Company. They signed with Ode in 1968 and released *Spirit* to poor sales and critical acclaim for their ability to play together in a loose yet structured way. Their only chart success was the Top Thirty single, 'I Got A Line On You' (1969). After *The Family That Plays Together* (1969) and *Clear* (1969) they moved to Epic for the uneven *The Twelve Dreams Of Dr Sardonicus* (1970), following which Andes and Ferguson formed Jo Jo Gunne and California released *Kaptain Kopter And The Twirlybirds* (1973) before re-forming a short-lived Spirit for *Spirit Of 76* (Mercury, 1975).

Spooky Tooth was formed in 1967 by Gary Wright, an American living in Berlin (keyboards, born April 26, 1945), Mike Harrison (keyboards, born Sept. 3, 1945), Luther Grosvenor (guitar, Dec. 23, 1949), Greg Ridley (bass, Oct.

23, 1941) and Mike Kellie (drums, March 24, 1947). A popular club band in the progressive rock era, it proved to be less successful on record. Signed to Island, *It's All About* (1968) and the highly regarded *Spooky Two* (1969) were released before Ridley left to join Humble Pie, being replaced by Andy Leigh.

From this point on, the band started to lose direction as Wright left to form Wonderwheel and three ex-Grease Band musicians (Chris Stainton, Henry McCullough and Alan Spenner) joined for the fourth album. Spooky Tooth disbanded between 1970 and 1973 while Harrison and Wright pursued unsuccessful solo careers. Re-forming, they cut two further albums and were joined by vocalist Mike Patto for the final record, *The Mirror* (Goodear, 1974).

Bruce Springsteen, born on Sept. 23, 1949, was hailed as the latest 'new Dylan' on the release of his first Columbia album, *Greetings From Asbury Park* (1973). The heaped similes and endless rhymes of his evocative songs about New York street life were strongly reminiscent of Bob Dylan's work in the *Highway 61 Revisited* era.

The Wild, The Innocent And The E Street Shuffle (1974) included 'Sandy', successfully covered by the Hollies, and found Springsteen developing a more individual style. He integrated a wide variety of musical elements – rock and Latin rhythms, blues hollering, classical motifs – into mini-operas capturing the chaotic energies of the teeming metropolis.

At this point, critical acclaim, at times counterproductive in its hyperbole, was not matched by commercial success. The recording of *Born To Run* (1975) was protracted, with former *Rolling Stone* critic Jon Landau being called in as co-producer to complete it. Promoted with all the resources at Columbia's disposal, both the single and the album were substantial American hits, and Springsteen commenced large-scale touring with his hard-edged E Street Band: Clarence Clemons (tenor sax), Roy Bittan (piano), Steve Van Zandt (guitar), Gary Tallent (bass) and Max Weinberg (drums). For the first time in his career he united critic and consumer alike.

The Stairsteps. From the Teenagers through to the Jackson 5, black music has always abounded in vocal teams featuring the quavering voices of pubescent youth. The Stairsteps were originally formed as the Five Stairsteps, a family group arranged by their father, Chicagoan Clarence Burke. Discovered by soulman Curtis Mayfield in 1966, the group – Clarence, James, Aloha, Kenny and Dennis Burke – were recorded on a series of densely orchestrated songs ranging from lilting dance songs to poignant love ballads that were released, all with soul chart success on Mayfield's Windy C label, as by the Five Stairsteps and Cubie. Transferring to Buddah in 1967 ('Something's Missing') and to Curtom in 1968 ('Baby Make Me Feel So Good') it was when the group finally split from Mayfield that they experienced their biggest hit, the beautiful, Stan Vincent-produced 'O-o-h Child' in 1970 (for Buddah). Family arguments saw the group disintegrate by 1973.

The Staple Singers are a family gospel quartet, noted for the striking guitar phrases of Roebuck 'Pops' Staples (born Dec. 28, 1915 in Winona, Mississippi) and featuring the emotive voice of his daughter, Mavis, leading her sisters Cleotha and Yvonne (who replaced her brother Pervis). After 15 years of recording they found international success as a 'soul' act without denying their roots or compromising their reputation. Following a single on United (1954) they recorded original ('Uncloudy Day', 'Help Me Jesus') and traditional ('Will The Circle Be Unbroken', 'Swing Low') gospel for Vee Jay records of Chicago (1956–59), before Riverside tried unsuccessfully to broaden their appeal (1960–64) and Epic partially succeeded by recording their interpretations of 'Why (Am I Treated So Bad)' and 'For What It's Worth', both produced by Larry Williams.

In 1968 they were signed by Stax. After two years of unsuitable releases, producer Al Bell began moulding the sound that climaxed with 'Respect Yourself' (1971) – the million-selling hit that introduced them to a mass public. Subsequent hits ('I'll Take You There' – 1972, 'If You're Ready' – 1973, 'City In The Sky' – 1974) and appearances in the films *Wattstax* and *Soul To Soul* have reinforced their popularity.

Alvin Stardust's extraordinary success story gave heart to every ageing rocker dreaming of a comeback. Born Bernard Jewry in London in 1942, his first break was passing an audition for BBC radio's *Saturday Club*. He and his group (which included Bobby Elliott – later of the Hollies – on drums) became Shane Fenton and the Fentones, an energetic quintet in silver lamé, who had a hit with 'I'm A Moody Guy' on HMV (1962) and made a reasonable living until they were beaten back by the Beatles.

He returned with the rise of rock'n'roll nostalgia and was working the Northern club circuit (still as Shane Fenton) when Peter Shelley of Magnet Records persuaded him to release 'My Coo-ca-choo' under the name Alvin Stardust. It rocketed to the top of the charts in 1973 and so did five follow-ups, all Shelley compositions featuring more tape echo on the voice than had been heard since Gene Vincent. His image alternates between being a moody guy in black leather and a big brother to his youthful audience. When interviewed about his good fortune, he always seems bemused by it. In 1976, Roger Greenaway replaced Shelley as his writer/producer.

Ringo Starr. Despite predictions that he would suffer most from the break-up of the Beatles in 1970, Ringo has successfully developed his cheerful, popular persona acquired in the group's seven years of stardom. *Sentimental Journey* (Apple, 1970) and *Beaucoups Of Blues* (1970) were pleasant collections of childhood favourites and country standards respectively. Both reached the American album charts and *Sentimental Journey* entered the British Top Ten.

Next, Ringo established himself as a major singles artist with a series of his own songs, including 'It Don't Come Easy' (1971 – his declaration of independence from the

Beatle image), 'Back Off Boogaloo' (1972) and 'Photograph' (1973 – co-written with George Harrison). The *Ringo* album included the gold record 'You're Sixteen' and involved Nilsson, Marc Bolan, Martha Reeves and members of The Band as session musicians.

Ringo was produced by Richard Perry, as was *Goodnight Vienna* (1974), which provided further hit singles with 'Only You' and the title track. His film career developed from cameo roles in *Candy* (1967) and *The Magic Christian* (1970) to a much-acclaimed starring role in *That'll Be The Day* (1973) and a less satisfactory directorial debut in the Bolan documentary *Born To Boogie.* He also achieved brief fame as a furniture designer.

Status Quo are Francis Rossi (guitar, vocals, born May 29, 1949), Rick Parfitt (guitar, vocals, Oct. 12, 1948), Alan Lancaster (bass, vocals, Feb. 7, 1949) and John Coghlan (drums, Sept. 19, 1946). As the Spectres, they recorded unsuccessful singles for Pye in the early Sixties with organist Roy Lynes (born Nov. 25, 1943), later becoming Traffic Jam, then Status Quo.

Rossi's 'Pictures Of Matchstick Men' (Pye) provided them with a British Top Ten hit in 1968, and 'Ice In The Sun' was equally popular later in the year. Later singles flopped, Lynes left, and Status Quo's brief moment of glory seemed to have passed. But they transformed their uncertain, ornate pop style into basic four-square boogie and returned to the charts in 1970 with 'Down The Dustpipe'. Moving to Vertigo in 1972, they consolidated their position with further single hits (including 'Paper Plane' and 'Caroline' in 1973) and the albums *Piledriver* and *Hello.* Status Quo are a major live attraction in Britain in the mid-Seventies and, surprisingly, have become a major influence on younger British bands.

Stealers Wheel came to international prominence during 1973–74 with two Top Ten hits on A&M, 'Stuck In The Middle With You' and 'Star', produced by Jerry Leiber and Mike Stoller. The group was formed in 1972 by two Scottish folk-club singers, Gerry Rafferty and Rab Noakes. The latter soon left to pursue an unsuccessful solo career with A&M and Warner Bros. Rafferty, formerly with comedian Billy Connolly in the Humblebums, teamed up with another Scot, Joe Egan, to form a fruitful writing partnership.

Egan had previously sung harmonies on Rafferty's solo album for Transatlantic, *Can I Have My Money Back?* (1971). The pure strong harmonies were perfected on *Stealers Wheel* (1972) and *Ferguslie Park* (1973), named after a district of Paisley, their home town. A series of problems with backing musicians led to the duo forgoing live appearances, which may have contributed to the poor reception of their 1975 album, *Right Or Wrong*. Musically, it continued the Rafferty–Egan synthesis of Sixties rock in a Seventies framework.

Steeleye Span was formed in 1969 by Ashley Hutchings (bass), formerly with Fairport Convention, traditional folk singers Tim Hart (guitar) and Maddy Prior and Gay and Terry Woods (guitar, concertina), who had previously worked with Sweeney's Men, an early folk-rock experiment.

For the first two years, Steeleye Span remained a part-time band, as most of its members continued solo work in the folk clubs. As a group they set out in Hart's words to be 'not a rock band but traditional musicians working with electric instruments'. The first line-up didn't appear live and cut one album, *Hark! The Village Wait* (RCA, 1970), before the Woods left to form their own band.

They were replaced by the renowned folk guitarist and singer Martin Carthy and by violinist Peter Knight. During 1971, this line-up toured extensively and cut two albums for B&C, *Please To See The King* and *Ten Man Mop*. They also performed in Keith Dewhurst's play, *Corunna*, reaching new audiences beyond the folk scene.

At this point Hutchings left to pursue his more purist concern for English traditional music in the Albion Country Band and his partnership with Shirley Collins. Differences over whether the replacement should be another electric bassist or a multi-instrumentalist led to Carthy returning to solo work, which he continues. Two musicians with a rock orientation were brought in – Rick Kemp (bass) and Bob Johnson (electric guitar).

Manager Sandy Roberton was also supplanted by Jo Lustig, who signed them to Chrysalis and planned the strategy which made Steeleye Span a major international group in the mid-Seventies. On *Below The Salt* (1972) and *Parcel Of Rogues* (1973), the dynamics of electric instruments were explored and arrangements were tight and dramatic. *Now We Are Six* (1974) saw the introduction of hard-rock drummer Nigel Pegrum.

The group's stage act, featuring five-part harmonies and focusing on Maddy Prior, was well-choreographed but almost predictable. In 1973, Steeleye Span added mummers' costumes to their act and the next year Hart presented a brief mummers' play on stage, to mixed reactions. 1975 saw another change of management (to Tony Secunda) and an unusual choice of producer for *All Around My Hat* – the Wombles' Mike Batt. Retaining their totally traditional repertoire, the group experimented with reggae backings and seemed to be increasing the heavy rock content of their sound at the expense of its folk roots. 'All Around My Hat' was a surprise Top Ten hit at the end of 1975.

Steely Dan was formed in 1972 after producer Gary Katz had brought New York-born songwriters Walter Becker and Donald Fagen to America's west coast as staff writers for ABC-Dunhill. Very few artists or bands were picking up on their material and so it was suggested that Becker and Fagen, who played bass and keyboards respectively, record an album themselves with the help of established session musicians. After the success of *Can't Buy A Thrill*, and the two singles taken from it, 'Do It Again' (a Top Ten hit in 1972) and 'Reelin' In The Years', drummer Jim Holder and guitarists Denny Diaz and Jeff Baxter joined on a permanent basis, although the same policy of using outside people was followed through on all the later albums: *Countdown To Ecstasy* (1973), *Pretzel Logic* (1974) and *Katy Lied* (1975).

The band's sound is a marriage of styles, east coast Latin-influenced R&B to Californian rock, all of which are shot through with a quirkiness – the group's name comes from William Burroughs – that stems from their jazz background. Frequently cynical, sometimes obscure but consistently interesting, Fagen and Becker's lyrics have been central to the group's success. Although they profess to enjoy jazz more than rock, Fagen and Becker have created in Steely Dan a rock band in which creativity and technical excellence play equal parts. Baxter and Holder left the band in 1974, the immediate effect of which can be heard on *Katy Lied* (ABC), a slightly below-par album, but there was good reason to suppose that the band would overcome the difficulties posed by their departure, particularly if musicians of the calibre of Rick Derringer and Elliott Randall continued to record with them.

Ray Stevens was born in Clarksdale, Georgia in 1939. Beginning as a session singer and writer for the Judd label in the late Fifties, he has since followed an unconventional musical path straddling country and pop. His first record, the comic 'Sergeant Preston Of The Yukon' (1959), sold well before it had to be withdrawn following a lawsuit brought by the owners of the radio programme of that name. In 1961, Stevens signed to Mercury, recording several popular comedy tunes, 'Ahab The Arab' (a Top Five Record in 1962) being the most successful. Incidentally, Ahab's camel was named Clyde in honour of Clyde McPhatter who was present when the song was recorded. Moving to Monument, he wrote and recorded the powerful social comment of 'Hey Mr Businessman' (1968) and the parody 'Gitarzan', a Top Ten pop hit in 1969. Further success followed with Kristofferson's 'Sunday Morning Coming Down', 'Everything Is Beautiful' (Stevens' first No. 1), and the traditional country song 'Turn Your Radio On' on Barnaby, the label owned by Andy Williams. A brief return to comedy led to the topical international hit 'The Streak' (1974), recalling his 1971 success with 'Bridget The Midget'. Stevens switched back from comedy with the follow-up, a witty, countrified arrangement of the pop standard, 'Misty' (Janus, 1975).

John Stewart was born in San Diego, California. He was a founder member of the Cumberland Three folk group in the late Fifties, joining the Kingston Trio as replacement for Dave Guard in 1961. With the Trio, Stewart cut numerous albums for Capitol before he left the group in 1966.

As a solo artist, he cut an album with Buffy Ford of his own songs, *Signals Through The Glass*, followed by *California Bloodlines* (Capitol, 1969). Produced by Nik Venet, this album is regarded by many as Stewart's finest achievement. The twin themes of the album – love for a woman and love of rural America and its past – run through all of Stewart's subsequent records.

After *Willard* (1970), he moved to Warner Bros for *The Lonesome Picker Rides Again* (1971) and *Sunstorm*. The former included Stewart's own version of his 'Daydream Believer', a hit for the Monkees in 1967. *Cannons In The Rain* (RCA, 1973) was produced in Nashville by Fred Carter Jr., and was followed by *The Phoenix Concerts* (1974), a live double album. As a songwriter, Stewart's version of the folk/country synthesis stands somewhere between those of John Denver and Johnny Cash, although he has yet to reach the large audiences either can command.

Rod Stewart, born in North London on Jan. 10, 1945, resolved an early conflict between ambitions in soccer and music when he abandoned his apprenticeship at Brentford FC to busk around Europe. He sang and played harmonica with Jimmy Powell's Five Dimensions for a short time in 1963 before joining Long John Baldry's Hoochie Coochie Men as second singer early in 1964. He made a solo single, 'Good Morning Little Schoolgirl' (Decca), released that October, and performed with the Soul Agents in the period between the disbandment of the Hoochie Coochie Men and the formation of Steampacket in mid-1965. He played harmonica on Millie's 'My Boy Lollipop'.

Heavily influenced by Sam Cooke's vocal style, he recorded 'Shake' (Columbia), backed by Brian Auger, in 1966, and after leaving Steampacket that summer he joined Shotgun Express, singing alongside Beryl Marsden, with Peter

Green (guitar), Peter Bardens (keyboards), Dave Ambrose (bass), and Mick Fleetwood (drums).

As a founder member of the Jeff Beck Group early in 1967, he began a longstanding and fruitful association with Ron Wood. After a disastrous start in London, the group did well in America, and Stewart overcame his shyness on stage in vocal duels with Beck's guitar. By the time he and Wood left to join the Faces in 1969 he had developed a unique and spectacular stage act. He signed a solo recording contract before joining the Faces, and his first big success, *Every Picture Tells A Story* (Mercury, 1971), which was also his first solo production, was not as a member of the group. After the cult following of the previous *An Old Raincoat Will Never Let You Down* (Vertigo, 1969) and *Gasoline Alley* (Vertigo, 1970), both of which demonstrated his interpretative powers, *Every Picture*'s enormous popularity and that of the accompanying single, 'Maggie May' – for one week the single and the album were top of their respective charts in both Britain and America – immediately made him a star.

His concentration on a solo recording career became a factor in the patchiness and increasing rareness of the Faces' recordings, and by the time they disbanded in 1976 they existed almost solely as a performing band. Perhaps his strangest hit was in 1972 as Python Lee Jackson with 'In A Broken Dream' (Young Blood) which was a British Top Five record and small American hit – Stewart had added a vocal to a backing track.

Never A Dull Moment (Mercury, 1972), the compilation *Sing It Again Rod* (1973) and the long-delayed *Smiler* (1974), using a nucleus of Ron Wood, his occasional co-writer, and Ian McLagan from the Faces, Martin Quittenton (mandolin and acoustic guitar) and Mickey Waller (drums), consolidated his position as one of the world's most successful artists. Perhaps disappointed by the poor public and critical response to *Smiler*, he changed the formula in 1975 to record the Tom Dowd-produced *Atlantic Crossing* (Warner Bros, 1975) in America, where he moved the same year, using Muscle Shoals and Memphis session men and the

Meters, from New Orleans. It included two hit singles, 'Sailing' and 'This Old Heart Of Mine'.

Stephen Stills, born in Dallas, Texas on Jan. 3, 1945, worked the New York folk circuit with limited success, before moving west to found Buffalo Springfield, for whom he wrote 'For What's It's Worth', still a painfully accurate account of the contradictions of social confrontation. This theme – the need to fight with new weapons rather than the old – was to run through his subsequent music alongside an approach to relationships that was desperately determined.

Stills, unlike Neil Young, earned a reputation as a musician rather than a songwriter, and appeared with Al Kooper and Mike Bloomfield on the 1968 *Supersession* album, one of the earliest teamings of individual talents from separate groups. In the same year, he formed CS&N and played most of the music on their album – electric and acoustic guitars, bass, and keyboards. With the addition of Young, Stills could better fulfil his role as a guitar virtuoso, shown to fine effect on the live *Four-Way Street.* On his two solo albums (Atlantic, 1970, 1971), and the two with Manassas, *Manassas* (1972), *Down The Road* (1973), Stills' wide musical vocabulary has come more to the fore, expanding the basic West Coast sound to accommodate country music, Latin rhythms, and harder rock'n'roll. His lyrics have been uneven, occasionally climbing to peaks in anthemic songs like 'Carry On', 'So Begins The Task', and 'Sugar Babe' which have simplicity allied to a reverberating depth. His major talent, though, remains in his guitar-playing. He has learnt much from the likes of Hendrix and Clapton, and since the former's death is the foremost exponent of the wah-wah pedal, just one part of his formidable stylistic range as a guitarist. In 1975 Stills had signed to Columbia, cut his fifth post-CSN&Y album (*Stills*) and formed a new touring band of whom only percussionist Joe Lala remained from the Manassas line-up.

Sly Stone, the extraordinary superdude of black music, has more than any other single artist irrevocably altered the face of Sixties and Seventies soul music, while at the same time showing rock music the rhythmic potential of 'funk' when transferred from riffing horns to electric keyboards and wah wah guitars. Born Sylvester Stewart in Dallas, Texas on March 15, 1944 he was a child prodigy, recording 'On My Battlefield For My Lord' at the tender age of four. At high school he was lead singer of a doowop group, the Viscanes ('Yellow Moon') before, quitting music college, he split his time between deejaying on San Francisco radio and working as a record producer for Autumn Records.

The discs he wrote and produced for Autumn ranged from uptown soul (Bobby Freeman) to plaintive harmony pop (the Beau Brummels) as well as intriguing instrumentals of his own like 'Buttermilk'. But Sly was being exposed to an environment totally different from the insularity of mainstream ghetto life. Firmly entrenched in the San Francisco psychedelic trip, with his backing band, formed in 1966 as the Stoners, he became ambassador extraordinary of the new drug and youth revolution cultures bringing elements of the West Coast white rock bands into their music. Sly and the Family Stone were spotted by Columbia/Epic's head of A&R, David Kapralik, and launched on the rock scene with the release of the *A Whole New Thing* album. But it was the issue of a classic dance single 'Dance To The Music' that took the band to the top of the charts. More pulsating fusions of wah wah guitar, undulating bass rhythms and chanted vocals followed: 'Everyday People' and *Stand*, the latter an album which contained the apocalyptic 'I Want To Take You Higher' – the number Sly performed at the 'Woodstock' concert with shattering effect. In 1970 pop music's most extrovert personality released one single, the double gold 'Thank You (Faletinme Be Mice Elf Again)'. Sly's huge success was damaged by frequent non-appearances at gigs but as late as 1971 his shattering 'new direction' album 'There's A Riot Goin' On' killed the critics and the public and possibly Epic's finances (it being rumoured to have cost a cool million dollars to make despite featuring Sly on most instruments). An increasingly frenetic private life, and public one (with a brief marriage), and the coolly received *Fresh* and *Small Talk* albums seem to show a decline for Sly Stone. But Sly Stone's past triumphs and immense influence on just about every black rock band of the Seventies are already a matter of history.

Stories, formed in 1972 by Michael Brown, the brilliant but erratic talent behind the Left Banke, originally included Ian Lloyd (vocals and bass), Steve Love (guitar) and Bryan Madey (drums). Their first Kama Sutra album was hailed as a promising debut (a single, 'I'm Coming Home' reached No. 42 in the charts), and their second was hailed as one of the classics of the pop revival, although none of the singles released from it ('Darling', 'Top of the City', 'Circles') became hits. It was a subsequently released cover version of Hot Chocolate's 'Brother Louie' that became a surprise No. 1 hit for Stories, just after Brown's departure from the group.

By then bassist Kenny Aaronson had joined from Dust, and by early 1974 Love had been replaced by Rich Ranno. With Lloyd's odd, raspy voice and the group's moody orchestral sound, they became a popular concert and television act, but a third album and several singles resulted in only one minor hit, a cover of the Pop-Tops' 'Mammy Blue' in 1974. The bisexual theme of 'Another Love' proved too controversial, and by the end of 1975 they had disbanded.

The Stylistics are a five-man Philadelphia soul group, featuring the distinctive falsetto lead of Russell Thompkins Jnr., whose every record has been a smash, thanks mainly to the expert guidance of writer/producer/arranger Thom Bell. Formed in 1970 from the remnants of the Monarchs and the Percussions, two unsuccessful local groups, the group comprises Aaron Love, James Smith, Herbie Murrell, James Dunn and Thompkins. Their first record, 'You're A Big Girl Now' (Sebring), was picked up and turned into a national hit by Avco, who then teamed them with Bell. He gave them nine straight hits (co-written with Linda Creed), each a skilfully orchestrated slice of romantic imagery that by 1973 had made them a top international attraction. Among his best creations were 'You Are Everything' (1971), 'You

Make Me Feel Brand New' (1974), and one untypical dance track 'Rock'n'Roll Baby' (1973). In 1974 Van McCoy became arranger for the group under the production of Avco bosses Hugo and Luigi. Although these collaborations have been less memorable than Bell's, the Stylistics' hits continued unabated and their *Greatest Hits* anthology had unprecedented sales in Britain for a black vocal group.

Sutherland Brothers and Quiver. Gavin and Ian Sutherland had recorded two albums, *The Sutherland Brothers Band* and *Lifeboat* (Island, 1972) and worked with a band, as a duo, and with session men, before teaming up in 1973 with Quiver – Tim Renwick (guitar), Bruce Thomas (bass), Willie Wilson (drums), and from the time of the coalition, Pete Wood (keyboards). Quiver had themselves made two albums for UA, played the opening night of the Rainbow, and lost co-founder and songwriter Cal Batchelor. The Sutherland Brothers and Quiver's first session together produced '(I Don't Want To Love You But) You Got Me Anyway', which became an American Top Twenty hit as they toured America supporting Elton John in September, 1973. They failed to match its success or that of a slightly reshuffled American *Lifeboat* with subsequent releases, though the pop-rock harmonies of *Dream Kid* (1973) were critically well received. When Bruce Thomas left in mid-1974 and Pete Wood early in 1975, neither was replaced as Gavin Sutherland switched to bass and the line-up was trimmed down to a four-piece. After *Beat Of The Street* (1975) SB&Q left Island for Columbia and released *Reach Out For The Sky* (1975). Gavin Sutherland's 'Sailing' was a 1975 hit for Rod Stewart.

Billy Swan was born in Cape Girardeau, Missouri in 1942. In the mid-Fifties, he joined Mirt Mirley and the Rhythm Steppers and travelled to Memphis where Bill Black's Combo recorded his composition, 'Lover Please', which two years later in 1962 was a Top Ten hit for Clyde McPhatter. By that time Swan had moved to Nashville where he divided his time between working at the city's various studios and occasionally being a roadie for country stars like Mel Tillis. In 1969 he joined Monument as a producer, being responsible for Tony Joe White's Top Ten hit, 'Polk Salad Annie'. As a recording artist, he released the lilting rockabilly-style 'I Can Help' in 1974, and it was a surprising transatlantic No. 1. Subsequent singles, such as 'I'm Her Fool' (1975), were not so successful, but his albums, *I Can Help* (1974) and *Rock'n'Roll Moon* (1975), are a pleasantly archaic mixture of rock'n'roll and relaxed country music.

Sweet was formed in 1968 by Brian Connolly (vocals), Frank Torpy (guitar), Steve Priest (bass) and Mick Tucker (drums). After unsuccessful singles for Fontana and Parlophone, the group were taken under the wing of Nicky Chinn and Mike Chapman in 1970. By this time, Torpy had been replaced first by Mick Stewart and then by Andy Scott, whose career had included a period backing Scaffold.

The group was transformed into infallible hitmakers via a string of Chinnichap songs between 1971 and 1974, beginning with 'Funny Funny' (RCA, which reached No. 13), and typified by such alliterative titles as 'Co-Co' (1971), 'Wig Wam Bam' (1972) and the heavier 'Blockbuster' (1973, their first No. 1). The tight, punchy production, owing much to classic American bubblegum records, was by Phil Wainman.

The group's stage image underwent several transformations, including banning from some venues for too suggestive performances and their cheerily androgynous style adopted in the wake of David Bowie. Their new songs included the powerful 'Ballroom Blitz' and 'Hellraiser', and Chinnichap's philosophizing about the youth revolution, 'The Six Teens'. By 1974, they had become restive at the total control of their career exercised by Chapman and Chinn, and elected to leave them. Sweet's first original composition, 'Fox On The Run' (1975), became their second No. 1 and showed how much they had learned from their former masters. Moreover, unlike their fellow British trend setters, by 1975 they had begun making strong inroads in America.

Sylvia scored her biggest solo hit in 1973 with the sensual

'Pillow Talk' (Vibration), just 23 years after her first release. Born in New York on March 6, 1936, Sylvia Vanderpool recorded as Little Sylvia for Columbia, Savoy, and Jubilee before teaming with guitarist Mickey Baker in 1955. For six years, Mickey and Sylvia tackled anything from rockers to wistful calypsos, like the million-selling 'Love Is Strange' (Groove, 1957), until they separated in 1961 after playing on Ike and Tina Turner's 'It's Gonna Work Out Fine' (Sue) and a last hit on their own Willow label the same year, 'Baby You're So Fine'. Solo releases on Sue and Jubilee in the mid-Sixties were unsuccessful, but in 1968 she emerged on the other side of the fence as co-owner of the All Platinum label with husband Joe Robinson. After a slow start the company has become one of the most successful independents in north-east America, hitting with heavy soul (Linda Jones), smooth vocal groups (the Moments, the Whatnauts), and disco-stompers (Shirley and Co, the Rimshots, Rhetta Young).

Philip Goodhand Tait was born in Hull on Jan. 3, 1945. With the Stormsville Shakers, a popular London club band, he backed American musicians including Larry Williams and Johnny 'Guitar' Watson. With the advent of the underground, they became Circus, a beads, droopy moustaches and kaftans band.

Leaving Circus shortly before they recorded for Transatlantic, Tait signed with Dick James Music as a songwriter. He embarked on a solo career, cutting four pleasant and workmanlike albums for DJM between 1970 and 1973. Their lack of success was partially attributable to comparisons drawn between Goodhand Tait and Elton John. His backing group – Andy Latimer (guitar), Andy Ward (bass) and Doug Ferguson (drums) – left in 1972 to form Camel with Peter Bardens. That group's *Snow Goose* (Deram, 1975) made them one of the most successful newer British bands of the year.

Tangerine Dream was formed by Edgar Froese (born on June 6, 1944) in West Berlin in 1967. The group – at present

Chris Franke (born April 4, 1942) and Peter Baumann; Steve Schroyder, Claus Schultze, Conny Schnitzler, Udo Dennebourg and Roland Paulyck having been members at one time – began playing music that was heavily influenced by West Coast acid rock (especially the Doors) and the Pink Floyd. However, in the following years as the line-up settled down, they gradually dispensed with conventional instrumentation in favour of synthesizers, mellotrons, pre-set tapes and other electronic aids and the music became a texture of electronic drones and waves of shifting tones and volume. Their early albums, *Electronic Meditation* (Ohr-Musik, 1970), *Alpha Centauri* (1971, released in Britain by Polydor) and *Zeit* (1972) were 'conventional' experiments in electronic music, but by the time of *Phaedra* (Virgin, 1974), *Rubycon* (1975) and Froese's solo albums, *Aqua* (Virgin, 1974) and *Epsilon In Malaysian Pale* (1975), the group was creating sounds that veered from the romantic to the ethereal without any referent whatsoever: *Phaedra* for example starts not from the myth but from the moods associated with parts of its action. As a result, Tangerine Dream have taken the brunt of the attacks on 'kraut rock'.

Bernie Taupin, born in Lincoln on May 22, 1950 began his partnership with Elton John when they met through a Liberty talent competition in 1967. His earliest lyrics were saturated with poetic aspirations but on *Elton John* and *Tumbleweed* he emerged as a superb craftsman of romantic ballads with a fascination for old Americana and leanings towards a bed-sit or sophomore mentality much in evidence on his solo album *Taupin* (DJM, 1971). His superficial profundity reached full flower on *Madman Across The Water* but he switched to a more direct, jaunty style with *Honky Château* and turned from cowboys to film stars on *Goodbye Yellow Brick Road.* An obsessive fan, he produced David Ackles' classic *American Gothic* in 1972, and drew on his early experiences with John for the bitter autobiographical *Captain Fantastic And The Brown Dirt Cowboy* (1975).

Chip Taylor, younger brother of actor Jon Voight, is probably best known as composer of the Troggs' 'Wild Thing'. From New York, his songs have also been recorded by Chet Atkins, Waylon Jennings, Tammy Wynette, Eddy Arnold, Bobby Bare, Floyd Cramer and dozens more. In the late Fifties he recorded rockabilly for King but it wasn't until 1966 that Chip had his first (minor) hit as a singer, 'You Can't Grow Peaches On A Cherry Tree', the same year the Hollies hit with his 'I Can't Let Go'. 'Wild Thing' was then picked up by the Troggs and, later, by Jimi Hendrix and Fancy. His songs received wide circulation, and the next to make the charts was 'Angel Of The Morning', covered by Merrilee Rush (Bell, 1968). Prior to that, Billy Vera and Judy Clay had recorded Chip's 'Storybook Children' (Atlantic, 1967) and 'Country Girl, City Man' (1968), while Jackie De Shannon cut 'I Can Make It With You' (Imperial, 1966).

Together with Al Gorgoni and Trade Martin, Chip formed the well-received trio of Gorgoni, Martin and Taylor, who recorded two albums for Buddah. Taylor went on to cut one solo album for Buddah, *Gasoline* (1972). In 1973 he joined Warner Bros and cut *Chip Taylor's Last Chance* which was critically praised, especially for the opening track '(I Want) The Real Thing' but sold relatively poorly. A year later came *Some Of Us*, which once again featured exquisite back-up by artists like the Jordanaires and Van Morrison's former guitarist John Platania. Chip's third album for the company, released in mid-1975, was the uneven *This Side Of The Big River*.

James Taylor was born on March 12, 1948 into a musical Boston family, and started to play guitar at an early age. In 1965 he met Danny Kortchmar, with whom he formed the Flying Machine in New York, some two years later. The group didn't do too well, and James, with a heroin addiction to cope with, went to England in 1968 where old acquaintance Peter Asher got him an album contract with the newly formed Apple. When *James Taylor* was released in 1969, a heroin-free James returned to the States for a second sojourn in a mental institution.

His second album, *Sweet Baby James* (Warner Bros, 1970) and the single from it, 'Fire And Rain', catapulted him to a stardom from which he has never really recovered. The simple world-weariness of the music seemed entirely apposite for the post-Kent State feelings of American youth. The music was basically acoustic folk-blues guitar; the lyrics were open to the point of vagueness. The tone of voice was the dominant factor: resignation and the sadness of a hopeless quest. James Taylor had fused together the simple pessimism of country music and the portentousness of much Sixties folk, so reflecting the 'failed hopes' ethos of the early Seventies.

Mud Slide Slim and *One Man Dog* followed in 1971 and 1972, featuring songs mostly dedicated to the salvations of love and the highway. Particularly noteworthy were the dignified 'Highway Song' and the huge hit 'You've Got A Friend' from the former, and the suite of songs that closed the latter. In late 1972 James married fellow-singer Carly Simon with whom he had a Top Ten hit with 'Mockingbird' in 1974.

Two further albums appeared, *Walking Man* (1974) and *Gorilla* (1975), the latter featuring some harmony singing from Crosby and Nash. Taylor's songs have not declined over the years, but their relevance as more than one man's music, or more than a pleasant sound, seems to have been superseded both by events and his unwillingness to exploit his own talent to the extent it deserves.

Ted Templeman, a leading house producer for Warner Bros Records in Burbank, grew up in Northern California and played drums with various R&B and jazz outfits before joining the immensely successful Harpers Bizarre. The group were signed with Warners and Templeman became friends with their producer, Lenny Waronker, now head of Warners A&R. When the group split, Templeman became a staff producer for Warners, joining the company in September, 1970. His first assignment was the Doobie Brothers' debut album, followed shortly by Van Morrison's *Tupelo Honey.* Since then he's produced everything for the Doobies and

Morrison, plus albums by Little Feat, Captain Beefheart, Montrose, Lorraine Ellison and others. Templeman is noted for the consistent cleanliness and sophistication of his recordings and for the sizeable role he has played in achieving a distinctive sound for groups such as the Doobie Brothers and Little Feat.

10cc, formed in Manchester, comprises Eric Stewart (vocals, guitar), Lol Creme (vocals, guitar) and Kevin Gogley (vocals, drums) who had played together as Hotlegs, a group which had a surprise British Top Five hit with 'Neanderthal Man' (Fontana) in 1970, and Graham Gouldman (vocals, bass), a successful songwriter of the Sixties who had written hits for the Yardbirds and Hollies among others.

All from Manchester, the group were based at Strawberry Studios, where they recorded a series of self-produced hits on Jonathan King's UK label: 'Donna' (1972), 'Rubber Bullets', 'The Dean And I' (1973) and 'The Wall Street Shuffle' (1974), all of which showed total mastery of previous rock styles, performed with a wit and polish that marked a new self-consciousness in British rock. All the members of the group write and produce equally.

In 1975, after two equally fine albums, *10cc* (1973) and *Sheet Music* (1974), they left UK for Mercury where they had a transatlantic hit with the ambitious *The Original Soundtrack* and the single from it, 'I'm Not In Love', a fragile ballad that epitomized both their inventive use of the studio as a musical instrument and their craftsmanlike attitude to song construction. Their second Mercury album, *How Dare You* (1976), which was even more ambitious, saw them less sure of themselves. None the less, it and its single, 'Art For Art's Sake', were enormously successful.

Ten Years After was formed in late 1966 by Alvin Lee (guitar, vocals, born in Nottingham on Dec. 19, 1944), Chick Churchill (organ, born Jan. 2, 1946), Leo Lyons (bass, born Nov. 30, 1943), Ric Lee (drums, born Oct. 20, 1945). Brought up in Nottingham on his father's extensive blues collection, Alvin Lee established a successful local trio with

Leo Lyons, journeying to Hamburg directly after the Beatles, where they established the direction that ultimately surfaced as Ten Years After. Working in London in a West End production they met Ric Lee, a music scholar, and subsequently Chick Churchill, also well versed in musical styles.

As Ten Years After they first gained attention at London's Marquee Club, soon signing a contract with Decca's Deram label, who released an album in 1967, *1st Album*, without the benefit of the then obligatory establishing hit single. American promoter Bill Graham booked them into his Fillmore Auditoriums on the basis of this recording and they soon became a major concert attraction in the United States. In 1968 they gained major English and European attention, but it was their fast and furious rendition of 'I'm Going Home' in the *Woodstock* film that established them as a top world attraction. Many of their subsequent audience, however, viewed this one song as their only style and were unprepared to accept anything else. The group officially disbanded in 1975.

In early 1974 Lee played a solo concert at London's Rainbow Theatre, subsequently performing a world tour as Alvin Lee and Co. before retiring once more to his country mansion-cum-studio, where he produced bands that interested him, such as FBI. The other members were similarly engaged in solo projects.

Richard and Linda Thompson. The quiet genius in Fairport Convention, Richard Thompson, a highly accomplished writer and influential guitarist, left the band after their fifth album *Full House* (1970). Following session work with Sandy Denny, Ian Matthews and other folk/rock musicians, he resurfaced in his own right with *Henry The Human Fly* (Island, 1972). That album was sadly neglected, and it was only when he teamed up with Linda Peters, whom he was later to marry, that Thompson's career took off. Through two albums – *I Want To See The Bright Lights Tonight* (1974) and *Hokey Pokey* (1975) – his genuine love for English traditional and American country music gave the term 'folk/rock' new meaning. The recognition given to songs like 'The New St George', 'Calvary Cross', 'The End Of The Rainbow' and 'When I Get To The Border' and their dramatic stage performances, have enabled the Thompsons to make the difficult transition from folk clubs to large concert halls. *Pour Down Like Silver* (1975) continued the successful progress of the duo.

The Three Degrees, originally Linda Turner, Shirley Porter and Fayette Pickney, met manager Richard Barrett in their home town, Philadelphia. Signed to Swan, their first hit was '(Gee Baby) I'm Sorry' in 1965. Barrett then took the girls to Boston, concentrated on their stage act, and the group graduated to posh niteries and supper-clubs. Fayette Pickney, Sheila Ferguson and Valerie Thompson recorded with Warner Bros, Metromedia and Neptune before 'Maybe' was a Top Thirty hit with Roulette in 1970. Signing with Gamble/Huff's Philadelphia International in 1972, the trio finally hit big ('Dirty Old Man', 'Year Of Decision', 1973, 'When Will I See You Again', 1974, 'Take Good Care Of Yourself', 1975) though it's been the European rather than the American audience who've really warmed to their posturing, sequin-flashing cabaret-soul.

Three Dog Night's beefy vocal harmonies and solid (if unimaginatively heavy) instrumentation have contributed to their record of eleven gold albums and even more gold singles since 1968. Although criticized for not writing their own songs, they displayed an unerring talent for finding great songs by little-known composers (among the authors of their hits have been Randy Newman, Leo Sayer, Laura Nyro and Hoyt Axton) and their instinct for raw material (a perfect example being B. W. Stevenson's plain, folkish 'Shambala' which they transformed into a fully produced pop smash) seldom failed.

The group was formed by several veterans of the LA studio scene, primarily vocalists Danny Hutton (born Sept. 10, 1946), who'd almost hit on his own with 'Roses and Rainbows', and Cory Wells (born Feb. 5, 1944), whose band the Enemys were Whisky regulars, with the addition of singer Chuck Negron from New York, and instrumentalists Joe Shermie (bass), Jim Greenspoon (keyboards), Mike Allsup (guitar) and Floyd Sneed (drums), from various local bands including Dyke and the Blazers and the East Side Kids. Their first big hit was 'One' (Dunhill), written by then-unknown Harry Nilsson in early 1969, followed by 'Easy To Be Hard', Nyro's 'Eli's Coming' (1969), 'Celebrate', Newman's 'Mama Told Me Not To Come', 'Out In The Country', Sayer's 'One Man Band', Axton's 'Joy To The World', Russ Ballard's 'Liar', Paul Williams' 'An Old Fashioned Love Song', Axton's 'Never Been To Spain', Paul Williams' 'Family Of Man', 'Black And White', 'Pieces Of April', 'Shambala', Leo Sayer's 'The Show Must Go On' and Allen Toussaint's 'Brickyard Blues'.

Nicky Thomas, from Portland, Jamaica, is best remembered for his catchy, pop-reggae hit 'Love Of The Common People' – a British Top Ten hit in 1970 on Trojan. An ex-labourer, he became a full-time musician in 1968 cutting 'Run Mr Nigel Run' for Derrick Harriott and earning himself a Jamaican hit and the nickname 'Mr Nigel'. Settling in Britain, he continued to record lightweight tunes: 'God Bless The Children' and 'Have A Little Faith'; and albums, *Tell It Like It Is* and *Images Of You.* But, despite an accomplished vocal style, he was stuck with a one-hit-wonder stigma and consequently faded from the scene.

Thundermug, a Canadian group (Bill Durst, Joe De Angelis, Jim Corbett, Ed Pranskus) formed in 1968, became a critics' favourite in 1973 with two singles, 'Africa' and 'Orbit' that brought comparisons ranging from Roy Wood to Led Zeppelin. Their sound was basic heavy metal: fast, hard and full of dynamism, and ultra-produced in an advanced pop vein. Both records were hits in Canada, and the group released two albums which were combined by Epic for US release in 1974. Singles of 'Orbit' and 'I Wanna Be With You' skirted the charts, but Thundermug never caught on in America. A charming version of Neil Sedaka's 'Breaking

Up is Hard to Do' was subsequently a Canadian hit. In mid-1975 they signed with Mercury in the US.

Keith Tippett is a talented composer with eclectic tastes and a great gift for making musical friends. His reputation as a jazz-rocker is a product of these attributes. From his first recording, in 1969, Tippett's work has been a fascinating amalgam, not of *styles*, but of *people*. Gary Boyle, Elton Dean, Roy Babbington, Robert Wyatt and innumerable others from all over the musical scene have played his music at one time or another. He has also appeared on albums by King Crimson and Soft Machine.

It was both bizarre and logical that he should tie all this up in an enormous parcel called 'Centipede' (50 players = 100 feet) for which he wrote *Septober Energy*, a sprawling but compulsive work recorded for Neon (1972).

Tippett is married to the singer Julie Driscoll.

Toots and the Maytals comprise Frederick 'Toots' Hibbert (born in 1946), Jerry Mathias and Nathaniel Gordon. A vocal group from Kingston, Jamaica who came together in 1963, they were formerly known as the Vikings ('Six And Seven Books Of Moses') and V. Maytals ('Little Slea'). They recorded copiously for various producers: Prince Buster ('He Is Real'), Coxon Dodd ('Hello Honey'), Dynamic ('If You Act This Way'). With dissonantly harmonic, hymn-like songs they established themselves as ska favourites, eventually winning the Jamaican Song Festival in 1966 with 'Bam Bam'.

The group's subsequent successes included 'Pressure Drop', 'Monkey Man' and '54-46 That's My Number'. By the early Seventies, with Toots intact as leader and a recording contract with the fashionable Dynamic Studios of Byron Lee, they had notched up two further Festival hits – 'Sweet And Dandy' (1969), 'Pomps And Pride' (1972). Following an appearance in *The Harder They Come* film and the rock-style promotion of their over-produced set *Funky Kingston* (Island, 1974), they were widely acclaimed by Britain's rock media and *élite*, gigging at Hyde Park during their 1974 tour. The follow-up album, *In The Dark* (1975), was less enthusiastically received, but a definite improvement. Toots' superb vocal range remains one of the delights of reggae; Mathias and Gordon its perfect complement. In 1976 they entered the British charts with 'Reggae Got Soul'.

Allen Toussaint, born in New Orleans on Jan. 14, 1938, is almost single-handedly responsible for keeping the New Orleans sound prominent on today's pop music scene. The son of a railroad worker, he has been a major figure in the Crescent City since the early Fifties, when he was touring pianist with Shirley and Lee. In 1955 he was spotted by Dave Bartholomew, long-time partner and collaborator with Fats Domino, and hired as a studio session player, working with the likes of Smiley Lewis and Lloyd Price. In 1958, he was given his first recording contract by RCA and cut an instrumental album called 'Wild Sounds Of New Orleans' featuring Al Tousan, as he was then known. Unaware at that time of the importance of his publishing royalties, he signed away the rights to some of his best-known compositions, among them 'Java', which made New Orleans trumpeter Al Hirt a national star. Another trumpet player who benefited from Toussaint's writing talents was Herb Alpert, who recorded his 'Whipped Cream'.

Despite the elusiveness of public stardom, Toussaint was becoming known in professional music circles as a talented writer and session musician. Working behind the scenes, he established his reputation and learned the art of producing discs (for Minit Records) with artists like Ernie K-Doe, Joe Jones, the Showmen, Jessie Hill, Aaron Neville, and Irma Thomas. He was also busy producing sessions for Lee Dorsey, Chris Kenner, the Meters, Lou Johnson, Wilbert Harrison, Clarence 'Frogman' Henry, Betty Harris and Barbara George. It's the songs that Allen has written, though, that are apt to be the most familiar to the casual listener. He's responsible for more R&B classics than anyone would imagine could flow from the same pen: 'Ride Your Pony', 'Working In The Coalmine', 'Get Out Of My Life Woman', 'Holy Cow' (all for Lee Dorsey), 'Mother-In-Law' (Ernie K. Doe) and 'Ruler Of My Heart' (Irma Thomas). He also wrote under the *nom de plume*, Naomi Neville – really his mother's name. He recorded for Seville as Al Tousan (1959–63) and for Alon in 1965 as Allen Toussaint.

In 1965 Toussaint teamed up with Marshall Sehorn, a white man from Carolina and a former general manager for Fire and Fury records. Together they launched Sansu Enterprises and later opened Sea-Saint Recording Studios, now the leading studios in New Orleans. Toussaint's second solo album, simply titled *Toussaint*, was cut in 1971 for Tiffany Records and distributed by the New York-based Scepter Records.

In 1972 Toussaint signed with Reprise and cut *Life, Love And Faith*, a disappointing album featuring the Meters in support, which contained the popular disco single 'Soul Sister'. His second and best solo album for the company, *Southern Nights* (1975), again failed to sell well though the title track saw Toussaint in a new and more adventurous light, dabbling with contemporary chord structures and studio electronics. Out of the limelight, however, his talent still continues to blossom. Recent productions include 'Lady Marmalade' by Labelle, *High Life* by Frankie Miller, 'Right Place, Wrong Time' by Dr John, plus all the Meters' Reprise albums. Toussaint's songs have been covered by many artists outside New Orleans, and the lengthy list is headed by Paul McCartney, Ringo Starr, The Band, Little Feat, Maria Muldaur, Frankie Miller, Jess Roden, Bonnie Raitt, Joe Cocker, Esther Phillips, Hues Corporation, and Van Dyke Parks.

Tower of Power, founded by Emilio 'Mimi' Castillo, were formerly known as the Motown Soul Band. All white musicians with the exception of lead singer Rick Stevens, the band – originally Greg Adams, Stephen Kupka, Mic Gillette, Willie Fulton, David Garibaldi, Francis Peestia and Brent Byar – specializes in raunchy super-tight dance riffs somewhere between the old Stax houseband and Blood, Sweat And Tears. Picked up by impresario Bill Graham, they recorded an album (*East Bay Grease*) for his San Francisco label. In 1971, they joined Warner Bros, and released *Bump City* (a track from which, 'You're Still A Young Man', was their first hit). After various personnel changes, Lenny Williams, an experienced West Coast soul singer, joined as vocalist. *Tower Of Power* came out next, including the massive ballad hit 'So Very Hard To Go'. *Back To Oakland* followed in 1974. Williams has now left for a solo career.

Robin Trower, born in Catford on March 9, 1945, was an original member of the Paramounts, a Southend R&B group of the early Sixties. He joined Procol Harum just as they were making their first album in 1967 and stayed with them until 1971. Then after *Broken Barricades*, the first Procol album to be dominated by guitar rather than organ (most notable on Trower's tribute to Hendrix, 'Song For a Dreamer'), he left, finding the group's range too narrow for his taste. He formed the short-lived Jude with Frankie Miller (vocals), Clive Bunker from Jethro Tull (drums) and Jimmy Dewar from Stone The Crows (bass). Next, the Robin Trower Group, with Dewar taking the vocals and Reg Isadore from Quiver replacing Bunker after Miller quit, released *Twice Removed From Yesterday* (Chrysalis, 1973). On *Bridge Of Sighs* (1974) and *For Earth Below* (1975), when Bill Lordan replaced Isadore, both of which sold very well (particularly in America), Trower successfully built upon his R&B roots to create an atmospheric modern guitar sound that owed much to Hendrix.

Uriah Heep was formed in 1970 when guitarist Mick Box (born in London on June 8, 1947) and singer David Byron (born in Epping on Jan. 29, 1947) left the Stalkers after meeting Ken Hensley (keyboards, born Aug. 24, 1945). For two years their rhythm section fluctuated – bassists Paul Newton and Mark Clarke (born July 25, 1950) and drummers Al Napier, Nigel Olsson, Keith Baker and Ian Clarke passing through the band – until in 1972 Gary Thain (bass) and Lee Kerslake (drums) joined permanently.

The title of their first album, *Very 'eavy, Very 'umble* (Vertigo, 1970) indicated their musical aims, and it was significant that it was in Germany and then America (as the latest British heavy band) that they were first successful.

Demons And Wizards (Bronze, 1972) and *Magician's Birthday* (1972) both went gold in America and marked the beginning of a gradual acceptance in Britain that grew further after *Wonderworld* (1974). Ken Hensley released a solo album, *Proud Words On A Dusty Shelf*, in 1973, and Gary Thain was replaced by John Wetton, formerly of Family, in 1975.

The Wackers, objects of a strong cult and critical following, were among the most promising American rock bands of the early Seventies. The nucleus of the group was Bob Segarini and Randy Bishop, formerly with Family Tree and Roxy, who made one album for Elektra.

When that group dissolved in 1970, the two brought in Bill 'Kootch' Trochim from the Family Tree and drummer Ernie Earnshaw to form the Wackers. This band, produced by Gary Usher, recorded three highly acclaimed albums for Elektra. Their music ranged from Fifties raunch to effete Beatles harmony, although in fact they were best known as a no-frills, pure rock'n'roll outfit and fell out with Usher over his attempts to excessively sweeten their music. A fourth album, *Wack And Roll*, was recorded in Montreal and withheld by Elektra, after which the Wackers left the label and moved to Canada permanently. Bishop subsequently went solo and Earnshaw returned to California, while Segarini and Kootch added David and Ritchie Henman, Brian Greenaway, Wayne Cullen and Leon Holt (all from various Canadian bands) to form All The Young Dudes, which was shortened to the Dudes. This group became one of Montreal's biggest attractions in 1974, and were signed by Columbia Records in early 1975.

Loudon Wainwright III was born on Sept. 5, 1946 in Chapel Hill, North Carolina. He came to the fore in the late Sixties with his harsh voice, acoustic guitar, and tragi-comic sense of reality. His two Atlantic albums (*Album I*, 1970, *Album II*, 1971) were starkly humorous, while his later records for Columbia were more mellow in their high irony. Loudon Wainwright is never more serious than when he's at his funniest, as in the song 'Dead Skunk', in which the skunk 'stinking to high heaven' rapidly becomes a metaphor for many a more offensive happening.

His songs of love are marked by the same attitude, centring on such activities as crawling under the snoring wife's bed in search of a cigarette in the middle of the night. In the process he manages to say more about relationships than many a more serious-minded writer.

His music increased in complexity through the second and third Columbia albums, *Attempted Moustache* (1973) and *Unrequited* (1974), with the addition of a backing group. He is married to songwriter Kate McGarrigle.

Rick Wakeman was born in Perivale, London on May 18, 1949. A former student of the Royal College of Music, he went on to construct some of the most commercially successful fusions of classical and rock music of the Seventies. After session work and spells with the Strawbs and Yes, he launched a series of ambitious solo works in 1973 with *The Six Wives Of Henry VIII* (A&M), inspired by a television drama series.

Journey To The Centre Of The Earth (1974) involved keyboards, orchestra and narration by David Hemmings of Jules Verne's story. Even more grandiose was *Myths And Legends Of King Arthur* (1975), premièred on ice at Wembley Pool. That year, he also wrote the score for Ken Russell's *Lisztomania.* The immense popularity of the amiable Wakeman confused critics, who were unable to accept him as a master of contemporary light orchestral music.

Jerry Jeff Walker was born on March 16, 1942 in Oneonta, New York. A singer and songwriter in the 'new Nashville' mould, he is probably most important for his pivotal position in the growing Austin, Texas music scene of the early Seventies.

Walker's best-known song is 'Mr Bojangles' (a Top Ten hit for The Nitty Gritty Dirt Band in 1970 and a minor hit for him in 1968, a tribute to a New Orleans street-dancer. He has recorded three albums for Atco (notably *Five Years*

Gone, 1969), one each for Decca and Vanguard and, most recently, for MCA. Previously he had led, with Bob Bruno, Circus Maximus, a five-piece rock group. In 1973, he had a hit with 'LA Freeway' (MCA).

Joe Walsh was born in New York and raised in New Jersey. He formed his first band, the G-Clefts, at school before joining the Nomads as bassist. He joined the Measles before moving on to the James Gang in April 1969. He shot to fame with them (aided by praise from Pete Townshend) and when it was clear that his talents exceeded the capabilities of the rest of the band, he left in November, 1971.

Six months later he formed Barnstorm with Joe Vitale and Kenny Passarelli, releasing the *Barnstorm* album (Dunhill, 1972) which confirmed his status as both an inventive guitarist and a talented writer. The 'Rocky Mountain Way' single success brought gold status to his next album, *The Smoker You Drink, The Player You Get* (ABC, 1973). After extensive touring, he felt that the band had reached its limits and he did his next album, *So What* (1974), with various friends. 1975 saw him touring with Bryan Garofalo, Paul Harris, Ricky Fataar and David Mason, with whom he recorded a live album. He has also produced Dan Fogelburg's *Souvenirs* (Epic, 1974) and Joe Vitale's *Roller Coaster Week End* (Atlantic, 1974).

War – Harold Brown (drums, born March 17, 1946), Howard Scott (guitar, March 15, 1946), B. B. Dickerson (bass, August 3, 1949), Charles Miller (saxes, flute, June 2, 1939) and Lonnie Jordan (keyboards, Nov. 21, 1948) – were an instrumental group working the West Coast club scene of the Sixties under various names including the Creators, the Romeos ('Precious Memories', Mark II Records, 1967) and Señor Soul ('It's Your Thing', Whiz Records, 1969). As the Night Shift they linked up with Eric Burdon, changed names again and toured as his backing band, having been joined by Papa Dee Allen (percussion, born July 19, 1931) and Lee Oskar (harmonica, March 24, 1948). The *Eric Burdon De-*

clares War album on MGM was followed by *Black Man's Burdon* on Liberty.

Leaving Burdon, War's solo albums, *All Day Music* and *The World Is A Ghetto* (United Artists, 1971), went gold and established a potent new voice in progressive soul music, their style embracing jazz/funk, Latin, rock, and R&B. Their sometimes mellow, sometimes percussive sound appealed equally to black and white audiences though they lost ground when disputes with their management in 1974 meant a year's lay-off and the release of a relatively mediocre live album. Their problems resolved, they went on to a hit single and album, *Why Can't We Be Friends.* In 1976 they scored their first British Top Twenty hit with 'Low Rider' (Island), an American hit for them in 1975.

Clifford T. Ward is responsible for some of the most productive moments in the British pop ballad form pioneered by Paul McCartney. From Kidderminster, Worcestershire, he played in various local groups including the Secrets, who were signed to Andrew Oldham's Immediate label. As a solo artist he recorded *Singer Songwriter* for Dandelion in 1970.

With the demise of the label, Ward joined Charisma, having a Top Ten hit with his first single, the lyrical 'Gaye', in 1973. Three albums followed – *Home Thoughts* (1973), *Mantle Pieces* (1973) and *Escalator* (1975). The latter produced his second hit, 'Jigsaw Girl'. His writing is melodic and whimsical, leavened with social comment and (occasionally over-elaborate) witty metaphor, reflecting his former career as an English Literature teacher.

Lenny Waronker is head of Warner Bros Records A&R and chief producer. He has found and developed many of the artists who are now the backbone of the label. In his early thirties, Waronker was born in Los Angeles and introduced into the music business by his father, who owned Capitol Records. The first single he produced for Warners in early 1967 was 'Feeling Groovy' by Harpers Bizarre. The group featured Ted Templeman, now a fellow Warners house producer.

Waronker went on to produce a string of successful albums by the Everly Brothers, Ry Cooder, Arlo Guthrie, Randy Newman, Beau Brummels, Van Dyke Parks, Gordon Lightfoot, the Doobie Brothers (co-produced with Templeman), Maria Muldaur (co-produced with Joe Boyd) and James Taylor. Waronker is centrally concerned with melody in his production techniques. He has been described as a 'sound sweetener', and uses strings, vocal harmony, even moog, to give a fuller flavour to melodies. His work with Lightfoot is typical of his general approach.

Watts 103rd Street Rhythm Band. Part of the frenetic whirl of the West Coast R&B scene of the mid-Sixties was the Fred Smith-produced instrumental group, the Soul Runners (whose 'Grits And Cornbread' was a 1967 R&B hit on Mo Soul Records). Changing their name to the Watts 103rd Street Rhythm Band, they hit with a churning Booker T-style disc, 'Spreadin' Honey' (Keymen, 1967) before bringing in a vocalist, Charles Wright (one-time doowop singer with the Shields and producer of Little Caesar and the Romans' 'Those Oldies But Goodies') and in 1969 had a Top Twenty 'pop' hit with the funky 'Do Your Thing' (Warner Bros). Despite Wright's singing in a raucous bellow, their compulsive funk gave Warner Bros more Top Twenty hits with 'Love Land' in 1970 and 'Express Yourself' in 1971. Charles Wright eventually left the group (which seemed to change its personnel every year) to join ABC Records, where he struggled to establish himself as a solo soul name. Among the members of the group have been Melvin Dunlop (bass, born in 1946), Al McKay (guitar), Bernard Blackman (guitar), John Rayford (tenor sax, born in 1943), Bill Cannon (tenor sax, born in 1939), Ray Jackson (trombone), Gabriel Flemming (trumpet, born in 1943) and James Gadson (drums).

Weather Report. Formed in 1971 by Joe Zawinul (ex-Miles Davis and Cannonball Adderley pianist, born in Vienna on July 7, 1932) and Wayne Shorter (ex-Davis and Art Blakey saxophonist and composer, born in New Jersey on August 25, 1933), Weather Report epitomizes the style of music associated with graduates of Miles' band. Their most characteristic approach is to build a performance from melodic fragments, weaving them into shifting patterns and textures, often of great subtlety and charm. Their records from *Weather Report* (1971) to *Tale Spinnin'* (1975) are carefully constructed artefacts which frequently achieve a rather cold and formal beauty. In person Weather Report take more risks and sometimes sacrifice coherence in the process.

Jimmy Webb, born in Elk City, Oklahoma, on Aug. 5, 1946, moved to California in the mid-Sixties where he briefly worked as a contract writer for Motown's Jobete Music. In Los Angeles in 1966, he met Johnny Rivers, who was then in the process of setting up his Soul City label, and wrote a couple of songs for him – including 'By The Time I Get To Phoenix'. Rivers teamed him up with the Fifth Dimension and his 'Up Up And Away' gave them their first hit in 1967. Then Glen Campbell decided to cut 'Phoenix'. Campbell's success with that and his even greater success with Webb's 'Wichita Lineman' (1968) and 'Galveston' (1969) – both Top Five records – and Richard Harris' with 'MacArthur Park', a Top Three record in 1968, established Webb as a writer – and made him his fortune as version after version poured from the recording studios of America.

Dissatisfied with other people's performances of his material, in 1970 Webb began touring as a performer and in 1971 signed with Reprise Records. While the resulting albums, *Words And Music* (1971) – which includes the plaintive 'P. F. Sloan' – and *And So: On* (1971), were uneven they showed him to be a much more thoughtful writer (and singer) than his earlier hits suggested. *Land's End* (Asylum, 1974) saw him produce himself, again with mixed results. In 1975, he produced the debut album of his sister, *Susan Webb* (ABC).

Barry White is one of the most enigmatic and controversial figures in black music, whose work raises the question: where does soul stop and easy listening begin? White was born in Galveston, Texas, in 1944 but has spent most of his life in Los Angeles. After a stint in the church choir, White joined an R&B group, the Upfronts. At 17 he did his first arranging, for Rampart Records (recording as Lee Barry), learned how to produce and spent some time as road manager for Bob and Earl. In 1966, White was made head of A&R at Mustang/Bronco Records. He worked with artists like Felice Taylor, and also did some singing on 'All In The Run Of A Day', a failure on Bronco.

When Mustang folded, White met up with three girl singers he dubbed Love Unlimited. Their first single, 'Walking In The Rain With The One I Love', was a worldwide hit on Uni. Signing in 1972 (together with his protégées) to 20th Century Records, White began to sing again himself and 'I'm Gonna Love You Just A Little Bit More Baby' like all his subsequent discs used an invigorating blend of Isaac Hayes-influenced lush 'sophistisoul' production and a driving rhythm track with extraordinary 'presence' in the guitar and drums. White enjoyed a run of million-selling singles ('Never, Never Gonna Give You Up' and 'You're My First My Last My Everything') and albums (*Stone Gon'*, *Can't Get Enough* and *Just Another Way To Say I Love You*). He also hit as leader of the instrumental Love Unlimited Orchestra with 'Love's Theme'. However, it's his heavy-breathing vocals which have gained most success. His growled and vivid descriptions of his sexual appetites have driven girls wild and caused scenes of hysteria, while never alarming the menfolk; it would appear that as husbands can't see White's appeal, he doesn't constitute a threat.

Tony Joe White, born in Oak Grove, Louisiana on July 23, 1943, came out of the swamplands in 1969 with an internationally successful funk-country-soul hit song, 'Polk Salad Annie'. This and other Monument recordings like the hit 'Roosevelt And Ira Lee' had a 'laid-back', sparse, muffled electric sound behind mumbled vocals of the best Presley variety. White qualifies as one of the earliest of the new-style country singer/songwriters, but his records did not sell in the country market, unlike those of Bobbie Gentry who had emerged in similar style two years before. 'Annie', however, has become a contemporary standard recorded by Presley and by Tom Jones among others. Other singles included 'Soul Francisco' and 'Old Man Willie', while other artists successfully covered songs of his such as 'Rainy Night In Georgia' (Brook Benton) and 'I've Got A Thing About You Baby' (Elvis Presley).

Joining Warner Bros in 1971, Tony Joe White's music continued to be distinctive though it diversified somewhat from the heavy swamp rhythm without regaining his commercial acceptance. White appeared in the film of Jack Good's *Catch My Soul.* He remains an important artist in the development of Southern music during the past decade.

Norman Whitfield was born in New York in 1943, and joined the Motown Corporation in Detroit soon after its inception to take up writing, arranging and production duties. Among his earliest Motown successes as a writer was Marvin Gaye's 1963 Top Ten hit, 'Pride And Joy'. After following mainstream Motown styles with songs for Kim Weston, Marvelettes, Velvelettes, etc., and scoring a giant hit with 'I Heard It Through The Grapevine' – a million-seller in successive years (1967–68) for Gladys Knight and the Pips and Marvin Gaye – Norman, with his collaborator Barrett Strong, transformed the Temptations into Motown's answer to psychedelia. The result was a series of Top Ten hits including 'Cloud Nine', 'I Can't Get Next To You' and 'Psychedelic Shock' during 1968–70. The group then took his beautiful ballad 'Just My Imagination' to the top of the charts in 1971, and a year later he shattered pop musical conventions with 'Papa Was A Rolling Stone', a masterpiece of near-symphonic proportion. The tune began life as a twelve-minute Temptations album track, and an edited version soared to the top of the charts, thanks to its disco pulse.

Whitfield was also enjoying limited success with a protégé male/female vocal group, Undisputed Truth. Following his split from the Temptations he has concentrated his efforts on this group with a series of musical experiments. Commercial success has been limited and the musical content has been a universe away from his R&B/gospel roots.

Jerry Williams Jr. was born on July 12, 1942 in Portsmouth, Virginia. He emerged in 1970 – after several years as a straightforward soul balladeer on V-Tone (1963), Southern Sound, Academy (1964), Laurie, Musicor, Dynamo (1967), and Cotillion (1968–69), with one minor hit, 'Baby You're My Everything' on Calla in 1966 – as the multi-talented and quite unique Swamp Dogg. Writing, producing, arranging, and playing keyboards, he has masterminded superb records for many soul girls (including Doris Duke, Sandra Phillips, and Irma Thomas) as well as half a dozen of his own extraordinary albums and a scattering of obscure singles for a variety of companies, including Canyon (1970), Elektra (1971), Cream (1972), Stone Dogg (1973), Brut (1974) and Island (1975). Because of his healthy disregard for commercial trends he has not yet received widespread recognition, although he's becoming increasingly known for the powerful imagery of songs like 'I Don't Care Anymore', 'Mama's Baby, Daddy's Maybe', 'Did I Come Back Too Soon?', and 'The Mind Does The Dancing While The Body Pulls The Strings'.

Paul Williams, a singer-songwriter in the same easygoing vein as Harry Nilsson and John Denver, worked in films and as a skydiver before taking up music professionally. After a short period of collaboration with Biff Rose he teamed up with lyricist Roger Nichols and the partnership has since produced a number of much-recorded songs. Although prone to excessive sentimentality, he is a superb song craftsman and much of the Carpenters' initial success can be directly attributed to their choice of such Williams-Nichols songs as 'Rainy Days And Mondays' and 'We've Only Just Begun' for single release. In 1975, he starred in a cult movie, *Phantom Of The Paradise*. Of his albums, *Inspiration* (A&M, 1973) is probably the best. He is the brother of record producer Mentor Williams.

Tony Williams, born in Chicago on Dec. 12, 1945, joined the Miles Davis Quintet on drums at an absurdly early age. The album *Miles In Europe* (Columbia, 1964) has a 19-year-old Williams bringing off extraordinary feats of rhythmic balance and, more often than not, dictating the course of the whole band's performance. While with Davis he made two albums under his own name for Blue Note which revealed his fascination with the tonal qualities of percussion instruments.

His involvement in rock, with his band, Lifetime, has, for the most part, been a disaster. Apart from a brief association with Jack Bruce and John McLaughlin (on the album *Turn It Over*, Polydor, 1970) his enormous gifts have lain dormant for lack of any real challenge.

Jesse Winchester, a singer/songwriter, born in Shreveport, Louisiana on May 17, 1944, and a rock'n'roll guitarist from his mid-teens, fled to Canadian exile as a draft-dodger in 1967, and became a solo performer. Robbie Robertson of The Band produced and played on his first album *Jesse Winchester* (Ampex, 1970), which breathes an air of wistful nostalgia for an older America on haunting ballads like 'Biloxi', 'Yankee Lady', 'Black Dog', and 'Brand New Tennessee Waltz', as well as breakneck rockabilly numbers like 'Payday'. It immediately established Winchester as a major and original talent, and with *Third Down, 110 To Go* (Bearsville, 1972) he was acclaimed by the critics as a 'genius' and had songs covered by Joan Baez, the Everly Brothers, and others. Mellower than its predecessor, *Third Down* celebrates domestic virtues with an oblique wit and earthy wisdom. His accommodation to exile and family life is cemented in the aptly titled *Learn To Love It* (1974) which, if not quite justifying the earlier critical hyperbole, comfortably consolidated his position as a writer and performer of the first rank.

Pete Wingfield was born on May 7, 1948. As a member of Jellybread, Wingfield made two Blue Horizon albums, *First Slice* (1969) and *Sixty Five, Parkway* (1970), the first while still at Sussex University. He continued to play sessions for label chief Mike Vernon after the band split up, playing keyboards with Freddy King, Van Morrison, Bloodstone, Colin

Blunstone, and many others. In 1975 Wingfield released a solo single, 'Eighteen With A Bullet', which made the British Top Ten and the American Top Twenty with a 'novelty' tag due to its clever, sustained music-biz metaphors and doowop style. His album *Breakfast Special* revealed a highly cultured soul performer tackling music areas never before essayed by a British white artist. This was reinforced by the release of a competent MGs-style album by the Olympic Runners – rhythm band on *Breakfast Special – Out In Front* (London, 1975).

Johnny Winter, an albino, was born in Beaumont, Texas, February 23, 1944 of a musical family. He started playing clarinet at five, but changed to ukelele and then guitar at eleven. Going through teen bands he made a short pilgrimage to Chicago in 1962, returning to Texas to join brother Edgar's band for three years. Settling in Houston in 1966 he determined to emulate the success of other white blues guitarists then emerging. With John 'Red' Turner (drums) and Tommy Shannon (bass) he started playing original blues-inspired rock in the local clubs, slowly gaining a devoted following.

In 1968 a rave *Rolling Stone* article attracted New York club owner Steve Paul. Masterminding a record-breaking contract from Columbia Records, Paul helped catapult Winter to stardom with albums like *Johnny Winter* (1969) and *Johnny Second Winter* (1970). In 1970 the band dissolved and the McCoys – Rick Derringer (guitar), Randy Hobbs (bass) and Randy Z (drums) – joined for *Johnny Winter And* (1970). The pressures of imminent superstardom and endless tours caused the band to turn to heroin and by 1972 Winter had hospitalized himself to recuperate. In 1973 he returned to performing with *Still Alive And Well*, utilizing his brother's touring crew to make short, civilized tours possible. His band now includes Randy Hobbs and Richard Hughes (drums).

Wishbone Ash was formed in the winter of 1969 from a nucleus of Steve Upton (drums, born May 24, 1946), Martin

Turner (bass, Jan. 10, 1947) and his brother Glen (guitar), who had been playing together in bands in Torquay. Glen retired due to ill-health and was replaced by Andy Powell (born Feb. 19, 1950). With Ted Turner (born Feb. 8, 1950) they decided on the twin lead guitar line-up, a style of presentation previously attempted only by Jimmy Page and Jeff Beck in the last phases of the Yardbirds. Though not a media favourite, they quickly established a large popular following and in mid-1972 their third album, *Argus* (MCA), reached No. 3 in the British charts. They failed to fully capture the dynamic live qualities of their act on record, however, and consolidation of their success eluded them, though in Britain and (especially) the United States they continued to be a major concert attraction. In June, 1974, Ted Turner decided to retire from the music business; he was replaced by Laurie Wisefield, formerly of Home.

Bill Withers, born in Slab Fork, West Virginia on July 4, 1938, spent some nine years in the US Navy, leaving at the age of 26 to join IBM as a computer operator. Withers made a demonstration tape as a singer/guitarist, using his own material, and hustled his wares around numerous west-coast record companies before being signed to Sussex by Clarence Avant. His debut disc produced by Booker T. Jones, a plaintive, sparsely funky 'Ain't No Sunshine', was a million-selling Top Ten hit in 1971. The following year the subtle, gospelly 'Lean On Me' topped the American charts and the embryonic street-funk of 'Use Me' was a No. 2 hit. Subsequent releases proved progressively less successful, however, and Withers joined Columbia in 1975.

Bobby Womack, now an international star in his own right, for ten years was recognized only as the originator of the Stones' first major hit, 'It's All Over Now', and a shadowy composer/session guitarist behind countless other stars, including Sam Cooke and Wilson Pickett. Born in Cleveland on March 4, 1944, he first recorded with his brothers Harris, Cecil, Curtis and Friendly (on Cooke's Sar label), singing gospel under their own name and then R&B as the Valentinos – including 'Looking For A Love' (1962), a Top Forty hit for the J. Geils Band in 1971, and 'It's All Over Now' (1964). Solo releases on Him, Checker (1965), Atlantic, and Keymen (1967) were largely ignored, but on Minit/Liberty (1967–70) he began attracting attention with an unusual mixture of original songs ('What Is This', 'It's Gonna Rain', 'More Than I Can Stand') and rearrangements of MOR hits (including 'Fly Me To The Moon', 'I Left My Heart In San Francisco').

Encouraged by Sly Stone, he reached wider audiences by adopting a looser more personalized format, including raps and extended instrumental passages, that earned him the nickname 'The Preacher'. Recording for UA since 1971, his best performances include 'Communication', 'That's The Way I Feel About Cha' (1971), 'Harry Hippie', 'I Can Understand It' (1972), 'Theme from Across 110th Street' (1973), 'You're Welcome, Stop On By' (1974), 'Check It Out' (1975), and new interpretations of several of his early songs.

Stevie Wonder first achieved fame as a child prodigy but continued to develop musically until by the mid-Seventies his vast audience spanned black and white, pop and rock. He was born Stephen Judkins on May 13, 1950 in Saginaw, Michigan, and was blind from birth. Taking up harmonica from an early age, he was brought to the notice of Berry Gordy by Ronnie White of the Miracles in 1960.

A year later Gordy set up his own label and recorded 'Little Stevie Wonder' as a falsetto R&B screamer and harmonica player. His third single, 'Fingertips Part 2' (Tamla) reached No. 1 in 1963 and for two years he was promoted as the Boy Genius, proclaiming his admiration for 'Uncle Ray' (Charles) and enjoying a series of minor hits including 'Hey Harmonica Man' (1964) and 'High Heel Sneakers' (1965).

'Uptight', a Top Ten hit in 1965, marked a change in style towards a more orthodox Motown sound and, as his voice deepened, his singles veered towards the romantic balladry of 'I Was Made To Love Her' (1967) and 'For Once In My Life' (1968). Like most of his early hits, the former was part written by Wonder and his producer Henry Cosby, while the latter typified the middle-of-the-road reputation Wonder was beginning to acquire: it had previously been recorded by Tony Bennett.

With the release of the *Where I'm Coming From* album (1971), he abruptly turned towards the progressive rock music of the time, making extensive use of moog synthesizer and writing philosophical lyrics. In the same year he married Syreeta Wright and renegotiated his relationship with Tamla, for the first time retaining full artistic control over his work.

Music Of My Mind (1972) and *Syreeta* (which he masterminded in the same year) were consummate examples of his new style of 'black rock'. On *Music*, he played every instrument, perfecting the interplay between a variety of electronic keyboard sounds, production techniques and his light, clear vocals. *Talking Book* (1972) and *Innervisions* (1973) confirmed Wonder's major status, and he recovered from a near-fatal automobile crash to release *Fufillingness First Finale* in 1974. If that album was thought by some critics to be somewhat repetitive, his best songs during the Seventies ranged from the raunchy rock of 'Superstition' through the serene lyricism of 'I Believe (When I Fall In Love With You It Will Be Forever)' to the compassionate social comment of 'Living In The City'. In 1975 he re-signed with Motown for the biggest ever advance, a massive 13 million dollars.

Roy Wood was born Ulysses Adrian Wood on Nov. 8, 1946, in Birmingham. In his early teens he learned guitar and started forming and joining bands: the Falcons, the Lawmen, Gerry Levine and the Avengers, Mike Sheridan and the Nightriders and finally, in 1964, the Move. A year later his composition 'Night Of Fear' was a British Top Five hit.

In 1970 Wood and fellow Move member Jeff Lynne began formulating the idea of an Electric Light Orchestra to expand in the direction suggested by the Beatles' 'I Am The Walrus'. This didn't reach fruition until 1972, by which time Wood and Lynne's working relationship had become uneasy. Wood thereupon left and formed Wizzard late that year.

After an initial hit, 'Ball Park Incident' (Harvest, 1973), Wood unleashed his re-creation of Phil Spector productions with 'See My Baby Jive', appearing in multicoloured fright wig and warpaint to promote it. With Wizzard he continued to mine this successful formula – 'Angel Fingers' was another No. 1 and later he even produced a Christmas record *à la* Spector, 'I Wish It Could Be Christmas Everyday'. Simultaneously, he cultivated a solo career. He recorded *Boulders* in 1970 (released in 1973). Apart from playing all the instruments he also produced, engineered and designed and painted the cover. Subsequently he recorded 'Forever' as a tribute to both Neil Sedaka and the Beach Boys which he followed with sporadic singles, equally indebted to the Beach Boys, and in 1975 a second solo album. By then he had more than twenty-five hit singles to his credit; though none of the albums in the last five years made the British charts. 1975 saw Wood for the first time turn his attention seriously to America where he (and his group) were only known in cult circles.

Link Wray, born of Shawnee Indian stock in North Carolina in 1930, recorded the classic 'Rumble' for Cadence in 1958 and enjoyed a huge hit that he could not follow despite recordings made over the next five years for Alpine, Epic – the Top Thirty 'Rawhide' (1959) – and Swan, 'Jack The Ripper' (1963).

For the most part of a decade, Wray dropped from the major labels to resurface on Polydor in 1971 with *Link Wray*. This renewed interest brought to light privately supervised recordings for Vermilion and Record Factory.

Betty Wright, born in Miami on Sept. 21, 1953, and signed at the age of eleven by Miami writer/producers Willie Clarke and Clarence Reid, was used for session work and solo releases on Deep City and Solid Soul before the duo took her to Henry Stone's TK Organization in 1967.

The following year, 'Girls Can't Do What The Guys Do'

(Alston), gave her the first of several romantic hits ('Pure Love', 'I've Found That Guy' – 1970, 'I Love The Way You Love' – 1971) until the funky 'Clean Up Woman' (1971), featuring Little Beaver's crisp guitar work, introduced a new mature image. Now considered a classic of its type, 'Clean Up Woman' was followed by similar themes ('Is It You Girl', 'Babysitter' – 1972, 'Let Me Be Your Lovemaker' – 1973, 'Secretary' – 1974) and even more successful pop hits ('Shoorah Shoorah', 'Where Is The Love' – 1975) that have made her one of the best known of TK's family of artists.

Robert Wyatt, former drummer with Soft Machine, emerged as one of the more imaginative presences in British rock during the Seventies. An able and sardonic lyricist, the tone and title of his first solo album – *End Of An Ear* (CBS, 1970) – presaged what was to follow. He formed Matching Mole (from the French for Soft Machine – *machine molle*) with David Sinclair (keyboards), Phil Miller (guitar) and Bill MacCormick (bass). Two exceptional but commercially unsuccessful albums on CBS included the lyrical 'O Caroline'.

Wyatt became a central figure in the loose circle of British *avant-garde* and jazz-rock musicians, appearing on Keith Tippett's 'Centipede' albums, and encouraging Henry Cow. He had a surprise hit in 1974 with a deadpan, cockney-style version of 'I'm A Believer', but was confined to studio and occasional live work following an accident which left him partially paralysed. He continues to record for Virgin (*Ruth Is Stranger Than Richard*, 1975) and is an influential figure with the London *avant-garde* rock scene.

Tammy Wynette, born on May 4, 1942, in Itawamba County, Mississippi as Wynette Pugh, worked in a beauty parlour before turning to country music. She secured a residency on the *Country Boy Eddy Show* in 1965, briefly sang with Porter Wagoner after Norma Jean left and before Dolly Parton joined him, and worked as a song plugger before Billy Sherrill signed her to Epic Records in 1967.

Her first record, produced by Sherrill, 'Apartment No. 9',

was a country hit and her second, 'Your Good Girl's Gonna Go Bad', inaugurated a string of country chart toppers, mostly written by Sherrill, Glen Sutton and herself. However, it was only when 'D-I-V-O-R-C-E' and 'Stand By Your Man' (a British No. 1 when it was re-released in 1975), paeans to the traditional virtues of Southern family life brought to life by Wynette's searing vocals and Sherrill's Spectorish productions, entered the American Hot Hundred in 1968, that she became a major force in country music.

Her marriage to George Jones in 1968 (she divorced him in 1975) and the slew of country awards she won that year, confirmed her position as the Queen of Nashville. Despite her success in the pop market, Tammy Wynette has doggedly refused to alter either the content of her songs – 'Don't Liberate Me' and 'Joy To Be A Woman' are representative titles – or her vocal styling, which remains uncompromising and countrified beneath the banks of strings with which Sherrill supplies her.

Yes had, by the mid-Seventies, established themselves among the leading practitioners of symphonic rock, alongside their former keyboards player Rick Wakeman. The group was formed in 1968 by Jon Anderson (born on Oct. 25, 1944 in Accrington, Lancashire), former singer with the Warriors, and Chris Squire, bass (born on March 4, 1948 in London).

With Peter Banks (guitar), Tony Kaye (keyboards) and Bill Bruford (drums), they signed to Atlantic. The first album (*Yes*, 1969) showed the influence of Keith Emerson's playing and the Fifth Dimension's harmony singing. *Time And A Word* (1970) continued this approach, notably in the group's arrangements of other people's songs.

Soon afterwards, Banks left to form Flash, a more conventional rock band, with vocalist Colin Carter. Apart from a minor American hit with 'Small Beginnings', the band had little success. He was replaced in Yes by Steve Howe, the former Tomorrow guitarist (born on April 8, 1947). *The Yes Album* (1971) marked the beginning of the later Yes sound, with Kaye introducing moog synthesizer and all the songs written from within the band.

Kaye was then replaced by the former Strawb, Rick Wakeman, whose mastery of classical keyboard styles – the result of an education at the Royal College of Music – had a liberating effect on the group on *Fragile* (1971). Yes, astutely guided by manager Brian Lane, were now ready to attempt the lengthy song-cycles and symphonic pieces on *Close To The Edge* (1972) and *Tales From Topographic Oceans* (1974), both of which featured drummer Alan White (born June 14, 1949), formerly with the Plastic Ono Band, who had replaced Bill Bruford in 1972. Though Anderson's lyrics veered towards incoherence, both were full of contrasting passages, in time, volume and tone, thrust together in powerful collages of sound. *Yessongs*, a triple live album, was released in 1973 and *Relayer* in 1974, when Rick Wakeman left to pursue a successful solo career with extended works like *The Six Wives of Henry VIII* (A&M, 1973) and *Journey To The Centre Of The Earth* (1974). He was replaced by the Swiss musician, Patrick Moraz, who had previously played with Brian Davison and Lee Jackson in Refuge. Kaye's group Badger had by this time fallen apart. By 1976 the individual group members were involved in solo projects and producer Eddie Offard had severed his relationship with the group.

Faron Young is a country singer with a smooth vocal style who has scored several popular ballad hits like 'Hello Walls' in 1961 and 'Four In The Morning' in 1971. He also appeared in several western movies like *Hidden Guns* in the mid-Fifties, but basically his career has been within country music.

Born in Shreveport on Feb. 25, 1932, he was a product of the popular Louisiana Hayride radio show and recorded with Capitol from 1953 to 1962, enjoying hits like 'Goin' Steady' (1953) and 'Country Girl' (1959). His later Mercury recordings include 'Unmitigated Gall' and 'Wine Me Up', typical hits from his rather uneventful roster of recordings. He is, additionally, publisher of Nashville's country paper

Music City News, and a pillar of the country music establishment.

Neil Young, born on Nov. 12, 1945 in Toronto, Canada, made his initial impact as a Dylanesque folksinger in Toronto's Yorkville in the mid-Sixties. He also played in folk-rock electric groups such as Neil Young and the Squires, before heading west to help form Buffalo Springfield in Los Angeles, early in 1966. He played lead guitar, wrote, and occasionally sang lead for the group.

His songs, for the Springfield and on his first solo album, *Neil Young* (Reprise, 1969), were notable for their blending of adult melancholy and childlike wonder and paranoia, their melodic invention, and the fluency of his guitar-playing. However, it was in 1969–70 that he came to the fore as a singer, with the albums *Everybody Knows This Is Nowhere* (1969) and *After The Goldrush* (1970). His high straining voice perfectly caught the mood of the Woodstock generation fighting a losing battle against political realities in a series of desperate love songs.

In summer 1969 he had joined Crosby and Nash and rejoined Stills in CSN&Y, a grouping that lasted little over a year in recording terms, but which has been sustained as an amorphous institution ever since. His time with CSN&Y saw some of Young's best songs – notably 'Helpless' and 'Ohio' – and a chance to recreate on stage the twin guitar battles with Stills which had marked the Springfield's live performances and which Young had emulated with Danny Whitten on *Everybody Knows*.

The two years that followed the splitting of CSN&Y saw Young making an unsuccessful film, the soundtrack of which was eventually released as *Journey Through The Past* (1973) and preparing *Harvest* (1972), amidst trying to come to terms with the pressures of stardom and the interrelated death of friend Danny Whitten, caused by drugs overdose in 1972. These two themes – the contradictions of stardom and death by drugs as a consequence of them – would henceforth rank with love and politics among the themes of his music.

Harvest, his most uneven and his best-selling album, also

marked a new musical direction, away from the angry sadness of his lead guitar and graceful voice-dominated music. The new input was Ben Keith's pedal steel playing, which provided a fatalistic tinge to the music from then on, as well as a sense of light and space to counterpoint Young's peculiarly repressed-anger style of lead guitar playing. On *Harvest*, 'A Man Needs A Maid', a song that dealt in role-playing in relationships with a depth and insight unthought of in previous years, marked the end of love as a major theme in his music.

The next three albums since released – *Time Fades Away* (1973), *On The Beach* (1974), and *Tonight's The Night* (1975) – have explored three different aspects of Young's world-view. *Time Fades Away*, a live album, presents the positive persona, the determined dreamer and self-righteous moralist, featuring both solo performances on piano and Young's own blending of hard rock and country instrumentation. *On The Beach* is a more sombre album, less overtly personal, a despairing tour through Nixon's America. The lyrics verge on the surreal, the music dark and heavily restrained. *Tonight's The Night*, the last to be released but recorded between the other two, is the most personal, a collage of songs centring on junkie death. The lyrics are alternately obscure and lucid, the music a starker and rougher version of the *Time Fades Away* style. Surprisingly, that album was a big American hit, as was *Zuma* (1975), which was only marginally lighter in tone.

Throughout his career Young has never eschewed the deep sense of pessimism that seems inseparable from the clarity of his insight.

Zager and Evans. In a classic example of the one-hit wonder, Denny Zager and Rick Evans sold over a million copies of 'In The Year 2525' (RCA) in mid-1969. After years of playing separately in various groups around Omaha, Nebraska, the two worked together for three years before their surprise hit, which was written by Evans (in less than thirty minutes!). An allegorical song inspired by the then-current 'future shock' fad, it mentioned a number of fairly predictable technological innovations, placing them thousands of years in the future, with a pleasant acoustic rhythm and harmony singing reminiscent of the early Sixties hootenanny sound. None of the duo's follow-ups managed to excite the public's sense of wonder in quite the same way, and they rapidly faded from sight.

Z.Z. Top. Formed in late 1970 from remnants of various Texas punk groups, Z.Z. Top (lead guitarist Bill Gibbons from the Moving Sidewalks, drummer Frank Beard and bass player Dusty Hill from the American Blues) joined the growing numbers of Southern guitar boogie bands, playing constantly and building a solid following. Their second album on London Records (*Rio Grande Mud*, 1972) produced a small hit, 'Francene', and propelled them onto the national tour circuit. Two albums followed, and the group's popularity grew steadily.

INDEX